TRACKS IN THE AMAZON

Tracks in the Amazon

The Day-to-Day Life of the Workers on the
Madeira-Mamoré Railroad

Gary Neeleman and Rose Neeleman

THE UNIVERSITY OF UTAH PRESS
Salt Lake City

The Defiance House Man colophon is a registered trademark
of the University of Utah Press. It is based on a four-foot-tall
Ancient Puebloan pictograph (late PIII) near Glen Canyon, Utah.

This book was first published in a Portuguese-language edition in 2011
by BEÍ Comunicação Ltda with the title *Trilhos na selva: O dia a dia
dos trabalhadores da ferrovia Madeira-Mamoré*.

18 17 16 15 14   1 2 3 4 5

LIBRARY OF CONGRESS CATALOGING-IN-PUBLICATION DATA
Neeleman, Gary.
  Tracks in the Amazon : the day-to-day life of the workers on the Madeira-Mamoré railroad /
Gary Neeleman and Rose Neeleman.
    pages cm
  "This book was first published in a Portuguese-language edition in 2011 by BEI Comunicao
Ltda with the title Trilhos na selva: O dia a dia dos trabalhadores da ferrovia Madeira-Mamoré."
  Includes bibliographical references.
  ISBN 978-1-60781-275-3 (pbk. : alk. paper) — ISBN 978-1-60781-276-0
  1. Ferrovia Madeira-Mamoré—History. 2. Railroads—Brazil—Rondénia (State)—History.
  I. Neeleman, Rose. II. Title.
  HE2930.M2N44 2013
  331.7'61385098111—dc23
              2013026892

Printed and bound by Sheridan Books, Inc., Ann Arbor, Michigan

*This book is dedicated to the thousands of forgotten men
who died while building a railroad in one of the most challenging areas of the world.
They came from countries around the globe, and they died and were laid to rest
in the Porto Velho Cemetery and along the 366-kilometer railroad track
on the banks of the Madeira River.*

Contents

Foreword

WADE DAVIS

The Indians called it *caoutchouc,* the weeping tree, and for generations they had slashed its bark, letting the white milk drip onto leaves, where they could mold it by hand into vessels and sheets, impermeable to the rain. On his first voyage, Christopher Columbus encountered Arawakans playing games with strange balls that bounced and flew. Thomas Jefferson and Benjamin Franklin found that small cubes of the stuff were ideal for erasing lead-pencil notations, and since they believed the plant hailed from the East Indies, the substance became known as India rubber. In fact, it came from the Amazon, and there the king of Portugal had already established a flourishing industry that made rubber shoes, capes, and bags. In 1823 a Scot, Charles Macintosh, dissolved rubber in naphtha and made a pliable coating for fabric, which led to the invention of the world's first raincoat.

All of these products, however, had a major flaw. In cold weather, the rubber became so brittle that it cracked like porcelain. In summer heat, a rubber cape was reduced to a sticky shroud. Then in 1839—quite by accident—an inventor from Boston, Charles Goodyear, dropped a mixture of rubber and sulfur onto a hot stove. It charred like leather and became plastic and elastic. This was the birth of vulcanization, the process that made rubber impervious to the elements, transforming it from a curiosity to an essential product of the industrial age. Over the subsequent thirty years, annual production of wild rubber in Brazil soared.

In 1888 John Dunlop invented inflatable rubber tires so that his son could win a tricycle race in Belfast. Seven years later in France, the Michelin brothers stunned critics by successfully introducing removable pneumatic tires in the Paris-Bordeaux car rally. By 1898 there were more than fifty American automobile companies. Oldsmobile, the first to be commercially successful, sold just 425 cars in 1901. Less than a decade later, the first of fifteen million Model Ts rolled off Henry Ford's assembly line. Each vehicle needed rubber, and the only source was the Amazon.

By 1909 merchants were shipping five hundred tons of rubber downriver every ten days. A year later, rubber accounted for 40 percent of all Brazilian exports. In 1911 production peaked at 44,296 tons. It was worth, at a conservative estimate, more than two hundred million dollars.

The flash of wealth was mesmerizing. In Pittsburgh steel tycoon Andrew Carnegie lamented, "I should have chosen rubber." In London and New York, men and women flipped coins to decide whether to go after gold in the Klondike or black gold in Brazil. At the height of the rush, five thousand men a week adventured up the Amazon.

Manaus, situated at the heart of the trade in Brazil, grew in a few years from a seedy riverside village into a thriving city where opulence reached bizarre heights. In this city cut off from the world, flaunting wealth became sport. Rubber barons lit cigars with hundred-dollar bank notes and slaked the thirst of their horses with silver buckets of chilled French champagne. Their wives, disdainful of the muddy waters of the Amazon, sent linens to Portugal to be laundered. In 1907—even as the events described in this remarkable book unfolded—the citizens of Manaus were the highest per-capita consumers of diamonds in the world.

The great symbol of excess—celebrated to this day—was the Manaus Opera House, a monumental Beaux Arts extravaganza designed by a Portuguese architect and built over a seventeen-year period ending in 1896. The builders, rejecting construction materials of local origin, imported ironwork from Glasgow, marble and gold leaf from Florence, crystal chandeliers from Venice, and sixty-six thousand ceramic tiles from Alsace-Lorraine. Even the massive murals depicting local jungle scenes were painted in Europe and shipped to Manaus. Operating expenses included subsidies of more than $100,000 per performance, the cost of luring established performers across an ocean and a thousand miles up the Amazon to a lavish venue built in the midst of a malarial swamp.

All of this wealth derived from the latex of three closely related species of wild *Hevea* that grew scattered across two million square miles of tropical rain forest. In this vast expanse—an area the size of the continental United States—there were perhaps three hundred million individual trees worth exploiting. Finding them was the challenge. Rubber trees usually grow widely dispersed in the forest, an adaptation that insulates the species from its greatest predator, the South American leaf blight. This disease, found only in the American tropics, invariably proves lethal once trees are concentrated in plantations. This accident of biology shaped the fundamental structure of the wild rubber industry.

To make a profit, merchants had to establish exclusive control over enormous territories. Once their lands were secure, they needed workers—thousands of them—to gather the latex from the wild. Impoverished peasants were imported from northeastern Brazil and absorbed into an atrocious system of debt peonage. Then the rubber men turned to the Indians, unleashing a reign of terror unprecedented in the Amazon. As a priest famously wrote of the rubber trade on the Río Putumayo, the river of death, "The best thing that could be said of a white man was that he did not kill his Indians for sport."

While the Indians died, rubber production soared. In twelve years that one infamous rubber baron operated on the Putumayo, four thousand tons of rubber worth $7.5 million sold on the London market. During that time, the native population on the river fell from more than fifty thousand to less than eight thousand. For each ton of rubber produced, ten Indians died, and hundreds were left scarred for life.

But as this noteworthy book makes clear, in the frenzy of the rubber boom, it was not only the indigenous people of the Amazon who suffered and died. Constructing the Madeira-Mamoré Railroad, conceived to provide a transportation corridor along which Bolivia could export the bounty of its forests directly to Europe—especially rubber—resulted in the death of some ten thousand workers. Nothing like it had ever been attempted. In an era when building railroads represented the very height of commercial enterprise and engineering prowess, no one had ever penetrated such an expanse of unknown rain forest.

Every tool and machine, every length of track—along with sufficient supplies to maintain an army—had to be shipped hundreds and, in many instances, thousands of miles merely to reach the project. Conditions in the work camps rivaled in their misery those in Panama during the construction of the canal. Malaria and yellow fever, dysentery and beriberi were rampant. In the first ill-fated attempt, thousands of men managed in five years to lay only three miles of track. When construction finally resumed in 1908, it took another four years to complete a line that ran from Porto Velho 224 miles into the forests of Bolivia, bypassing the treacherous and impassable rapids of the Río Madeira and giving that landlocked nation a direct route to the sea.

In the end, however, the Madeira-Mamoré Railroad was doomed to commercial failure by events that unfolded halfway around the world, a development that in the end brought an end to the merciless exploitation of the Indian people of the Amazon. Since the late nineteenth century, the British had tried to break the

Brazilian rubber monopoly. Rubber can be derived from as many as a hundred different species of plants, and they had tried them all. But nothing could match the quality of *Hevea brasiliensis*. On several occasions, the British had attempted to obtain seeds, but invariably they fermented and died during the slow ocean voyages.

But in 1876, the first modern steamship sailed up the Amazon, and a British planter managed to ship seventy thousand seeds back to England. Met in Liverpool by a special royal train, the precious cargo was brought to Kew Gardens, where the seeds were sown. Altogether 2,800 plants sprouted. The first shipment of seedlings left England a month later, bound for Ceylon.

It took some years of experimentation, but in time rubber became widely established throughout British colonies in Asia—lands free of the South American leaf blight. By 1907 plantations containing ten million rubber trees grew on 300,000 acres of land in Ceylon and Malaya. Production doubled every twelve months. By 1909 Malaya had planted more than forty million trees, each spaced just twenty feet apart in neat rows that allowed a single worker to tap more than four hundred trees a day. Each tree produced eighteen pounds of rubber a year, roughly five times the yield of even the most prolific wild *Hevea* in the Amazon. The cost of production was a fifth of the expense in Brazil.

With the success of the plantations in the Far East, the Amazon rubber boom imploded. In 1910 Brazil still produced roughly half of the world's supply. Within two years, however, the output of the Far East equaled that of Brazil. By 1918 the plantations produced more than 80 percent of the world's supply of rubber. In 1934—largely in response to the increasing demand for automobile tires—international production surpassed a million tons for the first time. In that year, plantations covering eight million acres in the Far East produced 1,006,000 tons of rubber.

In South America, the industry was dead. Total production for the entire continent did not exceed ten thousand tons. By 1940 Brazil was producing only 1.3 percent of the international rubber supply, and the nation had become a net importer of the product she had given to the world.

Today the era of the rubber boom seems very much like ancient history. Its horrors and its wonders have been largely forgotten. But it was a seminal period in the history of the Amazon: dramatic, grand, almost imperial in the scale of the ambitions and achievements of those who so desperately sought wealth and power. That the latex of a tree—this white blood of the forest—would lead men to spill their blood and that of many others so freely is one of the most remarkable sagas in the history of South America.

The Madeira-Mamoré Railroad is in many ways the ultimate symbol of both the glory and folly of those who entered the forest with such dreams. Today it has been largely forgotten. The last traces of its tracks—along with the rapids and cataracts of the Madeira it was built to surmount—are about to disappear beneath massive reservoirs that will inundate entire valleys. Thankfully we will at least have this splendid book as a record of just what was achieved by these remarkable engineers and workers who lost their lives and are today still buried along the right-of-way of this astonishing ribbon of steel.

WADE DAVIS is an explorer-in-residence at the National Geographic Society; his work as an anthropologist, writer, photographer, and botanical explorer has taken him throughout the world. His many books include *One River: Explorations and Discoveries in the Amazon Rain Forest* and *The Wayfinders: Why Ancient Wisdom Matters in the Modern World*. His latest book, *Into the Silence: The Great War, Mallory, and the Conquest of Everest* won the 2012 Samuel Johnson Prize.

Preface

On the afternoon of May 10, 1869, a lone telegraph operator sent a one-word message across the United States—"Done!" He was referring to the driving of the last spike—a golden one that joined the rails from the East Coast to ones from the West Coast to form the first transcontinental railroad in the United States.

This momentous event was recognized and celebrated throughout the world as one of the greatest engineering feats in history. According to *Golden Spike National Historic Site,* a booklet by Rose Houk, "Across the nation guns fired, bells tolled and whistles blew in jubilation as the final spike was driven in the first railroad that spanned the continent. America was now linked by a 1,776-mile ribbon of iron."[1]

Although thousands of pages in books and articles have been written over the years about this extraordinary event, a similar project was under way at approximately the same time more than eight thousand miles away under conditions even more challenging, and few people ever heard about this accomplishment.

The Madeira-Mamoré Railroad in the heart of the Amazon basin began in 1867, but the golden spike on this project was not driven until August 1, 1912. This railroad—later named the Devil's Railroad, Railroad of the Dead, the Ghost Train, or Mad Maria—was built by American engineers along the banks of the Madeira River deep in the Amazon jungle. It spanned 366 kilometers (224 miles) of treacherous rapids on the Madeira River, and its purpose was to bring Bolivian rubber and other products to Porto Velho, Brazil, the largest city in the upper Amazon Basin, and then down the Amazon River to the Atlantic Ocean and the markets of the United States and Europe.

Bolivia had lost its war with Chile and—as a landlocked country—had no access to the Pacific Ocean. The country envisioned the Madeira and Mamoré rivers as a hydrobyway to the Atlantic and a solution to its problems.

The president of the United States, Theodore Roosevelt, who himself was fascinated with the Amazon, called the Madeira-Mamoré project one of the great feats in the development of this part of the world. Thousands of men worked on the project, and it is said that more than ten thousand of them lost their lives in its construction. Workers came from the United States, Germany, Scotland, Portugal, Spain,

Greece, India, the Caribbean Islands, Denmark, and China. In all, fifty-two nations were represented among the workers. It is calculated that every crosstie represented the loss of one human life. The workers died from malaria, yellow fever, insect bites, wild animals, Indian attacks, and brawling among themselves.

In 1867 the Bolivian government recruited Colonel George Earl Church—previously an officer in the Union Army during the Civil War and then living in Mexico—to engineer and build the railroad. In spite of the fact that Church was warned that it was impossible to conquer the "green hell" of the Amazon, he was undaunted and moved forward. He raised a lot of money in Europe and in 1871 traveled to the United States to accumulate additional funds. He started construction on the railroad out of Porto Velho that same year, but by 1879 Church had laid only 7.5 kilometers of tracks. Even more discouraging, his investors had lost confidence in the project, and he was forced to abandon his company and the project.

The railway languished in the jungle until 1882, when the Brazilian government expropriated the project and initiated a new effort to complete it. Again the railroad lay dormant for the next twenty-one years. But then on November 17, 1903, Bolivia and Brazil signed a new treaty, and Brazil promised to complete the railroad within four years. There was renewed interest in the Amazon because of its vast resources. The possibility of having a hydrobyway to move Amazonian products, such as rubber, wood, medicinal plants, and foodstuffs, attracted speculators from many parts of the world.

Finally, an American by the name of Percival Farquhar negotiated a new contract with the Brazilian government. Farquhar, who was an entrepreneur and had experience in projects of this kind, immediately imported thousands of foreign workers when he assumed control of the railroad. Some called the project Farquhar's "Foreign Legion of the jungle."

Many of these foreign workers—including engineers and laborers—were veterans of building the Panama Canal and other projects around the hemisphere. There was also a group of ex-Confederate soldiers from the United States who had settled in the interior of the state of São Paulo in 1866, following the end of the American Civil War. One of the key figures in this group was Oscar Pyles, a descendent of one of the original Confederate emigrant families. He was an engineer and was invited to join the Farquhar management team to help complete the railroad. Judith MacKnight Jones, a granddaughter of one of the Confederate families that immigrated to Brazil, found the collection of photos in this book of the railroad under construction in Oscar Pyles's belongings.

When the Confederate soldiers left the United States in 1865–66 after the Civil War, they traveled to Brazil by steamship at the invitation of the Brazilian emperor, Dom Pedro II. They introduced the plow to Brazil and brought modern medical techniques, dental procedures, the buckboard, the kerosene lamp, and countless other innovations with them. This was what Dom Pedro II had hoped to achieve when he had invited these southerners to settle in Brazil. Most of the railroad's heavy equipment—the engines, cars, rails, and other machinery—was imported from the United States, and much of it had been manufactured in the Philadelphia Iron Works.

The Madeira-Mamoré Railroad received a lot of this equipment as did other narrow-gauge railroads throughout Brazil in the nineteenth and twentieth centuries. Farquhar was a tough negotiator, and in his dealings with the Brazilian government, he was able to secure a sixty-nine-year concession on the railroad, which included, among other things, access to thousands of acres of rubber trees. On August 1, 1912, the Farquhar Syndicate drove the golden spike to signify completion of the 366-kilometer Madeira-Mamoré Railroad. The ceremony took place at Guajará--Mirim on the Bolivian border.

It was not easy for the American company to complete this horrendous project begun by George Earl Church in 1867. Locomotive no. 12, one of the surviving pieces of equipment, bears his name and is currently housed in the Madeira-Mamoré rail yard in Porto Velho.

Acknowledgments

Dana B. Merrill, the railroad's official photographer, skillfully chronicled with his camera not only the construction of the railroad but also the lives and activities of the men who built it.

Frank Kravigny's diary as a seventeen-year-old worker on the rail line and later the editor of the *Porto Velho Times* recorded in minute detail the day-to-day events and people involved in the railroad's construction.

Judith MacKnight Jones, the descendent and historian of the U.S. Confederate community in Americana and Santa Bárbara d'Oeste, Brazil, was devoted to the history of her people and their contributions to their adopted land. She collected and preserved the photos of both Dana B. Merrill and fellow Confederate descendant Oscar Pyles to make this book possible.

We would also like to offer our thanks and appreciation to those individuals who helped us so much in preparing this book. Their willingness to help research and edit the book and offer suggestions was invaluable. These people include Alcides de Souza; Roy Webb and John Herbert of the University of Utah Marriott Library; Fernando Montes; Albert Henderson; our son, Dr. Stephen D. Neeleman; Daniela Spitzer; our granddaughter, April Hoyt; Steven Bartholomew; Andrew Moura; and Wade Davis, who kindly offered to write the foreword to this book.

We would also like to thank our friends at Editora BEÍ—especially Editor Laura Aquiar and Thomas Alvin—who published this book first in Portuguese.

And, of course, we also owe a debt of gratitude to acquisitions editor Peter DeLafosse; John Alley, who replaced Peter when he retired; Barbara Bannon, who patiently edited the final draft in English; and the staff of the University of Utah Press, who prepared the English-language edition of this book.

Looking south along the tracks at kilometer 53.
Photo by Dana Merrill from the Gary Neeleman collection.

Introduction

This is the story of a railroad unlike any other in the world. Most of the world's railroads built during the nineteenth and twentieth centuries crossed deserts, mountain ranges, vast plains, and forests, but no others faced the challenges of the Amazon, the densest tropical jungle on Earth.

The word "Amazon" sparks the imagination of human beings the world over. Although there are other jungles, the greatest is the Amazon. The Amazon River carries approximately 20 percent of all of the fresh water in the world, and the vast Amazon jungle has been called the "lungs of the world."

American President Theodore Roosevelt was fascinated with the Amazon Basin. In 1908—while still president of the United States—he began focusing on the Amazon and ultimately participated in a surveying expedition during which he contracted malaria and yellow fever, which ultimately contributed to his early death at sixty-one. Because of Roosevelt's interest in the Amazon, the Brazilian government contacted him and offered encouragement and support for his surveying expedition. Roosevelt ultimately descended the River of Doubt, assisted by his son, Kermit; Brazilian Army Colonel Rondon; and several others. The team was also supported by the Museum of Natural History in the United States, which happened to have been founded by the president's father, Theodore Roosevelt Sr. Roosevelt was very aware of the Madeira-Mamoré project, and in his book, *Through the Brazilian Wilderness*, he complimented "the American engineers who built the Madeira-Mamoré Railroad—a work which stands honorably distinguished among the many great and useful works done in the development of the tropics of recent years."[1]

Although many brief chronicles have been written about the Madeira-Mamoré Railroad over the years, in our extensive research, we discovered that most of these narratives barely scratched the surface of this incredible story. As a United Press International correspondent in Brazil from 1958 to 1966, I had heard of the railroad and even read *A Ferrovia do Diabo*, written by Brazilian journalist Manoel Rodrigues Ferreira. However, it was not until 1985, while I was researching *Farewell My South* about the southern Confederate settlers in Brazil, that I began fully to understand the audacity of this project.

Theodore Roosevelt in the Amazon with Colonel Rondon in 1913.
Photo courtesy of the Theodore Roosevelt Collection,
Houghton Library, Harvard University.

Tin can containing the photos and Marconigrams that Judith Jones gave to Gary Neeleman.
Photo from the Gary Neeleman collection.

Judith MacKnight Jones.
Photo from the Gary Neeleman collection.

On a warm, humid afternoon in 1985, in the little town of Americana, Brazil, I met with Judith MacKnight Jones, one of my main sources. During our meeting, Judith handed me a rusty tin canister, which contained 101 photos and ten original English-language newspapers, copies of the *Porto Velho Marconigram*. She told me that the family of a Mr. Oscar Pyles had given her the canister and pictures. She commented that she "really had no use for them at that time" and wondered if they would interest me.

Oscar Lee Pyles was born on March 16, 1880. He was the son of a U.S. Confederate immigrant family, which left the United States in 1866 and settled in the ex-Confederate community of Americana in the interior of the state of São Paulo, Brazil. At twenty-seven, Pyles traveled to Porto Velho, Brazil, and worked on the railroad. He apparently had a long association with Dana Merrill because he appears in several of Merrill's photos. In fact, we can assume that Oscar Pyles took some of the unidentified pictures in the canister.

In Judith MacKnight Jones's book, *Soldadodescansa!*, about the Confederate colony, she mentions that Oscar Pyles was married to Julia Seurlock, who died on October 23, 1966, and they had one son—Elmer Lee Pyles—who died on February 11, 1992. Oscar Lee Pyles died on July 21, 1953. All three are buried in the Cemitério do Campo in Americana, Brazil.

Dana Merrill sitting on an overturned Collins locomotive.
Photo from The Jungle Route by Frank W. Kravigny.

It wasn't until twenty years later that we began to look more carefully at these amazing photographs and read in detail the *Marconigram*s, which from 1909 to 1911 chronicled the final years of the construction of the Madeira-Mamoré Railroad. At that time, we became excited about this great story. Recently—since the announcement of the giant hydroelectric dam complex along the Madeira River in the Brazilian state of Rondônia—my excitement for this project became even more intense. The water from these dams will cover the remains of the old railroad bed, and the Madeira-Mamoré will become even more of a footnote in history than it already is.

Over the years, I have collected a bulging file of reports and documents about the old railroad. Recently, we took the 102-year-old photos and newspapers to the University of Utah Marriott Library, where the rare-documents division agreed to scan them with a high-definition scanner. The results were unbelievable.

Further research indicated that Dana B. Merrill, an American photographer, was employed as the official photographer of the Madeira-Mamoré Railroad from 1902 until 1912 and took thousands of photographs, including a good number of the ones in my collection from the tin canister. The fact that the photos in my collection survived in a tropical, humid climate for more than a hundred years is a tribute to Merrill's incredible technical skill. Rare-document experts at the University of Utah said the photos had been processed with an unusual silver gelatin compound. Combined with the old rusty canister, this technique helped keep the photos and

Dana Merrill (on the right) with American railroad engineers in 1910.
Photo by Dana Merrill, courtesy of the Foundation of the National Library of Brazil.

newspapers dry. In our effort to identify which photos were taken by Merrill and separate them from the ones taken by Pyles and others, we noted that the Merrill photos are numbered with India ink in the right-hand corner. The other photos are not.

At the turn of the century, Dana Merrill was a commercial photographer who spent his time working in the New York area. He operated out of the New York City Hall, where he returned after his time in Brazil, according to the bulletins of the Madeira-Mamoré Association. He later became one of the most well known and respected photographers in the United States with clients that included *House and Garden* (1933–34, 1938), *Vanity Fair* (1925, 1930), and *Vogue* (1929–30, 1932) from the Condé Nast magazine group.

Dana Merrill had accepted the challenge of documenting the construction of the Madeira Mamoré Railroad, and although some of his amazing photographs of the railroad have been published in books and periodicals, many of them were lost when the Brazilian military demolished large portions of the railroad and its files in 1971.²We also learned that many of Merrill's photos were destroyed by fire; before the discovery of the Pyles collection, it was estimated that only 189 photos had survived.

In our research, we managed to locate some personal albums that were apparently produced by Merrill and given as gifts to friends and associates. Most of the photos in this book come from the album Merrill gave to his friend Oscar Pyles. We found other albums in the National Library of Brazil in Rio de Janeiro, the Museu Paulista in São Paulo, and the New York City Public Library. We heard about a fifth album in Germany that had been purchased by Professor Franz Obermerir, a collector, when he contacted us after he heard about this book. When we examined the photos in Rio, São Paulo, and New York City, we found that they were not all the same.

Since the beginning of photography, it was a common practice to hire a photographer to document large construction projects and railroads. Brazilian photographer Pedro Ribeiro Moreira Neto, who completed his doctorate degree in social history at the University of São Paulo, says in his essay that closes this book,

> The photographic equipment Dana Merrill used was practically identical to what was available to most professionals at the time. The choice of the 13-by-18-centimeter negative format—considered small and light then—was best suited for frequent travel from one site to the next over difficult terrain. In addition to the more common glass plates, Merrill also adopted a chassis utilizing the recently developed film pack. These packs were composed of a plate with a flexible base and an emulsion coating; they were much lighter than glass plates and usually came in packages of a dozen plates. This choice considerably lightened the equipment weight for the photographer and made it much easier for him to change plates.
>
> However, the camera Merrill used was still a conventional one, more appropriate for traditional photography with the subjects placed at medium distance from the camera, carefully framed, and most often posed, a result of the necessary use of a tripod due to long exposure times.
>
> It appears that many of Merrill's surviving images fall into the category of early twentieth-century photography. However, Merrill was not a typical photographer but a pioneer, not bound by the technical limitations or aesthetic standards of his day. By taking the limits of his equipment to the extreme, he was able to explore a variety of camera angles and, in many

A group of North American and Brazilian engineers in charge of supervising
construction; Frank Kravigny is on the right with his trusty typewriter.
Photo by Dana Merrill, courtesy of Museu Paulista, University of São Paulo.

instances, did not conform to the photographic conventions of his era, for
example, when he purposefully used long exposure times for scenes involving
movement. He placed priority on not losing the moment.

His images suggest that he selected the point of view that best captured
the feelings that struck him at that moment, even though this often meant he
had to photograph from ditches, boats, or scaffolding, knee-deep in mud, or
from the tops of train cars or trees. Such practices—quite common in today's
photography—marked Merrill as a pioneer. The scenes in his images are so
dynamic that they seem to have been taken with a 35mm camera that didn't
even appear until twenty years later.

Merrill's job was to document the progress of the railroad construction.
Analysis of his photographs indicates that he did not have a planned routine.
He probably developed an arbitrary narrative in accordance with the oppor-
tunities that arose as the project progressed. Each negative—systematically

numbered in India ink—implies a chronological order, although this cannot be confirmed.

But the photographer—in addition to documenting the construction work—recorded the endless procession of every type of person who participated in the railroad project. Those not portrayed in groups, such as bureaucrats or the laundry or hospital staff, appear in individual photos or in pairs with the omnipresent background of their work environment. Others are depicted in individual portraits that highlight their physical attributes or distinctive traits.

The photographs in this book offer the reader a sample of Merrill's genius.

Frank Kravigny, a clerk who survived the difficulties of the railroad construction, tracked his experiences in his diary, *The Jungle Route,* which was published in 1940. Kravigny's diary and excerpts from the *Marconigram* newspapers in the metal canister we received from Judith MacKnight reveal a lot of what we know about the workers on the railroad. Kravigny was the first editor of the *Porto Velho Times,* which preceded the *Marconigram.* Unfortunately, there are no existing copies of the *Porto Velho Times,* but Kravigny quoted from some of the articles in his book.

When we showed our original copies of the *Marconigram* newspapers to the committee dedicated to preserving the old railroad and the Madeira River in Porto Velho, the members confirmed that they knew of no other copies of the newspaper. We were able to extract valuable information about Merrill's and Pyles's photos from these newspapers published from 1909 to 1911 and used that source to produce captions for the majority of them. The various publications where the Merrill photographs appear do not include detailed captions. Through our research, we have attempted to broaden the understanding of not only the Merrill photographs but those of Oscar Pyles as well.

The intention of this book is not to record in minute detail all of the political events and technical problems that plagued the construction of the Madeira-Mamoré Railroad. Rather, we hope to give the reader—through more than a hundred amazing photos and their captions—a better understanding of the daily lives of the thousands of railroad workers who lived, worked, and died in one of the most remote areas of the world.

Our trips to the Amazon Basin took us first to Manaus on the Amazon River, and then a nearly two-hour flight farther south to Porto Velho on the Madeira River. Our host in Porto Velho was Luiz Leite de Oliveira, a passionate organizer of

Fernado J. Torras.
Photo from the Gary Neeleman collection.

the committee to save the remnants of the Madeira-Mamoré Railroad and the Madeira River itself. Spending time with de Oliveira was like looking back in time as he recalled the days when the old train still operated. In fact, he told stories that years after the train had ceased operation, some people said they still heard it rumbling through town in the middle of the night. Even though he and his committee had some photos and documents, they had never seen most of our photos and told us there were no surviving copies of the *Porto Velho Times* or the *Marconigram*.

The Porto Velho de Oliveira showed us was considerably different from the town in 1907 before it officially became Porto Velho. Today it is the capital of the state of Rondônia, located on the border with Amazonas on the banks of the Madeira River. In 1907 the city only had a population of about a thousand people, but it grew to several thousand when it became a rubber boomtown and again during the World War II years from 1941 to 1946. Today approximately 400,000 people live in this capital city, and it is still growing from the families of the workers now building the two large hydroelectric dams on the Madeira River—the Santo Antonio and the Jirau.

Although we know very little about what happened to most of the railroad workers later in life, we can conclude that their experiences during the time they were in the Amazon certainly influenced the rest of their lives. Frank Kravigny was only seventeen years old when he arrived in Porto Velho, and the year he spent working on the railroad provided him with more life experiences than most young men his age gain in half a lifetime. Kravigny observed men at their best and their worst. He saw sacrifice and greed, sickness and death against a backdrop of one of the most difficult and challenging areas of the world.

In his diary, Kravigny said that when he boarded the riverboat *Oteri* that morning of June 4, 1910, he had the distinct feeling that this phase of his life had come to an end. In the beginning—as the time approached for his return to the United States—he had decided he would return to the jungle after a few months' rest. He later explained that the euphoria of returning to the United States caused him to drop his guard; as a result, "the careless use of a mosquito screen, and the sudden cutting down on the daily 30 grains of quinine, plus the temptation of a change in diet, took its toll."[3] By the time he reached the Atlantic Ocean and the port of Para ten days later, he had his first attack of jungle fever and the malaria that lasted seven years. Consequently, Kravigny never returned to the jungle.

We do know the story of one of the engineers, Fernado J. Torras. He was born on November 21, 1885, in Brunswick, Georgia, and attended Georgia Military Academy and the Georgia Institute of Technology, where he earned a degree in civil engineering. After graduating, Torras was recruited to work on the Madeira-Mamoré Railroad deep in the Amazon jungle. He was employed as a draftsman and was involved in designing rail bridges across rivers, swamps, and marshes.

This experience helped him in later life. After leaving the Amazon, he continued to travel around the world building bridges and roads across rivers and marshes using the techniques he had learned while working on the railroad. Torras returned to his hometown, Saint Simons Island, after World War I and found the area in an economic depression. Something was needed to boost the economy, and building a causeway was suggested. The experts in the area felt it could not be done, but Torras was undaunted; using the techniques he had learned in the Amazon, he built the causeway that today bears his name.

CHAPTER I

George Earl Church

Since the beginning of recorded history, mankind's relentless search for treasure has been legendary. For centuries both men and women have risked everything to pursue elusive riches, an endeavor that often cost their lives.

In the 1500s, Spanish and Portuguese explorers sailed to the New World in their quest for gold, silver, precious gems, and other treasure. The Spaniards found gold and silver in California; they conquered the native peoples of South America and plundered their riches. The British Empire girdled the globe for centuries, exacting whatever it could from the lands and people under its control.

When the Spaniards toppled the Inca empire and ruled South America, according to Neville B. Craig, the author of *Recollections of an Ill-Fated Expedition to the Headwaters of the Madeira River in Brazil*, "The silver deposits of Potosi [Bolivia] alone, from the time of their discovery in 1546 to 1864, are reported to have yielded the enormous sum of $2,919,899,400 [as calculated in 1907]," [1] not to mention millions more in gold, copper, and other precious metals. By the mid-1800s, the world was becoming increasingly aware of the vast wealth in not only the land-locked country of Bolivia but also the mysterious depths of the whole Amazon region—Bolivia, Brazil, Peru, Ecuador, and Colombia.

Craig continues, "Nor are these mineral resources by any means exhausted to-day [1907]. The almost impassable barriers to the transportation of machinery, the spirit of revolution, the indolence, ignorance, and poverty of the people, have all combined to render Bolivia's wealth unavailable, but that it exists to-day there is abundant proof." [2]

But, as Craig points out, Bolivia's wealth was not just buried beneath the earth.

Rich as Bolivia undoubtedly is in minerals, these constitute but a small part of her natural resources. She is possessed of a large area of remarkably fertile

11

George Earl Church.
*Photo from História Regional: Rondônia by Marco
Antonio Domingues Teixeira and Dante Ribeiro da Fonseca.*

land well watered by noble rivers and a climate that has almost every possible variation between the snow-capped peaks of the Andes and the tropical heat of her lowlands. Within her own borders she produces nearly all the cereals, vegetables, fruits, and meats one usually expects to find anywhere in the temperate or torrid zone.... Bolivian tobacco is incomparably superior to any other. India-rubber, cotton, sugar-cane, cinchona bark [the source of quinine], cacao, vanilla beans, the coco plant, gums, dye-woods, various medicinal plants, and many kinds of ornamental wood, highly prized by the cabinet-maker, are familiar products of her soil.[3]

In 1873 ex-Union Army Colonel George Earl Church, who at the time was living in Mexico, presented the Church Plan, which consisted of a two-hundred-mile railroad along the banks of the Madeira River. The railroad would circumvent nineteen rapids and cataracts, which were considered the only obstacle preventing the enormous wealth of Bolivia and the Brazilian Amazon from reaching the markets of the world.

On December 6, 1873, one of Philadelphia's newspapers published a long interview with Colonel Church, concluding with these words:

It is to remedy this (the commercial isolation of Bolivia) and to open up to the world a land as fair as "the Garden of the Lord" that two Philadelphians

Brazilian Emperor Dom Pedro II.
*Photo from História Regional: Rondônia by Marco Antonio
Domingues Teixeira and Dante Ribeiro da Fonseca.*

are to overcome the rapids of the Madeira. "I am not visionary, but know whereof I speak," said Colonel Church, "that this once accomplished, the wealth of Australia and California will sink into insignificance beside the auriferous yield of the mountains and streams of Bolivia and the teeming products of her fertile plains and valleys."[4]

A correspondent from the *New York Herald,* in an article from Philadelphia on January 2, 1878, said,

A national interest centres [*sic*] in the voyage of this ship, for the reason that it is the first time in the history of this country that an expedition has been sent from the United States, equipped with American money, materials, and brains, for the execution of a great public work in a foreign country.... The party of engineers, fifty-four in number, is said to be the ablest body of men in this profession ever united in a similar expedition.[5]

On December 6, 1877, in an interview in the *Philadelphia Times,* Church added, "When finished it will be the only railroad outside of the United States constructed from end to end by Americans and ironed and stocked with American rails and rolling stock."[6]

Church pursued the project that promised to fulfill his dream. Craig continues,

> Later [in 1884], Colonel Church is said to have made a new proposal to the Emperor [Dom Pedro II] of Brazil for the construction of the projected railway. Mr. Mackie, who then represented Colonel Church at Rio, says that Dom Pedro "supported it earnestly and often talked to me, as Colonel Church's attorney, of his great admiration for and confidence in that indomitable man, but political sentiment was then averse to letting any foreigners build what Brazilians regarded as the key to the heart of South America. The shadow of the Republic was already spreading over Brazil and nothing definite resulted."
>
> Thus it happened that for many years the Madeira and Mamoré project has been held in abeyance. The quinine in the forests of Bolivia has been exhausted, but the rubber trade on the tributaries of the Amazon became so valuable as to cause a Spanish adventurer to proclaim the existence of the "Independent State of Acre," embracing disputed territory, bordering on Brazil, Bolivia and Peru, of much greater extent than the whole of New England.
>
> The obliteration of this ephemeral creation almost precipitated a bloody conflict between the three contiguous nationalities over their respective claims to the rubber forests, which constituted all there was of the evanescent republic. Happily these claims were all successfully adjusted by the treaty of Petropolis, signed in 1903 and ratified in the following year.
>
> Under this treaty, in exchange for territorial concessions, Brazil agreed to build the Madeira and Mamoré Railway within four years and to pay Bolivia £2,000,000 [pounds], which the latter accepted *"with the intention of applying it principally to the construction of railways and other works tending to better communications and to develop commerce between the two countries."* [italics in original] [7]

Although Brazilian Emperor Dom Pedro II considered Colonel Church an "indomitable" man, all of his energy and vision was no match for the mighty forces of nature and the quirks of South American politics. Church spent sixteen years

Locomotive from the Church era
after it had been cleaned up, restored, and put back in use.
Photo by Dana Merrill from the Gary Neeleman collection.

from 1868 to 1884 planning and promoting the railroad with the expectation of exposing the world to the riches and wonders of the vast Amazon Basin. Finally, the Church Plan to export engineering technology and heavy equipment to a foreign land as one of the United States' first endeavors died.

Although the lure of untapped riches in the jungle remained lodged in the imaginations of those originally involved, the daunting combination of Brazilian nationalism and the malaria-carrying mosquito was too much to overcome. For twenty-three years, the remnants of what was called "the ill-fated expedition" lay rusting in the jungle. Accounts tell that thousands of workers were only able to lay three miles of track during the first five years of the Church contract. Thousands of men died from fevers and the elements. Weary and sick, the workers drifted downriver to Manaus, where they begged local Brazilians for funds to return home to the United States and Europe.

In 1935 *Harper's* magazine columnist Earl Hanson reported,

A locomotive, originally intended for use in 1878 had been abandoned when the *"Ill-Fated Expedition"* gave up its ghost, and had lain in these jungles for

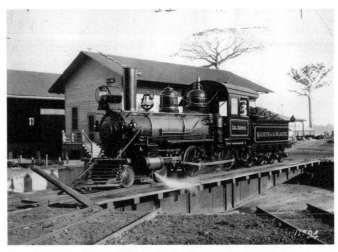

A restored locomotive from the Church era.
Photo courtesy of the Foundation of the National Library of Brazil.

over thirty years, during which time a tree had grown out of its wide flaring, wood-burning smoke stack. In spite of this, it existed until the day in 1911, when it was completely overhauled and actually went into service again on the new line, after a ceremonious christening under the name of Colonel Church, named for the original pioneer of this railroad development.

This was truly a story of the constant battle of the forces of the jungle to reclaim that which man had wrested from its clutches. Even before the days of the depression of 1929, these forces were at work and the economic debacle of those years has since contributed to providing practically the same fate for the completed railroad.[8]

CHAPTER 2

White Gold

While the original vision of Colonel George Earl Church mainly focused on finding a way to transport the riches of the Amazon to the outside world, the emphasis of the project changed dramatically in 1896. The industrialization of the United States and Europe had begun, and in that year, B. F. Goodrich manufactured the first automobile tires in the United States. Rubber was suddenly on everyone's mind, and "rubber madness" began sweeping the world.

In his book, *The Jungle Route,* Frank Kravigny describes the challenge facing rubber gatherers:

> While the process of rubber gathering is a simple one, the conditions under which it is performed are not. The work of the Seringuero [rubber worker] is not easy. His trek through the forests requires the constant hacking and hewing of new trails, which are rapidly overgrown. After completing his travels through the forests and swamps in search of trees which are often far apart, and successfully combating his insect and animal antagonists, he still has to battle with Old Man River, before a safe haven for the precious sap is found."[1]

The *seringueira* tree in the upper Amazon Basin, in the Brazilian and Bolivian jungle, produced the highest-quality natural latex in the world. Soon rubber barons were exploiting not only the trees that produced the rubber but also the workers who extracted it:

> The Seringueros are employed by the rubber firms who have secured concessions to exploit large rubber areas. The rubber gatherers turn in their collections at the warehouse and these are credited to their accounts, against which is charged the supplies they draw. In this system of practical peonage, these

Gathering rubber.
Photo by Dana Merrill from the Gary Neeleman collection.

men are always in debt and a gatherer who makes enough money to get out of the country is hard to find. Usually stolid and unemotional, the temperament of the Seringuero is such that he prefers the solitude of the jungle to any other place on the globe. Because of his uncommunicative and suspicious nature, the railroad men had almost as little contact with him as with the native Indian.[2]

Kravigny goes on to detail the way that rubber is extracted and processed.

The milk-like liquid of the rubber tree is not a true sap, but a secretion of the bark, and it is gathered by gashing the trunk of the tree and hanging a cup under the lowest point of the gash, the sharp edge of the tin being forced into the bark. At the end of the day the rubber gatherer empties the contents of the cups (about half a pint of liquid to each tin) into a large bucket and takes it to the smoking place. Here a fire fed by castanha [Brazil nut] shells is kindled under a funnel-shaped pipe about two feet high. Across the opening of the pipe is a pole, supported on a crotch at each end. While the fire is burning the sap is ladled out and slowly poured on to the pole at the place where it is hottest, and the pole is then kept rotating until a rubber ball is formed. The diameter of the ball increases until it reaches a thickness of about a foot, and a length of eighteen inches. During this process, the color of the ball changes from white to black. The ball is then forced off the pole and branded, at which time it weighs about fifty pounds.[3]

In 1910 the *seringueros* were paid about sixty cents a pound for the rubber, and it was sold on the open market for about five times that amount. By 1940 Amazon rubber was selling for only about seventeen cents a pound because most of the world's production had transferred to Southeast Asia.

The rubber then makes its arduous way downriver to civilization.

The rubber then starts its trip to market in a canoe, to a river port where it is picked up by a steamer. The canoes, loaded with rubber balls afforded a degree of safety to the men who shoot the rapids in them, as the balls will float, and in the event of the capsizing of a canoe will act as life preservers for the battalone men. Some of the balls float away during these accidents and wherever these are found the brand is examined and the owner located. His

Tapping Rubber.
Photo by Dana Merrill from the Gary Neeleman collection.

Smoking the rubber.
Photo by Dana Merrill from the Gary Neeleman collection.

property is returned to him after he has paid a fixed sum, as is the custom in the Amazon Valley. The reward is a substantial one, and the system operates in a most satisfactory manner.

All of the caoutchouc from the Amazon Valley is known as Para rubber and in the international rubber markets this product is considered the best.[4]

Dr. C. J. Wilson and Mr. J. C. McLean were employed by the Trans Andean Railway tunnel in South America. They described the difficulty in getting the rubber through the rapids in the *Porto Velho Marconigram*:

On the subject of rubber cultivation Dr. Wilson said: "There are thousands of miles of rubber trees, and the supply appears to be almost unlimited. But labor is still so scarce, and the distance so great and difficult, that you cannot get the stuff into the market except at a big price, and therefore there will be a good price for years to come."

Guiding a boat through the shallow
rapids of the Madeira River above lower Caldeirão falls.
Photo by Dana Merrill from the Gary Neeleman collection.

As soon as they got to into the rapids the explorers found the dangers foreshadowed for them. The water ran two or three miles in the open, and fifteen or sixteen miles an hour in the rapids. To navigate these they had only flimsy rafts, a few inches above the water surface. So that, with the heat of the sun and standing in the water, when they had done a few weeks of it their feet were swollen and their agony almost unbearable.[5]

The Treaty of Petropolis, signed on November 17, 1903, opened the door for a revived Madeira-Mamoré project, where rubber could be brought down the Madeira River past the nineteen waterfalls by train, then loaded into steamships to make the journey down the Amazon to the Atlantic and on to the United States and Europe. The new Brazilian Republic was anxious to take advantage of this windfall opportunity, and in 1907 signed a contract with another American businessman, Percival Farquhar, to build the railroad in four years. Farquhar was a shrewd negotiator and had railroad holdings and businesses in many other countries throughout the world. With the rubber boom now in full swing, he drove a hard bargain with the government of the young republic and secured a sixty-nine-year concession on

Moving the balls of rubber to the train station.
Photo by Dana Merrill, courtesy of the Foundation of the National Library of Brazil.

the railroad, which also included large areas of seringueira (rubber trees) along the Madeira.

There was never a time when the old adage "Time is money" was more appropriate. With construction on the Panama Canal beginning to wind down, Farquhar hired thousands of workers from that project. They came from the Caribbean Islands, Spain, Cuba, China, Germany, and the British Isles and were consequently sometimes called Farquhar's Foreign Legion.

An ad in *Engineering News* solicited railroad engineers with tropical experience of no less than one year. The pay ranged from $125 to $250 per month in U.S. gold, in contrast to New York, where wages were averaging about $75 per month. After the ad appeared, thousands of men traveled into the jungles of South America. According to Kravigny, most of them had absolutely no experience in the tropics and knew nothing about its perils; many never returned home.

The workers were transported south on the Amazon on small steamships—first to Manaus and then on to Porto Velho on the Madeira—1,650 miles from the Atlantic ocean and the port city of Para.

The Farquhar Syndicate hired New York photographer Dana Merrill to document the railroad when construction began. One of the albums Dana Merrill put together included his photos and a number of poems.[6] Some of these poems were also published in the *Marconigram* and its predecessors, the *Porto Velho Times* and

A map of the rivers of South America.
Courtesy of Andrew Moura.

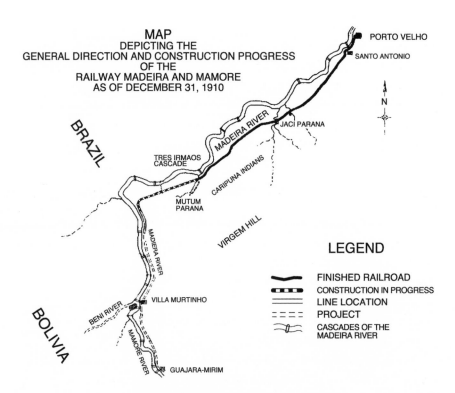

A map of the Madeira-Mamoré area.
Courtesy of Andrew Moura.

the *Porto Velho Courier*. A selection of these poems is included in this book. This is true, unpolished folk poetry, written by amateurs with no particular talent but plenty of vernacular style. Although some readers may find the poems difficult to read because of their frequent awkwardness and sentimentality, they are the surviving voice of the men who worked on the railroad and vividly capture their lives and labor. The poems express the frustrations and heartaches of individuals who worked and, in many cases, died in one of the most difficult regions in the world.

The Land of the Rubber-gum Tree
by R. S. Stout

It's a hot old zone, the Torrid Zone,
This land of the rubber-gum tree,
With its fever and chill that so often kill—
And its Rivers that run to the sea.

It's a hot old zone, yea hot as hell,
And it's not very far from here—
Where the devils roast their victim's ghost,
And dance around his bier.

Just over the way on the other side,
Of the Rio Mamoré,
The demon lives, Who ne'er forgives
And gloats the live long day.

You don't have to look at [it] this way or that,
To find little hell in Brazil—
You have to possess the lives of a cat,
And live on a quinine pill.

Its jungle is all you could wish for,
In the shape of bugs that can bite,
And the snakes, and the lizards and 'gators galore—
Can put up a pretty good fight.

It's funny we don't get religion,
Out here in the wilds of Brazil—
The name of the Lord is oft' spoken,
But not with a very good will.

Are we sorry we came to this country,
This land of the rubber-gum tree?
Where it rains every day—and well rather—
For it's home where we all long to be.

Will I leave it some day in the future?
Go back to the land of the Free?
Where there's shows and there's girls, and there's laughter—
And a sweetheart that's waiting for me?

Ask the 'squito that bites thru your stocking,
Ask the jigger you find in your feet—
Ask the red bug that itches like blazes,
Ask the "carne" at Mesa, they call meat.

It's great to be crazy they tell us,
(To use an expression not mine)
If we ever come back to this country—
For greatness, we'll all be in line.

For it's a hot old zone, the Torrid Zone—
This land of the rubber-gum tree,
With its fever and chills that so often kill,
And its rivers that run to the sea.[7]

Construction on the railroad was under way by 1908, and the Farquhar Syndicate drove the golden spike on August 1, 1912, in Guajará-Mirim, Brazil. The railroad began operating at peak capacity, and Brazil exported more than thirty million dollars' worth of rubber in that year alone (equal to half a billion dollars today). The railroad's top year was 1913.

Loading the balls of rubber on the train.
Photo by Dana Merrill from the Gary Neeleman collection.

By 1915 the Panama Canal was open for business, and Chilean ports became available to Bolivia, which severely restricted the viability of the railroad. The good times were not to last.

> The day of prosperity for the rubber gatherer departed when a British doctor successfully smuggled some of the seeds of the rubber tree to England; propagated them and sent them to the East Indies. The result of all this was the present [1940] groves of cultivated rubber trees that now exist in the East Indies under such ideal and healthful surroundings that the rubber is gathered there by labor willing and able to work for about two per cent of what the Amazon gatherer gets. Added to this was another advantage in producing rubber in this location. The transportation difficulties of the falls and rapids of the Amazon were eliminated and while the distance from the market was slightly greater, the water freight on ocean liners was not materially different from either of these two points.[8]

This American naval ship brought rubber tappers from the northeastern Brazilian coast to Manaus and Porto Velho on the Amazon river and took balls of rubber back down the river during World War II.
Photo courtesy of the U.S. Senate files.

The combination of these factors—the completion of the Panama Canal and mass production of rubber in the East Indies—killed the rubber business in the Amazon for many years. Then the 1929 financial crash made long-term recovery impossible.

Only during World War II, when the Japanese controlled the rubber groves in Malaya and other countries of Southeast Asia, did Amazon rubber gain, once again, worldwide importance.

> In 1942, Japanese troops swept through Indonesia and Malaya, occupying vast rubber plantations and cutting off the allies from 95 percent of the world's rubber supply. In the United States, rubber stocks were low and a synthetic rubber industry was in its infancy.
>
> From airplane tires to surgical gloves, rubber was crucial to the war effort. In desperation, the United States turned to Brazil. With as many as 200

million wild rubber trees in the Amazon, American experts calculated, Brazil could quickly increase its rubber production. With an injection of manpower, the Americans reasoned, Brazil could raise output eightfold, hitting 100,000 tons a year.

Soon recruiting posters for rubber tappers were appearing in Brazil's drought-stricken northeast, a traditional source of migrants to the Amazon. Referring to Brazil's expeditionary force in Italy, one poster made the patriotic appeal, "While our soldiers are fighting in Italy, you are fighting in the trenches for rubber."[9]

American navy warships—many on lend-lease from the United States—sailed nearly seventeen hundred miles up the Amazon River to the port city of Porto Velho on the Madeira River to deliver rubber tappers recruited from northeastern Brazil. They then picked up the rubber for transportation to the United States and Europe. Brazilian President Getúlio Vargas had negotiated a deal with the United States to provide rubber from the Amazon for the war effort, and this required many thousands of workers. The agreement between Vargas and the government of Franklin D. Roosevelt was signed on March 3, 1942, just three months after the Japanese bombed Pearl Harbor.

Most of these recruited workers knew nothing about the perils of the Amazon jungle. It has been determined that about fifty-five thousand workers from northeastern Brazil poured into the Porto Velho area. By the end of the war, as many as twenty-six thousand of these men had died from malaria, yellow fever, and hepatitis. Once again the frantic quest for "white gold" took a tremendous toll on human lives.

About twelve thousand of the workers returned to their homes in northeastern Brazil. Those who survived the jungle and did not return home settled in Porto Velho. Today hardly anyone born in the city of Porto Velho does not have a relative, a friend, or an acquaintance who was not a rubber soldier.

CHAPTER 3

Porto Velho

Much of our research concerning the Madeira-Mamoré Railroad had to be done in the United States because those who built the railroad were Americans. In 1912—when the golden spike was driven in Guajará-Mirim on the border with Bolivia—the railroad was said to be the only one built from start to finish by Americans outside of the United States. The engineering was American, the equipment was American, Porto Velho's newspaper was in English, and the editors were Americans. The hospital doctors and administrators were Americans.

Consequently, most of what we know about the construction of the Madeira-Mamoré Railroad comes from the diaries and photos of Americans who survived the jungle and returned to the United States to tell about their experiences. Few, if any, of these individuals spoke Portuguese, and they had only limited contact with authorities in the Brazilian government. Obviously, the workers came from all over the world, but the administration of the project was American. The money was both American and European.

Today, few rank-and-file Brazilians have heard of Porto Velho in the Amazon Basin, and fewer than one in ten thousand has visited the city. Porto Velho was the epicenter of the railroad construction. Although it was a community on the Madeira River settled by pioneers and the center of the Madeira-Mamoré Railroad operations as early as 1902, it was not officially named Porto Velho until 1914.

Frank Kravigny commented on the town,

> On my return, Porto Velho presented a very changed aspect from the town on my arrival. Buildings were being erected with some semblance of regularity, on what seemed to be an attempt at streets. The master mechanics' shop was now practically completed and on the northeastern end of the town had been built more living quarters for the men, but the clearing had not been

A group of railroad personnel at Porto Velho headquarters. Front row, left to right: William Voss, D. R. Palmer, L. E. White, R. E. Johnson, Dr. Stephen Smith; center row, left to right: H. W. Warner, William K. Runyon, John Y. Bayliss, C. M. DuBois, and an unidentified person; back row, left to right: R. G. Jenckes, E. M. Poole, Felder Furlow, E. A. Smith, D. J. Dodd, and Dana B. Merrill.
Photo by Dana Merrill from the Gary Neeleman collection.

Porto Velho, formerly called Los Pedros, about 1909.
Photo by Dana Merrill from the Gary Neeleman collection.

Porto Velho in 1909.
Photo by Dana Merrill from the Gary Neeleman collection.

Porto Velho in 1909.
Photo by Dana Merrill from the Gary Neeleman collection.

extended any further. Prominent on the landscape was a two-legged arrangement of telegraph poles made by utilizing some of the old, light weight steel
rails of the Collins Expedition of 1878. These poles had finally filled a need
that the wooden ones could not satisfy because of the susceptibility of wood
to insect attack and rot decay.[1]

The story of Porto Velho is one of triumph, defeat, sickness, and death. It is
an American story, a Brazilian story, and a world story. From no more than a village on the banks of the Madeira in 1907, Porto Velho exploded with activity as
heavy equipment, ships, construction workers, rubber tappers, engineers, doctors,
and hospital equipment descended upon this sleepy tropical town and changed its
face forever.

Frank Kravigny provides a detailed description of the railroad's administrative
quarters:

> The office building was a two-story structure situated on a slight ridge, about
> fifteen feet above and three hundred feet back from the river bank. The front
> of the first floor of this building was occupied by the timekeeper, paymaster,

The wireless station at Porto Velho.
Photo by Dana Merrill from the Gary Neeleman collection.

The office building at Porto Velho.
Photo by Dana Merrill from the Gary Neeleman collection.

cashier and the postmaster, each with his own office, and in the rear was the mess hall for the office force. Connected by a passageway was a small building used as a kitchen. On the upper floor were the administrative offices, except for one room which was reserved, but rarely occupied by Lombard, the camp messenger,...[2]

Even though Porto Velho was a relatively small community, it published its own newspaper. The purpose of the newspaper was to report the progress of the railroad to the workers and also entertain them. Although it was produced by a small staff originally on a typewriter, the English-language newspaper—first the *Porto Velho Times* and later the *Marconigram*—was considered by many around the world to be one of the best newspapers of its time.

In the *Porto Velho Marconigram*, published on November 19, 1910, we find this description of the paper that originally appeared in *The India Rubber World*:

The readers of *The India Rubber World* have been kept informed of indications of commercial progress of the Madeira river, which is destined to become an outlet to the world's richest natural rubber field—Bolivia. Not the least important of these indications is the regular publication, at the headquarters of the engineering corps at work on the Madeira-Mamoré Railway, by some of the bright young American employees temporarily exiled there of a newspaper—The Porto Velho *Marconigram.*

This remotely published little sheet is not as yet impressive in appearance, but it happens to be of the same size and general appearance as the earlier numbers of the *Sun,* which long has been one of the principal newspapers of New York. As indicating the up-to-dateness of the Madeira river newspaper, it may be mentioned that the latest issue received in New York mentions the new prices for automobile tires quoted by some of the leading American manufacturers.

But what is of very much more importance is the fact that a large part of the contents of the *Marconigram* is devoted to the work in progress for improvement in the sanitation of the Madeira Valley. It is evident that definite results are being attained in this work, and this is one of the most promising facts in connection with the great enterprise now developing for opening the Bolivian rubber field to the world.

It is not unreasonable to suppose that ultimately the Madeira region will become as habitable as the now populous Mississippi Valley in the United States, a region which Charles Dickens, in his "Martin Chuzzlewit," not longer than 65 years ago, felt called upon to warn the world against.[3]

In the same issue of the *Marconigram,* the editor expressed some sensitivity about criticism he received:

None but the initiated know the accuracy required in a printing office. The average reader who detects a misspelled word or letter upside down feels that his mission on earth is not accomplished until he has called the attention of the overworked editor to the glaring defect. He does not notice the thousands and tens of thousands of letters that are in place or the multitude of words correctly spelled, but his eagle eye is glued on the one that is out of place.

So it is with our deeds. Man does a thousand good deeds and no attention is paid to them, but if he makes one mistake it is flashed all over the world. A life-time may be spent in building up a reputation that may be wrecked in a moment. The world is a harsh critic, exacting to a fault.

Moral—Avoid that one mistake.[4]

American railroad workers celebrating the Fourth of July in 1909.
Photo by Dana Merrill, courtesy of the Foundation of the National Library of Brazil.

Kravigny took over the responsibility of the publication of the *Porto Velho Times* when the former editor fell ill. He continued to publish the paper using a typewriter for several weeks. Typing the issues was a very slow and tedious operation. The typist was limited to producing five or six copies at one time using carbon paper; making additional copies—while routine work—was always a problem. Only after Kravigny returned to the United States in 1910 did the newspaper become the *Marconigram,* from which we were able to identify many of the photographs in this book.

In *The Jungle Route,* Kravigny tells us that the newspaper got a new look for a specific festive occasion:

> Of particular interest in Porto Velho was the celebration of Independence day in this far off clime where the hearts of these American pioneers beat all the faster in the realization of the distance from their homeland, here in the impenetrable jungles. On this July 4th, 1909, we inaugurated and published for the first time in printed form, the *Porto Velho Times,* which had hitherto been issued in typewritten form, and which was now entered in the Post Office as first class matter....

"Modern" conveniences at the engineering camp: "You are next in the shower."
Left to right: Mauel, Kyte, Dodd, Schmidt, and W. H. Bennett.
Photo by Dana Merrill from the Gary Neeleman collection.

On the eve of the Fourth, hope for the scheduled appearance of the special edition was dimmed by the discovery that our printing press was of French make, unfamiliar to anyone, even to myself, who had had some experience with American presses. The difficulty was overcome finally by having one of the master mechanics take the press apart until we were able to lock the form on the bed of the press, and then re-erect it again. Some years later I saw a press of this type and was shown that there was a simple gadget that merely required the pressure of a finger to release the part that, at that time, would have saved several hours work for a locomotive mechanic in Porto Velho.[5]

By 1909 the Farquhar Syndicate had invested heavily in electrical power and shower and bathing facilities and had made sanitary improvements that did not exist anywhere else in the region. However, for the Farquhar Syndicate even to expect to capitalize on its huge investment, it had to anticipate and contend with the indomitable forces of nature.

Railroad supervisors Jekyll, Randolph, May, and Dose.
Photo by Dana Merrill from the Gary Neeleman collection.

A "white-collar" Sunday gathering on the railroad line. Left to right: F. J. Reedy,
R. B. Mantor, D. C. Cutler, Dr. Andrews, J. M. Robinson, H. F. Dose,
Marion Hills, A. McLeod Miller, Otto Schmidt, and E. A. Blakeslee.
Two men in the background of the photo are unidentified.
Photo by Dana Merrill from the Gary Neeleman collection.

Left to right: Willian Emriah and Dana Merrill in Porto Velho in 1909.
Photo by Dana Merrill, courtesy of the Foundation of the National Library of Brazil.

Mules trapped in high water during the rainy season.
Photo by Dana Merrill from the Gary Neeleman collection.

Candalaria Hospital in 1910 with this caption: "At Candelaris, on the bay,
/The home of the sick and the sore—/Where they go get well, from a fever spell,/
Or never leave there anymore."
*Photo by Dana Merrill, courtesy of the Miriam and Ira D. Wallach Division
of Art, Prints and Photographs, New York City Public Library.*

Farquhar himself lived in Rio and reportedly never visited Porto Velho. His construction supervisors for the railroad—May, Jekyll, Randolph, and Dose—lived in a camp based in Santo Antonio near the railhead.

Porto Velho lies in an area flooded by the Madeira River. During the wet season, the river rises forty-six feet and ocean-going ships can sail up it. In the dry season, however, only flatboats can be used. Kravigny wrote in his diary about another challenge created by the rainy season:

> Of course, no story of the Amazon jungles (or for that matter of the Long Island marshes or the Jersey meadows) would be complete without some mention of the mosquito. The principal weapon in fighting this menace was quinine—the watchword both in and out of Candelaria. This important drug was the product of the cinchona bark of the trees of the Bolivian and Peruvian jungle lands. First found there in 1881, its cost of $400 a ton was later greatly reduced when the East Indies successfully produced this product more cheaply. The reduced cost, a boon to the sick, was a heavy economic blow to the Amazonian gatherers. But with the death of the cinchona boom, began the contemporary rise of the rubber boom, which was destined to follow the same curve of depression when the East Indies again proved a more economical producer of this product.[6]

Candelaria Hospital.
Photo by Dana Merrill from the Gary Neeleman collection.

Porto Velho had its own hospital to contend with illnesses such as malaria and yellow fever from mosquitoes. The Candelaria Hospital, built to provide services for a city of seventy-five thousand people when the original worker population was only four thousand, was a sign of things to come. The hospital boasted modern medical equipment on a par with anywhere in the Americas.

The *Porto Velho Times*, of Sunday, August 15, 1909, described the hospital this way:

> Our hospital at Candelaria comprises at present, fourteen buildings, consisting of a doctor's residence, nurses' residence, officers' ward, surgical ward, three laborers' wards, small wards for septic and contagious diseases, kitchens, etc.
>
> The rooms of the officers' ward are spacious and well-appointed, containing twenty-five comfortable spring beds. About the building is a large corridor with a number of convalescent chairs which patients whose illness does not confine them indoors may occupy. Both medical and surgical cases are treated in this ward....

Convalesing at Candelaria.
Photo by Dana Merrill from the Gary Neeleman collection.

Candelaria Hospital building.
Photo by Dana Merrill from the Gary Neeleman collection.

The treatment received by the patients is the very best, the food excellent and the doctors and nurses and all employees of the hospital unite in their efforts to make it as comfortable and as cheerful as possible. Candelaria is a most desirable place for the sick, and judging by the reluctance with which most discharged patients leave it, it is also a good place for the well.[7]

The following statistics give an idea of the number of deaths at Porto Velho. Note, however, that the death rate decreases for each succeeding year:

Year	No. Employees	Deaths per Year	Per Thousand
1909	4000	500	125
1910	4000	417	90.65
1911	4600	390	84.78
1912	3142	222 (est.)	70.65 (est.)[8]

As the construction of the railroad progressed, many of the workers became infected with malaria and yellow fever. Very little was known at that time about these diseases. As a result, the railroad company set up quarantine areas for those afflicted, some of which were on islands in the Madeira River. Thousands died of these illnesses.

This poem succinctly describes the plight of many railroad workers.

Just a few simple words of comfort, to our fellow sufferers from Quarantine.
by R. S. S[tout]

Welcome, gentle strangers,
You've come a long way here—
To earn a little money,
In this land of fever drear.

Welcome, foolish strangers,
You're due to get real sick,
We're sorry, but we've been there too,
And it does no good to kick.

Welcome, homesick strangers,
You're due to get that too—
And soon all colors look alike—
They'll all have changed to Blue.

Three months later!

Farewell, ye homebound strangers,
Strangers—to your health—
But strangers not, to fever—chills,
BUT TO YOUR FORMER SELF.[9]

Quinine was the only known treatment for malaria, and the rail company imported a world record of twenty-five tons of quinine at one point to treat its workers. The workers were obliged to take up to thirty grains of quinine a day to avoid malaria, and the rule was that if someone did not drink boiled water and take his quinine, he would be exiled from the camp into the jungle, or "even shot." These iron-clad regulations were fiercely enforced to keep infections from spreading through the camp.

In fact, the *Porto Velho Times* of Sunday, June 6, 1909, and Kravigny's memoirs tell that arriving workers were taken to a quarantine island until the medical team could clear them.

> The Quarantiners were let off the Island on Wednesday last—twenty-two white men and one hundred and eighty-seven laborers.
>
> Dr. Emrich was in charge of the Island and reports that on the first day, Spanish cooks struck for cigars, cigarettes and beer, wine, and other little necessities of that sort. They claimed that they had been receiving all these things while en route, and they would cook no more unless they were supplied with them—"Caramba!," etc.
>
> The doctor led them gently to understand that they were not on a Sunday School picnic, although they could hardly be blamed for thinking so, seeing that some of the kindergarten candidates were along, and that if they would not cook, they certainly would not eat, and that with every kick they made, he would deprive them of some item of their daily bill of fare. When at last, with fresh meat and other little things of that sort denied them, they were living on bolacha, xarque and coffee, they became so tame that they came and ate out of the doctor's mitt. Give a Spaniard an inch and the sky is the limit.
>
> It became necessary, however, to make a dead line and place a guard around the white men's quarters at night, and when the Czar of all the Island made his rounds one evening, he found a certain young man fresh from his mother's side in the states, asleep and his rifle pointing toward China, instead of Spain in the dust. The other tenderfoot on guard, suddenly awoke and explained that he was keeping guard for both, but alas and alack, 'twas an empty gun that afforded protection to all those sleeping innocents.
>
> At another time, the camp was thrown into great excitement when an hombre unknowingly crossed the fatal line and Mr. First Time From-Home fired point-blank at him, but fortunately his knowledge of firearms came exclusively from the show windows on Broadway, and he succeeded only in frightening half to death that poor Spaniard who probably thought Uncle Sam had declared war on Spain.[10]

Cemetery at Candelaria in Porto Velho.
Photo by Dana Merrill, courtesy of Museu Paulista, University of São Paulo.

A medical doctor, Dr. C. J. Wilson, described the frequency of death from the fever like this:

> It was no rare thing for one-half of those making a trip in the fever area to be stricken and die in the course of a few weeks. In one case a party of forty started, and twenty-seven died during the journey.
>
> In another case the question of anchorage for the night was being discussed. Some of the crew were known to be dying. "No; don't stop here,"

Candelaria Hospital building.
Photo by Dana Merrill from the Gary Neeleman collection.

one trader responded to a suggestion. "There is a good piece of soft ground a bit higher up, and we can plant these fellows (the dying 'boys') more easily." They did so, and the graves were marked by a simple little wooden cross, replicas of which can be found all over the district, which has claimed so many victims. In that area Dr. Wilson found practically everyone suffering from a mild form of ague or fever, but he and his companion both came through without contracting the sickness.[11]

In addition to the hospital, many other buildings were erected in Porto Velho to house the railroad administration. Kravigny describes them this way: "the 'Mad House' Annex, which despite its name was a very pleasant two-story frame building, containing some twelve rooms on each floor, each with comfortable iron beds, two men occupying a room. The rooms opened out on to a fully screened verandah, that extended all around the building; the upper floor being a duplicate of the lower." There were other names given to buildings in the compound, such as the "Brain House," the "Bull Pen," and the "Wise House."[12]

Candelaria Hospital building.
Photo by Dana Merrill from the Gary Neeleman collection.

Life wasn't all bad in Porto Velho, even at the hospital, and an example comes from the *Porto Velho Marconigram* of December 31, 1910, entitled, "Christmas at Candelaria."

> To realize one was five thousand miles from home was a hard task for those that sat down to dinner at Candelaria last Saturday evening.
>
> To his reputation for the curing of physicals ills his guests unanimously presented all honors for the curing of the mental ailments as well.
>
> The evening was inaugurated by fourteen hungry but happy guests of Dr. Lovelace, and it wasn't many moments before all forgot their hunger through their happiness.
>
> Tributes must be paid to "Mamma's fair haired boy" who did his best to live up to his reputation, and succeeded, to the silent (?) members of "the cave" and last, but second only to our host, "The Ladies."
>
> After dinner, which all survived most beautifully, the balance of the evening was devoted to dancing and the celebration of the passing of another mile stone—(number 22) of one of the party.

About 9:30, the dancing was interrupted by a serenade to Dr. Lovelace by the Spanish and Barbadian laborers of the hospital, followed by the "not to be outdone" Chinese contingent, a trifle small in quantity but equal to all in quality and sincerity.

The dawn of Christmas, 1910, will long be remembered by the fifteen, who heartily agreed that life in Brazil is far from being as black as it is painted. The table: Dr. Lovelace, Miss Hardy, Mr. Garnett, Dr. Fitch, Mr. Foley, Miss M. Hardy, Dr. Whittaker, Mrs. Farrell, Dr. Forsythe, Mr. Smith, Dr. Walsh, Mr. Heflin, Dr. Garnett, Mr. Putland, Miss Irwin.[13]

One of the pastimes of the workers was to write poetry. Careful reading of these unique poems gives us an insight into the thoughts, hopes, dreams, and sometimes desperation that came from working on the line. Here are three poems that were written about Porto Velho.

My Babies
by R. S. S[tout]

I never see a baby, in
The Porto Velho Streets—
Of all the world, a baby is—
The sweetest of the sweets.

I never see a baby here,
But maybe it is best—
For babies lives are very dear,
And those who have them, blest.

I have a little nephew home,
And a darling little niece—
Each certainly is, the sweetest kid,
That life e'er gave a lease.

I love them, oh how dearly—
I'd give the world, if I
Could buy a great big airship,

And back to loved ones fly.

When I go home, I'll take them—
A lot of pretty things,
I think I hear them calling me,
Their childish laughter rings.

Ah, Home Sweet Home, that is the place,
Where all of us should be—
But sad to say, though 'tis the truth—
There's no "sweet home" for ME.[14]

The Greatest of All—Porto Velho
by R. S. S[tout]

Of all the countries that border the sea,
The greatest of all, it seems to me—
Is the one where marsh and swamp hole dank,
Place death by fever in very first rank—
In Malaria, Great—over all—First Rate—
Brazil.

Of all the rivers that run to the sea,
The greatest of all, it seems to me—
Is the one that is long, and deep, and wide—
Where you can't see across to the other side—
The Mighty—the Great, over all, First Rate—
The Amazon.

Of all the towns far from the sea,
The worst of all, it seems to me,
Is a place on Madeira—broad and long,
Where all things seem to be dead wrong—
In sickness, Great—over all, First Rate—
Porto Velho.[15]

A Porto Velho Awakening
by R. S. S[tout]

At just about this time of year,
In April and in May,
My thoughts are wont to wander—
Toward San Francisco Bay.

Just now, the rain's all over—
The sun is shining bright—
The ocean breeze blows fresh and strong,
All nature's at her height.

In fancy I am standing there,
Out near the Golden Gate—
I watch the sun sink in the sea,
Too soon the hour grows late.

I walk along the beach sways,
Communing with my thought—
When suddenly, o'er land and sea,
A miracle is wrought.

The silvery moon, has just escaped,
From out a Fleecy cloud—
All space is flooded in moonlight—
The earth takes on her shroud.

I'm dreaming of that scene sublime,
I'm happy as can be—
When I wake up, and look around,
And Porto Velho see.

My pulse takes on a score of beats,
My head aches, oh so mad—

My temperature goes up in leaps,
My stomach's awful bad.

And all of this, because I know—
I've got to stick it out—
For money's lure, has got me sure—
For me—no river route.[16]

CHAPTER 4

The Workers

When Percival Farquhar won his sixty-nine-year concession to engineer and build the Madeira-Mamoré Railroad in 1907, he wasted no time in pushing the project forward. Flush with investments from the United States and Europe, he hired thousands of workers from all over the world. The Panama Canal was nearing completion, and experienced tropical workers became available. Farquhar brought many of them up the Amazon River—more than seventeen hundred miles—to the city of Porto Velho on an old steamship called the *Estrada de Ferro Madeira--Mamoré.* Many came from Barbados, Trinidad, Cuba, and other Caribbean Islands. Men from Galicia, Spain, known as "hombres," were considered the hardest workers of all.

The boats carrying workers stopped along the way to pick up food products from native Brazilians. The workers even shot alligators as they moved upriver. Some of the boats were small steamships and had hammocks on the decks where the workers slept. In addition to the railroad workers, many of the passengers were *seringueiros,* who were employed to tap the rubber trees.

As the workers arrived in Porto Velho—after days on the Amazon, then up the Madeira—they soon discovered the river itself was one of their first great challenges. The river rose during the rainy season so that steamships could sail right into Porto Velho. However, in the dry season, men and equipment had to be ferried to port on flatboats.

The translation of *madeira* is "wood," and the river got its name because during the wet season, the high water literally swept the surrounding jungle of all fallen trees and undergrowth and carried it downstream into the Amazon.

When the foreign workers finally arrived in Porto Velho, they encountered their most difficult challenge: malaria and yellow fever. The workers soon realized the reality of their new world.

The steamship Estrada de Ferro Madeira-Mamoré.
Photo by Dana Merrill from the Gary Neeleman collection.

The chunky and dependable Madeira-Mamoré, a wood-burning, screw-propeller
steamship, starts her seven-day voyage upriver. Lashed alongside
is a barge carrying a hundred laborers.
Photo by Dana Merrill from the Gary Neeleman collection.

A small Amazon steamboat.
Photo by Oscar Pyles from the Gary Neeleman Collection.

Frank Kravigny relates the source of one national group of workers:

A new source of labor was sought by the railroad company, and it was proposed by a German engineer on the job that he should seek a supply of men
in Germany. Towards the end of 1909, preceded by many startling rumors,
one of the stern-wheelers arrived at Porto Velho with several hundred men
recruited from Germany on board. They were a good type of men as that
class of laborer goes, but of a more determined disposition than the Latins
and the blacks, to which we had become accustomed.

Apparently these men had gained the impression that they were going to
a veritable Garden of Eden to help build a railroad. At the various stops along
the Amazon River, their disillusionment had so increased that when they finally reached Porto Velho, they refused to disembark except under their own
terms, part of which were that the contractors would return all those unwill-
ing to remain, to Germany. The refusal to meet these demands was accompanied by notice that no further food would be issued to the boat. By this time,
organized and armed, the Germans announced that they were coming ashore
to take what food they needed, by force. It was then that I received orders to
repair to the material stores, where I was placed on guard duty with Rowlee
and one other man. We were given instructions to shoot to kill anyone who

American security guards.
Photo by Dana Merrill, courtesy of the Foundation of the National Library of Brazil.

attempted to enter the stores. A guard had been placed at all the other supply buildings as well. A parade of armed civilians in full view of the boat had its effect, and at this point, the authorities assumed a conciliatory attitude that satisfied some of the demands of the Germans, and saved us from participating in a civil war in the jungle.

Very few of the Germans elected to remain and a great part of them went down the river again by various means. One group of nine attempted to float down the river with the current, on an improvised raft. None of them were ever heard of alive, and the heads of five were later found floating on the river. Their chances of reaching the coast on a raft would have been slim in any case, in this land of the alligator and the deadly mosquito, even if they had not had to pass through the country of the unfriendly Paratintin Indians and the Acanga Pirangas (Red Heads) of the Jamary River. When word of this experience reached Germany, the German government put a stop to further emigration of this sort.[1]

About this same time, several other countries heard about the disease, death, and other problems and also banned emigrants from working on the Madeira--Mamoré Railroad. These countries included Portugal, Spain, Italy, and even Cuba.

A group of American engineers.
Photo by Dana Merrill from the Gary Neeleman collection.

An unknown worker penned this verse:

Way up in the jungle
Where the Madeira River flows,
Where tarantulas by the thousand
And the Palm and Rubber tree grows;
There's a gang of railroad builders
Working just as hard as can be,
To complete a railroad
To take the rubber to the sea;
They are working in the morning,
They are working still at noon,
And some nights you'll find them working
By the light of the bloomin' moon;
They're over in the tropics
In a country far away
But they're here to build a railroad
Called the Madeira-Mamoré.[2]

An ants' nest built of mud on the trunk of a tree.
Photo by Dana Merrill from the Gary Neeleman collection.

The vast array of personnel that worked on the Madeira-Mamoré Railroad between 1907 and 1912, when it was completed, was like a huge kaleidoscope of the human race. Although Americans were responsible for most of the engineering and administration, the construction workers came from all over the world. Some of them—like those recruited from the Panama Canal—were experienced in working in the tropics. Others, who came from countries in Europe and the United States in search of adventure and money, were not nearly as well prepared for the challenges of the jungle.

Some accounts told that the jungle was so dense along the Madeira River that it was almost silent during periods of the day. Other stories said that after night fell, workers were terrified by the howls and screams of jungle animals and birds, which not only affected their sleep and nerves but also created psychological problems.

American engineers and doctors.
Photo by Oscar Pyles from the Gary Neeleman collection.

The jungle is filled with the varied architecture of the ants. Some of their "buildings" stand four or five feet high. The challenges of Mother Nature in this unusual part of the world included ants as much as an inch long, spiders like crabs, and beetles as large as a man's hand.

The monkey population of the jungle was greater than any other animal life. Frank Kravigny tells us, "It was a very small type of monkey that I once observed that left me very doubtful of the authenticity of the statements that there were Indian tribes who practiced the shrinking of their human victims' heads."[3]

The number-one menace in the jungle was the malaria-carrying mosquito, which also caused yellow fever and blackwater fever, but the workers also suffered from beriberi, which they treated by eating oranges and grapefruit. The camp had a rule that every worker had to be in his mosquito-net-draped bed in his tent by 6:00 p.m. each evening, when the swarming insects descended on the camp, biting through clothes and covering the workers' hands and faces. Fleas and ticks, wasps and bees tormented the workers around the clock.

In the Madeira River lived fish called *paraíba* that were, in some cases, three meters long. These giant catfish attacked canoes and even men who were swimming.

Former Confederates at home in the Amazon. Many of them migrated to Brazil
from the American South between 1866 and 1910.
Photo by Dana Merrill, courtesy of the Foundation of the National Library of Brazil.

There were also alligators, poisonous snakes, piranhas, and electric eels that could
kill a man.

Among the workers from dozens of nations, it was reported that a group of
Freemasons came to work on the railroad. In fact, the Freemasons had a large gathering of their members on June 24, 1909, in Porto Velho. The fact that the Brazilian
emperor, Dom Pedro II, was a Mason, and the group of seven thousand U.S. southern Confederates who settled in Americana, Brazil, in 1866 were also Masons may
explain Porto Velho's association with Freemasons. In the little Cemitério do Campo between Americana and Santa Bárbara d'Oeste in the state of São Paulo, several
hundred Confederates are buried, and many of the tombstones have Masonic em-
blems. Although most of these southern U.S. Masons were also Southern Baptists,
they were very much involved in Masonry.

Many of the pictures in this book came from Oscar Pyles's belongings; he was
a descendent of the Pyles Confederate immigrant family, which settled in Amer-
icana/Santa Barbara about 1867–68. Colonel George Earl Church was a Union
officer in the Civil War, and obviously other young men from the Americana colony like Pyles were recruited because of their construction skills and experience.
It is well known that the transcontinental railroad in the United States benefitted

A section of track near camp 24.
Photo by Dana Merrill from the Gary Neeleman collection.

A Brazilian hunter.
Photo by Dana Merrill from the Gary Neeleman collection.

greatly from veterans of the Civil War—both from the North and the South. The Madeira-Mamoré Railroad most likely also profited from experienced U.S. Civil War veterans.

There was really no recorded practice of religion among the workers during the construction of the railroad. No churches existed in Porto Velho at that time, and with the huge diversity of races and nationalities, no one church could have served all of them. One administrator said, "Religion was not conducive in the jungle environment."

As the railroad moved forward into the jungle, workers traveled by foot, wagons, horses, and saddle mules. Once the tracks were laid, handcars on the rails moved men from camp to camp and provided a means for railroad administrators to visit camps along the line with less difficulty.

The daily diet for the workers consisted mainly of meat, rice, and beans. Eggs were rare and sought after. Kravigny reprints this poem that came from the August 15, 1909, edition of the *Porto Velho Times*.

Eggs!
(To be sung to the tune of Auld Lang Syne)

I had an egg, long, long ago,
'Way back in the days gone bye,
But now dear friends, I see no mo'
It almost makes me cry.

Chorus
Oh think of it and ponder long,
And wonder if we'd die,
If all the chickens in the world
Would come a'floating by.
But that's a flight of fancy, boy!
Come back to earth again
Just be contented with one look
From the track of a hospital hen.

II
They say that patients get fried eggs,

The Caripunan Indians carry all their personal belongs in crude bark canoes
on their nomadic migrations.
Photo by Dana Merrill from the Gary Neeleman collection.

A nest of alligator eggs found along the riverbank. The natives pick
up dead alligators and sell their hides downriver.
Photo by Dana Merrill from the Gary Neeleman collection.

To help them get robust,
But what's the use of grumbling so,
And trying to bust that trust.

(Now all together boys)
Oh think of it and ponder long, etc....[4]

Kravigny describes the diet that sustained him and the other workers in the camp.

Also attached to the camp was a Brazilian hunter, whose sole occupation was
to secure fresh meat from the jungle for our table. The most general diet was
one of tapir meat. I have also eaten in this camp, anteater *(Tamandua),* monkey, parrot, peccary, turkey, a small species of deer, armadillo, and a bird similar to the melanistic mutant pheasant, which the New Jersey Fish and Game
Commission has released in recent years in its game-stocking program for
hunters. Less frequently seen was the jacou, a near relative of the English
ring-necked pheasant, but of larger size. The jungle bird was a blackish one,
of the size and shape of our domestic Guinea hen. I found all the meat very

A family of Caripunan Indians.
Photo by Dana Merrill from the Gary Neeleman collection.

palatable, except that of the anteater. The greatest difficulty was the necessity for immediate consumption of all the meat. Because of the climate they were unable to age the meat and we were forced to have it cooked while quite fresh. In the case of the tapir meat particularly, this practice resulted in slight stomach disorders, but they seldom had any lasting effect.[5]

Although some reports claim local Indians in the region harassed the workers, other accounts state that the Indians in that area, the Caripunas, were by and large very peaceful and created few problems. In fact, the Indians liked trading with the workers and brought meat and fish to trade for shoes, clothing, and trinkets. Railroad administrators warned the workers not to trade for guns or alcohol as this inevitably led to problems among the Indians, as well as with workers on the line.

Caripunan Indians at Mutum Paraná.
Photo by Dana Merrill from the Gary Neeleman collection.

A group of Caripunan Indians at Três Marias.
Photo by Dana Merrill from the Gary Neeleman collection.

Here is a description of the Caripunan Indians from Kravigny:

> Mostly of plump figures, particular attention was drawn to their distended
> abdomens, a condition induced by their starchy diets and alternate feasts and
> famines. They did not possess the red skins of the North American Indians,
> but their complexion was that of the natives of the shores of the Mediterra-
> nean Sea. In many instances their features could be called negroid. Some of
> them had curly hair, but not kinky, although there were as many with straight
> hair, which was black in all cases.[6]

Kravigny also gives a good example of the workers' relationship with the Indians in his diary:

> At that time no one had any good pictures of the Indians or knew much
> about the Caripunas except from hearsay. The chief engineer was very anx-
> ious to get some pictures for his report and these he got when a Dutch supply

A Caripunan Indian family escorted by Dana Merrill (on the left).
Photo by Dana Merrill from the Gary Neeleman collection.

ship arrived in Porto Velho with railroad supplies. That captain, who knew the country into which he was going, had filled all his available cargo space with various sorts of supplies he thought would sell. He did a wonderful business, selling everything from champagne, shoes and clothing, to candy. Merrill had bought some wild-colored pyjamas from this ship's store, and as soon as the Caripuna chief had a look at them he was lost. The Chief got the pyjamas, and Merrill got some pictures as well as a much prized bow and arrows. The Chief donned the pyjamas at once, and became the envy of all his braves.[7]

Not only did the worker crews consist of men from many nations around the world, but there were also outlaws and criminals from the United States and other countries. In the words of one of the administrators of the railroad, "Here there is no law, and every man carries a gun." Because there was no formal way of prosecuting men who committed crimes, railroad officials administered harsh penalties such as crushing a finger or ear so people could recognize that the person was a criminal.

Every railroad worker carries a gun.
Photo by Dana Merrill from the Gary Neeleman collection.

Following is an example of the atmosphere in the camps from the English-
-language newspaper, the *Porto Velho Marconigram:*

> The Hon Mayor of the Mad House at Jaci resigned his office on Sunday in
> favor of sharpshooter Davis, a prominent member of the bridge gang, who
> immediately took the chair and a farewell reception was given the parting
> Mayor.
>
> The camp at Jaci is practically deserted as there is nothing left but the
> bridge gang, two Chinamen and a yellow dog.
>
> Nigger Richie and Eagle Eye Bill, two prominent members of the bridge
> gang are recuperating at Candelaria.
>
> The rattling of the air guns at Jaci is a sure sign that the bridge is drawing
> near to completion.[8]

Payday was the most important day of the month. Workers were paid $125–
$150 U.S. dollars per month in gold, and it was a tradition following payday that the
workers gathered in the camps and engaged in poker games. Many of the men lost

A line doctor, timekeeper, and members of a section gang head out
to protect the payroll from Caripunan Indians.
Photo by Dana Merrill from the Gary Neeleman collection.

their entire month's wages in these games, and it was a camp regulation that the ultimate winner had to resign his job and return to the United States.

Payday consisted of the paymaster and the timekeeper traveling up the line from the camp with several sacks of cash and the workers gathering around to receive their monthly salaries. Kravigny describes the experiences of paymaster Lombard, as published originally in the August 1, 1909, edition of the *Porto Velho Courier:*

> The difficulty in maintaining communications with the preliminary party of engineers was overcome by the expedient of a monthly trip by Lombard, who was a combination paymaster, dispatch bearer and liaison man. He made the trip on the tenth of each month and returned to Porto Velho just long enough to rest before starting out on the next trip. Lombard, a man six feet tall, weighing about 200 pounds, was of a genial, virile nature, and had been experienced as an express messenger on railroads near the Mexican border in Texas.

Authorities view a completed stretch of track.
Photo by Dana Merrill from the Gary Neeleman collection.

The comparative luxury he enjoyed on the first stages of these trips by
train travel soon became a different story, when after progressively utilizing
boats and mules, he was finally forced to travel on foot and search through
the jungle until he located the preliminary party which was constantly on
the move. Dana Merrill accompanied him on one of these trips and both became lost in the jungle. It was only the keen observation by Merrill of an old
guava jelly tin that he remembered having passed previously on the trail, that
brought them to the realization that they had been backtracking instead of
breaking through an old trail that had become overgrown at the point of
juncture to the one they were on.[9]

Three groups of men were involved in the construction of the Madeira-Mamoré
Railroad: the administrators, mostly Americans, a group that also included the engineers, as well as the surveyors and the medical personal who worked at the hospital and visited the camps; the construction workers, who lay track, culled the jungle,
built the bridges, and maintained the right-of-way. Finally were the rubber tappers,
who provided the reason for building the railroad in the first place.

Battelãos at Morrinhos falls delivering mail.
Photo by Dana Merrill from the Gary Neeleman collection.

It is reported that by 1909, nearly all the workers from the original group, who had started in 1907, had been replaced. The three d's—disease, desertion, and death—had taken their toll, but there were always other men to take their place.

One of the small luxuries of the men working up the line was highly anticipated mail from home. The mail *battelãos* braved the currents and waterfalls of the Madeira to deliver the mail to the camps. One up-line worker wrote about what he and many others dreamed of in the *Marconigram:*

The Woman Who Understands

Somewhere she waits to make you win,
Your soul in her firm white hands—
Somewhere the gods have made for you
The woman who understands.

As the tide went out she found him
Lashed to the spar of despair—
The wreck of his ship, around him,
The wreck of his dreams in the air—
Found him, and loved him, and gathered
The soul of him to her breast;
The soul that had sailed on unchartered sea—
The soul that had sought to win and be free—
The soul of which she was part;
And there in the dusk she cried to the man,
"Win your battle—you can—you can."

Helping and loving and guiding—
Urging when that was best—
Holding her fears in hiding
Deep in her quiet breast—
This is the woman who kept him
True to his standards lost—
When tossed in the storm and stress and strife,
He thought himself through with the game of life
And ready to pay the cost—

Watching and guiding—whispering still,
"Win—you can—and I know you will."

This is the story of the ages—
This is the woman's way—
Wiser than seers or sages,
Lifting us day by day—
Facing all things with a courage
Nothing can daunt or dim;
Treading life's path wherever it leads—
Lined with flowers or choked with weeds,
But ever with him—with him;
Guardian, comrade, and golden spur.
The men who win are helped by her.

Somewhere she waits, strong in belief,
Your soul in her firm white hands;
Thank well the Gods when she comes to you—
The woman who understands.[10]

Here are some more examples of poetry from Madeira-Mamoré Railroad workers written by contributors to the *Porto Velho Times* and the *Porto Velho Marconigram.*

In Far-Away Bolivia
by R. S. S[tout]

At the junction of the Beni-Mamoré
In Tropic South America, far away,
Villa Bella, sleeps and dozes—
Dreams again, and wakes—reposes,
A little Spanish town is she,
And hot as Torrid Zone can be—
In far-away Bolivia.

Full six hundred souls are there,
Counting men and babies bare—
And of foreigners, a few—
English, French, and German too
Three and twenty answer call,
And one American—that's all.
In far-away Bolivia.

MacTaggert is our hero's name,
He did not sigh for name or fame—
He simply was American true—
The same as any one of you—
And to him came a great desire,
That set his brain and heart afire—
In far-away Bolivia.

For Independence Day drew near,
The sixth of August every year.
The American's pride and honor stirred—
When from the other foreigners heard,
That no American Flag e'er flew,
O'er Villa Bella—sad but true,
In far-away Bolivia.

A flag he fashioned, so I'm told,
Just like our patriots of old—
Old Glory, never looked so quaint,
For Stars there were of pure white PAINT—
And Stripes of more than five full feet—
The only flag that ne'er was beat—
In far-away Bolivia

The sixth of August dawned that year,
With noise and patriotic cheer—
And wondering Villa Bella gazed—
As o'er the trees, old Sol just blazed—

Upon those Stars and Stripes of ours,
The grandest flag of all the Powers—
In far-away Bolivia.

Bolivian, French, and English-Dutch,
All loved their flags, and loved them much—
And waved to their heart's content,
But theirs were from their countries sent,
While ours, came from a heart and soul—
And never surer reached the goal—
As in far-away Bolivia.[11]

That Man Who Knows
by R. S. S[tout]

There's the man who knows your business,
Knows it better than you do—
And he's always butting into it,
He's one of those kind who—

If you happen to a doctor be,
You'll run across him often—
He knows all 'bout the only way,
To save you from your coffin.

There's the man who's always knocking,
And who never has a word,
Of good for any one or thing,
Now isn't he absurd?

He's your boss, as often happens,
And he'll rile you up for fair—
By butting into little things,
Till you don't give a care.

If you happen to be postmaster,
And try to do things right—
He'll break the rules, and meddle so—
You'll surely want to fight.

If you're a clerk, and sure have had—
Experiences galore—
There's always one with none at all—
Who thinks he knows much more.

We've got 'em here in Porto Velho,
We have them by the score—
We will not mention any names,
For fear that they'd get sore.

You'll find him everywhere and in—
All classes and condition—
He's too self-righteous e'er to sin—
He'll go to hell—perdition.

We might go on, and tell about
The faults of [sic] others own,
But then you see, we've many too,
Our wild oats were well sown.

So we'll stop here, and "never more"
As Klienpaul used to say,
Will faults of others trouble us—
Unless they stop our pay.[12]

Wood, Stone, and Rubber

When Mr. Stone met Mr. Wood,
One day on old Broadway—

They said "Hello," and stopped awhile,
To pass the time of day.

Just then a pretty damsel passed—
Each thought that he could love her—
Wood turned to Stone, and Stone to Wood,
And then they turned to Rubber.[13]

Here is another poem on a most unexpected subject:

[One of the least inspiring subjects for a poet would seem at first glance to be a railway time-table. But a poet who writes in *McClure's* has found the time-table freighted with "treasures golden" and "hot with passion."]

Lines on a Railroad Time-Table

How very reticent a page it is
To be so hot with passion, and so proud
With treasures golden, guarded, wonderful,
Won in an utter wrath of surging war—
That shrill, terrific war where gray old Time
Went fighting, beaten backward, while the field
Rang with the cries of hammers clamoring!
These leaves are light, but they are whirled before
The very tempest of that Victory.
It is a young, hot, eager, wind, of steel.
And hissing steam, black coal, and human will,
Bursting from cities, dusk Chicago's breath
And Pittsburgh's, panting

What a pageant,
A pomp of strength and moving majesty,
That gale of battle lays upon its path!
A hundred roaring trains go every day

With hasty hands stroking Niagara bridge—
As children stroke a cat November nights
To see the sparks—and leave the long beast purring.
Beyond, out in the Rockies, coupled engines
Stamp smoking up the great mood-flooded grades,
White miles of winter where the old Wind sits
To weave his tapestries in trailing snow,
And all alone he hears the loud train climb.
And morning after morning, when, aflame
And mighty, bent about the sturdy world,
Dawn like a maned sea-breaker rushes down
Off the Atlantic, all those pallid rails
Take heart before it and the brightness runs
To lead the day a three hours' westward chase.
Then farmers wake, and cities, and the land
Stands up, a tall young man in sun-dashed strength,
Son of the world, and turns to search for tasks.
So searched the Colorado when he flung
Away the flimsy bank ten thousand years
Builded and held against him, and peered down
Upon that crisp, embittered Salton land,
And filled himself an ocean for a toy.
—By Joseph Boardman,[14]

Trials of a Doctor on the Line
by A. C. Fitch M.D.

A maiden fair, with raven hair,
Went up the line to 'leven—
There to reside at her brother's side
With cousins, six or seven.

But human ills, such as fever and chills,
Draped in gloom the camp life quickly—

"Candelaris, for you, and P.D.Q.—
This is no place for a girl who's sickly."

To the Medicine man, the relatives ran,
Saying "whither she goeth, go we."
The Doctor said, "well go to Port'Vel—
Throwing all out, won't bother me!"[15]

The Call of the States
by R. S. S[tout]

Oh, for a sight of the USA—
Oh, for a stroll on old Broadway—
Or to linger a while, mid the State Street lights,
Or to promenade Market Street, Saturday nights.

There are only few cities that 'mount to much,
New York, and Chicago, and Frisco, and such—
But the country itself, is the one that is best—
She's better than any—she surely is blest.

For her mountains, and valleys, her plains, and her streams,
With the life of true freedom and glory it teems—
Where its men are more noble, and women more true—
To the Flag of their nation—the Red White and Blue.

So I hear the call sounding, thru thousands of miles,
The call of my country, in Brazil's dreary wilds—
So I'll hasten back shortly, on river and sea,
To the home of my choice—For June 6th, I'll be FREE.[16]

Men at work at kilometer 152.
Photo by Dana Merrill from the Gary Neeleman collection.

CHAPTER 5

Camps and Right-of-Way

Even with thousands of new foreign workers on the job, progress on the railroad was slow, and most of the work had to be done by hand while the workers were still contending with sickness and the ruthless pressure of the Amazon's natural elements.

Percival Farquhar was a tough taskmaster. With his concession contingent on his contract to finish the railroad in four years, he spared no expense. The new hospital with up-to-date equipment, more doctors, qualified engineers, and skilled workers began to make a difference.

Farquhar's plan was to establish work camps from Santo Antonio up the Madeira to the city of Guajará-Mirim, past the nineteen waterfalls. There were more than thirty camps about seven miles apart covering the two hundred miles.

During Colonel Church's ill-fated effort from 1873 to 1884, Robert Ripley claimed in "Believe It or Not: The Road to Ruin" that workers were only able to drive the railroad three miles into the jungle in five years at a cost of six to ten thousand lives, but this time would have to be different.

The first order of business was establishing a right-of-way through the jungle. Of course, the surveyors were the first step.

And then came the engineers.

Beginning in 1907, Farquhar crews began literally chiseling their way through some of the most formidable terrain on Earth. Clearing the right-of-way was rarely a straight shot. Mules had to carry tons of dynamite up the line to blast away mountainsides and huge boulders.

Finally, the critical right-of-way began to take shape. It and the rail bed became the point of reference for workers trying to find their way through the jungle. If they ever became disoriented moving from camp to camp in the dense jungle, it was essential that they find their way back to the right-of-way to avoid perishing.

American engineers.
Photo by Dana Merrill from the Gary Neeleman collection.

Rocks with hieroglyphics on the banks of the Madeira River.
Photo by Dana Merrill from the Gary Neeleman collection.

A view of camp 7 at kilometer 30.
Photo by Dana Merrill from the Gary Neeleman collection.

As fast as the bed was cleared and bridges built, worker crews laid the rails. With the rails in place, workers and engineers used handcars to move supplies and equipment up the line to the camps.

After many months of agonizing effort, there was enough rail to put a locomotive on the track, which could then move more and more supplies and workers from camp to camp—only then did the work begin to show real progress.

The native Brazilian wood was very susceptible to Amazonia termite infestation, which consumed the ties in a matter of months. As a result, not only did the railroad company import wood from Taiwan, but it also acquired eucalyptus trees from Europe and planted them throughout Brazil to use as fuel to power wood--burning steam engines on the narrow-gauge railways. The engineers also used eucalyptus logs for the railroad's crossties because the oil was a buffer against the native termites.

The *Marconigram* newspapers in the old rusty canister helped explain many of Merrill's and Pyles's photos, and the articles describe in detail the struggles of the workers. Although there were reports that the Indians in the area were hostile, the

A surveyor taking a measurement.
Photo by Dana Merrill from the Gary Neeleman collection.

The engineering draft room. Left to right: W. C. Miller, L. V. Manspeaker, Joseph Toplake, Leslie Miner, William Voss, F. J. Torras, and Meade Bolton.
Photo by Dana Merrill from the Gary Neeleman collection.

The quarry at camp 18.
Photo by Dana Merrill from the Gary Neeleman collection.

A cleared right-of-way, ready for tracks, at kilometer 72.
Photo by Dana Merrill from the Gary Neeleman collection.

Filling a washout with dirt.
Photo by Dana Merrill from the Gary Neeleman collection.

The end of the tracks.
Photo by Dana Merrill from the Gary Neeleman collection.

*Marconigram*s contained no account of any hostility demonstrated by the Caripunas. For example, see this story:

> The other day a score of "tame" Bolivian Indians stopped their battelão at Camp 25 and all filed solemnly up the river bank to see the locomotive and train come in. A box car was off the track and the train stood a hundred yards away from the camp, the air brake pump coughing away cheerfully and black smoke pouring from the stack. While the crew was working on the distant car the Indians stood in a silent, stolid group for a full ten minutes and then, being convinced that the thing couldn't move, after all, they all turned and marched in single file back toward the river. Just then the engine gave three shrill toots of its whistles. It was worth an admission fee to see that bunch whirl round and gaze in excited expectation toward the train. The engine backed up a few feet, the car eventually refused to go back on the rails and the train stopped. Still the Bolivians stood and waited. Minute after minute passed by and nothing moved. At last they all turned, as if at a secret signal,

Camp 15 haphazardly sprawls along the tracks.

Photo by Dana Merrill from the Gary Neeleman collection.

The finished tracks at kilometer 1A.

Photo by Dana Merrill from the Gary Neeleman collection.

A worker stands in a culvert at Porto Velho.
Photo by Dana Merrill from the Gary Neeleman collection.

filed down the bank to their battelão and, now thoroughly assured that the train was a humbug, paddled silently away.[1]

Another account from a *Marconigram* of October 22, 1910, explains the challenges the workers faced while in the camps:

At one o'clock Sunday afternoon J. E. James, Chief Timekeeper, and A. L. Marshall, Stenographer, started out on a short hunting trip intending to make a semicircle through the jungle from Porto Velho, coming out at Candelaria. They had made the trip together some time before, but this time they went a little deeper into the jungle—probably 2 kilometers from the river. About four in the afternoon, when they were headed back for Candelaria, Marshall grew suddenly faint and was able to go on only with the greatest difficulty, continually stumbling and falling. James urged him and encouraged him to keep up, but he finally collapsed and then, the fear of spending the night helpless in the jungle overcoming him, he became delirious. James had no *machete* but he built a rough palm bed for the sick man and a palm shack over him, using his bare hands to tear down the necessary vines

A Brazilian native at Três Irmãos.
Photo by Dana Merrill from the Gary Neeleman collection.

Temporary housing at the front end of the tracks.
Photo by Dana Merrill from the Gary Neeleman collection.

and palm. There they stayed all night. The matches were wet and he couldn't build a fire. Towards nine o'clock Marshall became violent and tried to tear down the hut, and from then until morning James struggled with him to keep him quiet.

At daylight Marshall was much worse and appeared to be dying. It became necessary for James to choose between staying at his side till help came or leaving him, unconscious and unprotected from the animals of the jungle, while he made his way in to the hospital for a doctor and assistants. Marshall's weight, about 180 pounds, put carrying him out of the question. He decided to make his way in.

There was no sign of a trail but he made good speed, although he had to stop continually and break down branches to leave a trail to mark the way back after he had secured a relief party. At about seven in the morning he reached the railroad a little above Candelaria where he met a gang working for Arthur Decker. Decker carried word to the hospital, and Dr. Garnett and seven laborers with *machetes* and a stretcher cut their way out to the sick

A mud slide and damaged tracks near Santo Antonio.
Photo by Dana Merrill from the Gary Neeleman collection.

man, James leading the way following the trail of bent and broken branches which he had left to mark a trail. They found Marshall in a serious condition. His heart had nearly ceased to beat and Dr. Garnett worked over him half an hour before they were able to carry him in to the hospital on the stretcher. His delirium continued on Monday and Tuesday. He failed to recognize Mr. Jekyll and Mr. Randolph, and even James appeared as a stranger to him.

Mr. Marshall had spoken of some slight heart trouble recently and it was probably a partial failure of the heart which caused his collapse. Mr. James was badly scratched and all his clothing torn by thorns and brambles, but otherwise he was none the worse for his harrowing experience.

This morning (Saturday) Dr. Lovelace reports that Marshall is getting along splendidly and that a few more days would find him fully recovered.[2]

Another article in the same issue of the newspaper describes the difficulties generated by the rainy season:

The beginning of the rainy season means something more to the men at the front than it does to us in Porto Velho. On the last trip of the Paymaster to camp 24 he saw something of the difficulties they are up against.

Train dispatcher Guilfoyle had told him at [camp] 18 that it had been raining up at [camp] 24 all afternoon, but as no serious difficulty with the track was anticipated the motor started at 8:30 in the evening and drew near 24 about two hours later. The ride over the last five kilometers was like a trip at sea, as the motor swayed and careened over the uneven track, but the rain had ceased. The supply of kerosene had run out at camp 24, so that when they arrived all was dark except for a candle light in a distant barracone [bunkhouse]. The money box, rolls, blankets and slickers were picked up and a start made to walk to the light. Then the rain came, and came hard. Slipping and sliding down the steep clay embankment in the darkness, stumbling over a little bridge and splashing through unseen puddles of water, they made their way to the barracone. A watchman showed where the cots were prepared for the party, and all night they could hear the steady, soaking downpour on the palm roof overhead. A tent next door became overloaded as the canvas sagged to the growing weight and sometime in the night one side fell in, with a crash and a rushing flood of water that startled the sleepers from their beds.

About four in the morning a locomotive whistled, and a minute later Conductor Higgins came in, dripping, and told how he had worked all night to get through from 18 with the swing train. They had stopped eight times with different cars off the track, and he had finally climbed on the engine and come on to 24 for help, leaving the train stuck in the mud near camp 23.

Daylight opened on a dreary and forlorn looking camp. The large open space before the barracones was flooded except for here and there an island of mud. The gray, gloomy sky seemed to rest on the tops of the giant trees and though the hard rain had stopped, there was still a dismal drizzle coming down. Things were a little better on the side track in the woods where Melver, Provo, Thorne, Fallaise, Horsey and other *chefes* slept. In their dry, comfortable box cars with windows and doors all fitted with screens they could laugh at the weather, as well as at the mosquitoes and flies. But they couldn't stay there long. A big gang of laborers was loaded on flat cars at daylight and Engineer Stipp and Conductor Higgins hauled them back toward

Oscar Pyles.
Photo by Oscar Pyles from the Gary Neeleman collection.

the abandoned swing train. This train, loaded with supplies, was due the night before; it did not get in until four the following afternoon.

Another gang, under Provo, was taken by Conductor Thorne and Engineer Nat Fraser over the newly laid rails toward [camp] 25, to continue track laying, but every hundred yards or so they had to stop and "pick up the track." An ambitious but inexperienced youth who had been sent out a few nights before to "pick up the track," took his mission very seriously and not only picked up the track, but brought it bodily *back into camp!*

No wonder one of his laborers exclaimed "Boss, you sure do know Railroadin'!"

This little operation is carried on slightly differently under Mr. Provo's supervision. The train of flat cars loaded with rails and ties is backed up slowly over the yielding track, the ties sinking one by one out of sight in the mud as the weight presses them, until a point is reached where the fill is softer than usual. There the train is stopped, the black laborers tumble off the cars and bring up poles from the piles of brush and lots left at the end of the right of way by the clearing gangs. Fifteen or twenty men take the largest of these and, using it as a lever, pry up one side of the track and hold it about a foot above the ground while other men roll smaller poles under the projecting

Tents at a railroad camp.
Photo by Oscar Pyles from the Gary Neeleman collection.

ends of the ties, laying them parallel to the rails. After a hundred feet or so of track has been so picked up, the train comes creeping over the bolstered rails and the gang rides on to the next soft spot. The end of track was about eight kilometers away. After working all the morning the track gang had only advanced two kilometers from camp. As most of the men were sent down the line in the afternoon to help rescue the stranded swing train, which finally got in at 4:30, the end of track was not reached at all that day.

Melver, limping around camp with a lame foot, was not able to get into all this. He had a chance to use up some of his repressed energy, however, when in the afternoon one of the tents by the track, where some laborers lived, took fire and burned up like a pile of hay. When the Paymaster left, Melver threatened to arrest every man loafing in the camp, tear down all the tents and put every workman on the job in the barracone.

Taylor, Lawton, Lindsay and some more very tired train men were at Camp 22 that night. Some of them had worked twenty hours through the rain and mud, without a bite to eat. And they didn't belly ache about it. Theirs is a man's job, and they all took hold and stuck to it, as Americans have a way of doing. And they got the train through.[3]

Men with a dead ant bear.
Photo by Dana Merrill from the Gary Neeleman collection.

Life in the camps was certainly not dull. It was not all work and no play, either. While not working on the rails, workers had some spare time to fish and hunt, and the fishing sometimes had unexpected consequences.

Much has been written of the many strange specimens contained in Brazilian Rivers. The whole world knows of the alligator but pays little attention to the other strange denizens that infest these inland waters.

The rivers of Brazil fairly teem with fish life, particularly so the Amazon and Madeira Rivers. Occasionally one of these strange specimens is seen or caught and attention is momentarily attracted.

At Candelaria this week a monster fish of the Pirihyba species was caught on a hook and line, that measured seven feet and weighed two hundred and seventy pounds. Shades of Isaac Whalton [sic], what a whopper! His disciples may well gather around and wonder. Several specimens over six feet long have been taken at different times, but this is the biggest on record.

This is no fish story and doubting Thomases may be convinced by a photograph which was taken by a member of the Medical staff and is on exhibition. It is to be turned over to Mr. Merrill, the photographer, for reproduction.[4]

It was difficult to know exactly what to anticipate in the jungle; the workers only knew they should expect the unexpected.

While making the return trip from Camp 16 to Porto Velho, on a hand car, on November 17, Road Doctor Garnett and Timekeeper Hirst were attacked by a vicious ant bear, who, being tired of walking in the heat of the day, decided to take possession of the car. At the first onslaught of the beast the crew on the hand car took to "the shade of the sheltering palms" and left the doctor and timekeeper to defend themselves as best they could. After a short decisive struggle the brute was defeated and put to rout and started to climb a tree, with the doctor, who was by this time thoroughly aroused, in hot pursuit.

Seeing that there was no hope of escape in this way the bear again took to the ground and started up the track, only to be headed off by Mr. Hirst. With Hirst in front and the doctor behind the animal became nonplussed; not so the doctor, seizing the opportunity and the bear's tail he had the enemy in his possession; however, after capturing the animal the doctor was

Men hold a snakeskin twenty-five feet long. Left to right: Knobel, White, Smith, Geraty, Pyles, Johnson, Palmer, DuBois, Poole, Warren, Wood, Merrill, and Hull.
Photo by Dana Merrill from the Gary Neeleman collection.

at loss what to do with him and the captive was all the while battling for his freedom with renewed vigor; he grappled with his captor and with one sweep of his mighty paw tore away part of the doctor's boot, inflicting a slight wound on his leg.

Seeing it was useless to attempt to take the brute alive, Mr. Hirst uprooted a nearby tree and with a few sharp blows on the head quickly dispatched him and the danger was over, but it is unlikely that either of the men will ever forget this thrilling encounter.[5]

Another report from the *Marconigram* on October 15, 1910, describes an equally exciting event:

On Thursday afternoon there was quite a little excitement created around the General Office and the Engineering Department, when four or five hombres were seen coming up the hill bearing the huge folds of a monster reptile.

Evidently his Snakeship intended to investigate what all this noise and hubbub meant and was on his way to Porto Velho. When he was first seen just below the barr[a]cones he was near the railroad on the edge of the Ig-arape. The police force was called out, but a shot from a Winchester did the work. The snake measured a little over 16 feet in length, and 24 inches around. After Sr. Knapp had photographed about twenty men holding the snake up, he was taken by Mr. Wilheim Vass, (who was in at the death), and his skin will go to increase Mr. Vass' collection of souvenirs of his skill with knife and rifle.

A great many expressions as to what would be done should a snake of that size be met with, were heard, and it is not a bad suggestion that some of us who have any fear of running into one, should "change the brand" or cut it entirely.[6]

One day, Dana Merrill, after traveling all day through the swamps with a group of men, offered to hurry ahead and

procure a hand car and crew to fetch the others into camp.... In order to make as good time as possible, he left his gun and other equipment with Dose and Hill.... He had not gone far ...when he was startled to hear something following alongside of him. He could think of only one thing that would keep pace with him in that fashion—and that was a tiger.

Merrill let the tiger approach quite near and then stopped and threw lumps of dirt, which were the only weapons he could find in the darkness, at the beast, shouting at the same time. This halted the tiger for a bit and gave him a chance to put some distance between himself and the animal. He finally reached the place where the ties and rails had been laid, and stumbled along the track. His progress was slow and painful on the unballasted bed, and when he tried to run outside the rails, he found himself rolling down the side of the fill. He found that the track was safer, but would have given anything for his gun, as the tiger came nearer. Suddenly, to his great relief, he saw the lights of the track camp ahead, and by the time he reached it, on the run, the tiger was gone.

The next day, when the resident engineer was riding over the line, looking for possible washouts, his mule either scented or saw the tiger, for he started back for camp and no matter how the engineer tried to stop him, he made straight for the corral.

"Tiger" skin.
Photo by Dana Merrill from the Gary Neeleman collection.

Dressing a wild hog killed by a native hunter near camp 21 in December 1909.
Photo by Dana Merrill from the Gary Neeleman collection.

Several days later one of the hombres shot the "tiger," and secured the pelt. It was a beauty, as I can testify by the photograph Merrill made of it.[7]

Even figuring out what to have for dinner sometimes turned into an adventure.

Great excitement prevailed in this camp on Sunday, October 9th, when Camp Foreman Yale decided on killing a hog for Sunday dinner. The question arose "who would do the killing," whereupon Foreman Doyle and fourth pusher Davis volunteered their services as chief executioners of said porker. Armed with Winchester rifles, loaded to the muzzle, they proceeded to the scene of action. Camp Foreman Yale wished to have hog killed in the pen—Foreman Doyle objected saying, "give him a chance for his life." The hog being turned loose Foreman Doyle raised his deadly rifle to his shoulder and taking deliberate aim at the hog's heart fired, the bullet penetrating the hog just below the tail. The hog becoming enraged at such treatment charged upon his tormentors. Davis hit the trail at a ten second clip, while Doyle

The drink wagon.
Photo by Dana Merrill from the Gary Neeleman collection.

took to the tall timbers climbing up a prickle palm so fast that the prickles did not have time to enter his hide. The hog becoming disgusted took to the railroad track, whereupon Doyle came down from his lofty perch and grabbing his trusty rifle yelled "turn him this way, until I get another shot at him." The last seen of the hog he was crossing the railroad track with Doyle and Davis in hot pursuit a safe distance behind. Doyle and Davis returned about 11 p.m., leg weary and heart broken saying they did not like pork anyway and the rest of the camp agreed with them in regards to *Hog Meat.*[8]

In a place where any kind of convenience was nonexistent, line workers relished every little pleasure—or at least dreamed of possible pleasures they were missing:

Dope

If only the dreams that we like to dream
Were the only dreams to come true;

I wonder what boys on the line would dream—
Just listen, I'll dope it to you;

They dream of a land with hills of crack'd ice
And huge geysers of scotch high-balls;
Of rivers of bourbon, and corn and such
And flunkies awaiting their calls.

Of valleys of bright green crème de menthe,
Where cows give absinthe frappes;
Of parts with fountains of sparkling gin-fiz
And pools of pousse cafes.

Of mint julep marshes, fringed round with green,
Near oceans of champagne clear;
Where rainstorms are naught but heavy downpours
Of amber-like cold German beer.

They'd dream such a dream—and enjoy it too,
As you would; and so too, would I;
But, alas! the heart aches when the sleeper awakes,—
Far better to dream on and die.
—The Black Sheep[9]

The Farquhar Syndicate's effort to provide better working conditions for the men in the camps up the line was recognized by *The India Rubber World* in 1910, as quoted in the *Porto Velho Marconigram*.

> The following article taken from *The India Rubber World* published in New York City is an illustration of the progress we are making in Journalism as well as Railroad Building....
>
> It is no secret that the high cost of rubber from the Amazon has been due largely to the sparse population of that region, and the fact that conditions of life there have been most unattractive to European laborers. Not the least unfavourable condition has been the difficulty of acquiring food of a suitable character and at reasonable prices.

A recent issue of the Porto Velho *Marconigram* devotes most of its space to the question of food supplies in the railway construction camps, where more than 4,000 men are employed, most of whom are from other countries and a number of them professional engineers. It is pointed out in this paper that satisfactory food conditions prevail already, and that there is a continued improvement in this respect. Fresh beef is served to all the camps, being slaughtered and dressed at Porto Velho. An ice making plant is operated successfully. While the vegetables used have been derived in canned shape from the United States, the *Marconigram* mentions: "Lately we have been getting fresh vegetables from a farm about a day's sail down the river and from present indications this farm will probably be able to supply quite a quantity of fresh vegetables. Eggs are brought in by the natives."

It must be taken into account that the successful sanitation and satisfactory food supply at Porto Velho have been due to the work in progress there being on a large scale and under capable scientific and financial control. If each engineer and dirt digger had to look out for himself probably the enterprise would have ended long ago in disaster. The lesson for the rubber interest in South America is the reorganization of rubber camps on a large scale instead of the work being conducted by *seringuieros* singly or in small groups. This change, by the way, is already in progress, and it is reasonable to suppose from indications already apparent that ultimately the food supplies on the better *seringaes* in the Amazon basin will compare favorably with those on farms in the United States. When this new regime becomes better established it is not to be doubted that rubber supplies will be increased, and the cost to consumers materially lessened, while still yielding an adequate profit to the producers.[10]

This poem exemplifies the optimism of at least one of the railroad workers:

Le Futur. With apologies to Kipling.
by B. A. deBourbel

When Earth's last railroad is builded,
And the rails are rotten with rust,
And the oldest "Chief" has departed,
And the youngest contractor is bust—

Preliminary "Farry's camp" at the front of the tracks.
Photo by Dana Merrill from the Gary Neeleman collection.

We shall rest, and faith we shall need it,
Lie down for a noon or two—
Till the master of all good workmen,
Shall put us to work a new.

And those that were good shall be happy—
They shall sit in a Morris chair—
With others to do the work for them,
And sweat and tear their hair.
They shall find the pick of the jobs are theirs
With men at their beck and call—
They shall never do any work again,
And never get tired at all.

And no one shall work for money,
And no one shall work for gain,

A train station along the railroad route.
Photo by Dana Merrill from the Gary Neeleman collection.

Porto Velho in September 1909. In the background is the blacksmith shop and
commissary on the riverbank with concrete piers for the superintendent's house.
Photo by Dana Merrill from the Gary Neeleman collection.

A big tree to the left of the rail line at kilometer 41.
Photo by Dana Merrill from the Gary Neeleman collection.

A camp along the right-of-way.
Photo by Dana Merrill from the Gary Neeleman collection.

A camp along the banks of the Madeira River.
Photo by Dana Merrill from the Gary Neeleman collection.

Straw and canvas houses at camp 29.
Photo by Dana Merrill from the Gary Neeleman collection.

Santo Antonio.
Photo by Dana Merrill from the Gary Neeleman collection.

And no one shall work for honor,
And no one shall work for fame,
But each shall really enjoy himself,
And each in his separate star—
Shall do whatever he wants to do—
Like a little "Tin God" in a car.[11]

Although early twentieth-century historians and those involved in the study of the Amazon have written about the Madeira-Mamoré Railroad, the discovery of more photos by Dana Merrill and unseen photos by Oscar Pyles from the American Confederate community of Americana/Santa Barbara, and the collection of the *Porto Velho Marconigrams* have shed a new, more personal light on the experiences of the railroad builders.

The accounts in this chapter, quoted from the *Marconigrams*, have not appeared in any previous publications about the railroad. These articles provide the reader with a new and colorful account of the day-to-day activities of the workers in the camps along the right-of-way.

CHAPTER 6

Water Challenges

Charles Darwin once said, "No man can stand in the tropic forests without feeling that they are temples filled with the various productions of the God of Nature and that there is more in man than the breath in his body.[1]"

The silk cotton tree is similar to other large trees in the Amazon. These trees as a rule are smooth barked, but they also have another peculiarity. Their roots leave the ground and create a convoluting ribbon effect. About ten feet from the ground, the convolutions cover a circle about fifteen feet in diameter. A fairly large man can stand within any of these larger trees and be well hidden.

When the idea of a two-hundred-mile railroad along the Madeira River was born in the mid-1800s, little was known about the formidable challenges the builders would face. The greatest challenge in the construction of the Madeira-Mamoré Railroad was the vast amount of water in the Amazon Basin. The description of the Amazon jungle as rain forest is an understatement.

The Amazon River carries approximately 20 percent of all of the fresh water in the world, and the Madeira River delivers 20 percent of the water in the Amazon Basin and carries 50 percent of the silt as it tumbles more than five hundred feet down from the base of the Andes in both Bolivia and Peru.

An article published in the *Porto Velho Marconigram* subtitled "Daring Trip by a London Doctor and His Friend—2,000 Miles Journey," begins with the warning given to Dr. C. J. Wilson and J. C. McLean: "You will never make the journey. If you try you will be drowned in the rapids. If you escape drowning you will be killed by Indians; and if you escape both the rapids and the Indians, you will die of the fever." ...

On the subject of rubber cultivation Dr. Wilson said: "There are thousands of miles of rubber trees, and the supply appears to be almost unlimited. But labor is still so scarce, and the distance so great and difficult, that you cannot get the stuff

Silk cotton tree near Três Irmãos.
Photo by Dana Merrill from the Gary Neeleman collection.

Near Mutum Paraná Geral.
Photo by Dana Merrill from the Gary Neeleman collection.

Rough waters nearing Teotônio falls.
Photo by Dana Merrill from the Gary Neeleman collection.

Teotônio falls.
Photo by Dana Merrill from the Gary Neeleman collection.

Near Jirau falls.
Photo by Dana Merrill from the Gary Neeleman collection.

into the market except at a big price, and therefore there will be a good price for years to come."[2]

The purpose of the railroad was to bypass the nineteen waterfalls on the Madeira River, but this task was easier said than done. Not only did the construction engineers and workers have to deal with the huge Amazon River—the first obstacle of their water challenge—but they also had to face and conquer endless swamps, marshes, and streams that crisscrossed the entire area and more than ten feet of drenching rain per year.

The Madeira River is the second-largest river in the Amazon Basin. It has been described as the "jewel of biodiversity" and one of the four most important rivers in the world. The Madeira is formed when the Guaporé, Mamoré, and Beni rivers converge.

> The Madeira, it will be remembered, is the Amazon's greatest tributary. It comes from Bolivia and furnishes about the only outlet for that landlocked republic. From where it enters the Amazon to San[to] Antonio, nearly 500 miles away, it is navigable by ocean steamers. Then come 250 miles of rapids, in which there are nineteen cataracts. When the water is high the big rubber

A view of Teotônio falls, looking down the river.
Photo by Dana Merrill from the Gary Neeleman collection.

scows, or *batelaos* [*sic*], are able to get through by floating part of the way and making portages around the falls, but shooting the rapids. These portages are furnished with narrow gauge tracks. The *batelaos* are unloaded, pulled upon a small truck, and dragged up over the hills, and then eased down on the other side. The return trip involves 25 portages, and three trips a year are all that is possible.

The enormous effort required in moving these heavy boats can hardly be imagined. Every season at low water new roadways must be made by clearing the great boulders out of the river bed, and then laying a corduroy road of green poles, over which the keel of the *batelaos* can slip. Where it is possible they use tackle block to help in the pulling, but sometimes everything must be done by main strength.

There is a loss of 10 to 15 per cent of the rubber sent down by the upsetting of the scows. Not only that but many men are drowned. The *batelaos,* by the way, are flat bottomed scows 30 feet long and 8 feet wide, and carry about 10 tons of rubber. They are manned by 16 paddlers, or *bateleiros,* and usually make the journey down in 20 days, while it takes 60 to return.[3]

Hauling a boat up at Teotônio falls.
Photo by Dana Merrill from the Gary Neeleman collection.

Once the railroad was completed, this same journey over the two-hundred-mile stretch took only twelve hours each way.

The railroad had to contend with all of these challenges under some of the most adverse conditions imaginable. Bridges had to be built, and rails had to be laid through the miles of snake- and insect-infested swamps and marshes.

Frank Kravigny gives us an idea of the engineering challenges:

Around July, 1909, the rails had reached Camp Number 8, fifty kilometers away, and construction was going on beyond Camp Number 16 on the Caricoles River, eighty-eight kilometers from Porto Velho. Definite engineering location of the line had been established beyond what was to be Camp Number 20, on a line inland from the Madeira River about even with Calderon del Inferno and Girau [sic] Falls. The preliminary, or tentative survey much

Hauling a boat up at Teotônio falls.
Photo by Oscar Pyles from the Gary Neeleman collection.

Repairing a washout at kilometer 72.
Photo by Dana Merrill from the Gary Neeleman collection.

Preparing to lay tracks at kilometer 76.
Photo by Dana Merrill from the Gary Neeleman collection.

Hauling battelãos around the falls at Geral.
Photo by Dana Merrill from the Gary Neeleman collection.

A caracolos.
Photo by Dana Merrill from the Gary Neeleman collection.

Porto Velho in 1910.
Photo by Dana Merrill from the Gary Neeleman collection.

further out in the jungle was still under way, no one having any definite idea of how this would eventuate. The usual difficulties of the pioneering engineer were augmented here by the swamps, some of them measured in miles, and by the heavy jungle undergrowth in which the level and transit men established the preliminary topographical facts by calling to their hidden companions, when sighting became impossible.[4]

The modern hospital at Porto Velho struggled to keep the railroad workers healthy.

The headquarters of the construction camp was not at San Antonio, but at Porto Velho, where were assembled from 4,000 to 5,000 men. Of these 300 to 400 were Americans. Here were built substantial quarters for the engineers, bunk houses for the men, an up-to-date thorough equipped hospital, an ice plant, and large storehouses. The company had also drilled wells for the water, and was making every effort to keep the men well. In spite of that

Pharmacy at the Candelaria Hospital.
Photo by Dana Merrill, courtesy of Museu Paulista, University of São Paulo.

there were sometimes nearly 300 men in the hospital, and seven to ten doctors and eight male nurses were constantly employed. The experiment of having female nurses were [*sic*] tried, but they were married and carried away so constantly that it was voted a failure.

The camp was under military discipline, and liquor was taboo. In spite of this the native laborers smuggled in more or less "cachaca" [a local alcoholic beverage]. The most troublesome diseases were *beri-beri,* black water fever, and dysentery. Quinine, of course, was the remedy generally used and most potent. It was bought by the ton, and three laboratory men were kept busy from morning until night making it up into pills.[5]

Quinine is a natural drug that comes exclusively from the bark of the cinchona tree. The Quechua Indians of Peru and Bolivia originally discovered the medicinal properties of the cinchona tree, and the Jesuits were the first to bring its benefits to

Europe. Quinine's fever-reducing, pain-killing, and anti-inflammatory effects were lifesaving for those working in jungle environments. Quinine was the first effective treatment for malaria beginning in the seventeenth century and remained the anti-malarial drug of choice until the 1940s.

One of the poems in Dana Merrill's collection sings the praises of the drug.

King Quinine
by R. S. S[tout]

When you have a great big headache,
And your back and legs grow tired—
And you think of home and mother—
Then King Quinine is required.

When you have a burning fever,
And your stomach's out of gear,
Take a dose or two of quinine,
And you'll have naught to fear.

When you have a little jigger,
Right in your great big toe—
Just take a dose of quinine,
It will relieve it so.

When you get a turndown letter,
From your sweetheart in the States—
Take mucho, mucho, mucho quinine,
Until that pain abates.

When e'er you have a trouble,
Of any sort of kind—
Take thirty grains of quinine,
And relief you'll surely find.

Take thirty grains—take thirty more—
You hear this left and right—

Boats at Santo Antonio.
Photo by Dana Merrill from the Gary Neeleman collection.

It is enough to make you sore,
And swear with all your might.[6]

Along the two-hundred-mile route up the Madeira past the waterfalls, workers were constantly confronted with the near-impossible task of laying the rails over swamps and marshes—some of them several miles long. Forward progress stood still until the workers found a way to stabilize the right-of-way so that the locomotive and railcars could safely move on. On many occasions, workers had to move outside the swamp to make the line secure. Once the route was stabilized, they linked up the two sections. To lay the tracks across swampy ground, workers cut down trees and placed them along the rail bed over tons of brush and debris.

Among the innovations that helped move the railroad forward was the wireless telegraph. Without this relatively new invention, communication with the camps up the line would have been impossible. With it the railroad supervisors in Porto Velho were able to track the railroad's progress along the two-hundred-mile stretch and attend to the sometimes-urgent needs of the workers.

The amazing wireless had other advantages as well. An article that appeared in the *Porto Velho Marconigram* on January 7, 1911, relates another valuable contribution:

Constructing a bridge at Mutum Paraná; the first bridge is wood to be followed by metal.

Photo by Dana Merrill from the Gary Neeleman collection.

The bridge at Jaci Paraná, ninety kilometers south of Porto Velho.
Photo by Dana Merrill from the Gary Neeleman collection.

On December 11th the old Gardener at Porto Velho reported to the General Office that he had been robbed the night before of nearly two contos of reis. He stated that he suspected his room mate who was missing that morning. As the *S.S. Campos Salles* had sailed late the night of the robbery the Manaos office was advised by wireless giving the man's description.

On arrival of the *Campos Salles* at Manaos Mr. Chambers, our genial Purchasing Agent was on the job and discovered a man that answered the description. He (the man—not Chambers) was turned over to the police and Porto Velho received the following wireless message:

"Refer to your telegram of the 12th. Spaniard with cut above nose and pox marked was arrested on arrival of *Campos Salles*. Gave name Joaquim Lagos, 23 years. Found on him 1,540$000 [cruzeiros] and 85 pesos. Also a hospital ticket bearing name of Manoel Rodriguez. Have you any evidence against him, otherwise will be liberated to-day."

In the meantime the Gardener had left for Manaos on *S.S. Madeira-Mamore,* not doubting the effectiveness of our force at Manaos and the eagle eye of that Chambers, Manaos was informed that evidence was on the way and Mr. Pox Marked was held.

Paredao.
Photo by Dana Merrill from the Gary Neeleman collection.

Jirau falls.
Photo by Dana Merrill from the Gary Neeleman collection.

On the arrival of *S.S. Madeira-Mamore* at Manaos, Emilio Perez, the victim, was met by Mr. Chambers and taken around to the police station where he identified the robber. The man confessed and Perez recovered his loss.

That must have been a surprised Spaniard. He had no doubt spent his entire time on the way down river figuring out what he could do with that bunch of wealth back in Spain and instead of his dreams he has been urgently requested to remain as a guest of the police at Manaos for 12 months.

We hope this will serve as a warning to all other would-be-get-aways, tin-horn sports and Get Rich Quick Wallings that may be on the job.

Oh you Wireless. Oh you Chambers.[7]

We end this chapter with another example from the poems collected by Dana Merrill.

Work
by B. A. deBourbel

Work, my brother, always work—
Work goes on forever—

A view of the river near Jirau falls.
Photo by Dana Merrill from the Gary Neeleman collection.

Work and work and never shirk,
Though your jobs may seem to irk,
And tempters ever round lurk—
Work goes on forever.

Work, my brother, while 'tis day—
Work goes on forever.
On this Madeira-Mamoré,
There never is a moment's play.
To pleasures always answer NAY—
Work goes on forever.

Work, my brother, 'tis thy doom—
Work goes on forever.
Work by light and in the gloom—
Work until you reach your tomb—
Other[s] soon will take your room,
For work goes on forever.[8]

Looking toward Porto Velho from Santo Antonio.
Photo by Dana Merrill from the Gary Neeleman collection.

A view of the rapids on the Mutum Paraná River, looking upriver from the
storehouse at Três Irmãos. An Indian in a canoe is in the background.
Photo by Dana Merrill from the Gary Neeleman collection.

CHAPTER 7

The Inauguration and Beyond

Since pre-dawn of history, before the first Abel bore sheep on his shoulders or a Cain garnered his primal harvest, one of man's principal considerations has been how to best slide, roll, push, drag, sail, or propel his possessions in the quickest, quietest, safest manner by the shortest or most feasible route.

Thus transportation has developed from the hand-paddled log to the *Lusitania;* from the thong backpack to the modern Mallet compound locomotive; from hard-beaten forest trails to systematic railroad extension until to-day [1910] man has built enough steel track to girdle the world at the equator twenty-five times. A fifteenth of this track (40,000 miles) stretches across South America, placing it fourth (including Australasia) among the world's continents in point of mileage....

The history of South American railroad development is preeminently a tribute to American engineers and captains of industry.[1]

After so many fits and starts, the railroad was finally completed and fulfilled a fraction of its destiny from 1912 to 1915. Local diaries and reports tell that many of the workers on the railroad—destitute, malaria ridden, or afflicted with other tropical diseases—drifted into Manaus downriver, begging on the streets for financial assistance so they could return to their homes. The infirmary in Porto Velho was packed with sick workers suffering with all kinds of illnesses, many of whom eventually died and are buried in the Porto Velho cemetery. According to turn-of-the--century records and diaries of the administrators of the railroad, three d's created most of the problems during the construction—disease, death, and desertion. The top year for the railroad's income was 1913. After that, it was all downhill.

When the railroad was completed in 1912, the demand for rubber was still high, so it would seem that Percival Farquhar was over the hump. He had boundless energy and a vision that matched that of his predecessor, Colonel George Earl Church. However, by the end of 1913, world events began to catch up with him. Much of

A steam engine.
Photo by Dana Merrill, courtesy of the Foundation of the National Library of Brazil.

Farquhar's capital came from Europe, where he had sold his idea of marrying European capital with American technology to exploit the wealth of the Amazon.

The Balkan War of 1913 and World War I that followed sent shock waves through Europe and brought the Farquhar companies to their knees. According to Farquhar's biographer, Charles Gauld, a combination of Latin American politics, French banks pulling credit lines, and rubber production being transferred to Asia created problems he could not foresee. Ironically, Farquhar did beat the jungle at a tremendous cost, but he could not overcome the tide of world events.

As Farquhar's companies floundered, his creditors sent a court-appointed administrator named W. Cameron Forbes, the former governor of the Philippines. Even Forbes was impressed with Farquhar and called him a genius.

Most of the problems with the railroad's long-term success were due to the completion of the Panama Canal in 1915 and Bolivia's reconciliation with Chile. With the Panama Canal operational, the Bolivians could reach the Atlantic markets from

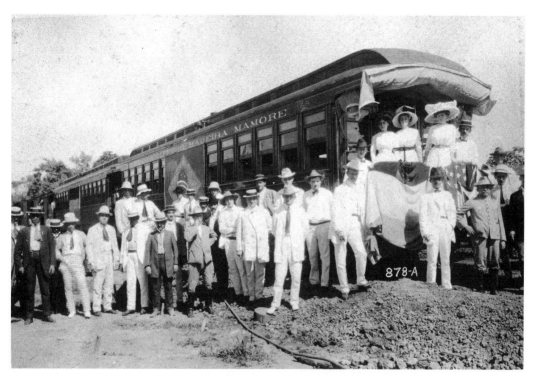

The railroad inauguration train and party.
Photo by Dana Merrill from the Gary Neeleman collection.

On August 1, 1912, the Farquhar Syndicate drove the railroad's
golden spike in Guajará-Mirim.
Photo by Oscar Pyles from the Gary Neeleman collection.

Inauguration day.
Photo by Oscar Pyles from the Gary Neeleman collection.

Handmade flags for the inauguration.
Photo by Dana Merrill from the Gary Neeleman collection.

the Chilean coast, and they no longer felt obligated to use the Madeira-Mamoré Railroad as their path to the sea.

Even though the railroad was in decline, it continued to operate as a regional form of transportation up and down the Madeira. During the 1929 world financial crash, however, the railroad suffered a fatal blow. In 1931 the Brazilian government took control of the railway; continual controversy and litigation between the government and the railroad company followed, each claiming the other had not carried out parts of the concession and contract. Under the new and final agreement of 1937, the 1909 contract between the two parties was rescinded. The government paid an indemnity to the company, and the company recognized the government as sole proprietor of the railway and all its property.

It took until 1937 to resolve all of the legal entanglements and problems and finally terminate—once and for all—the Farquhar concession. An article entitled "The Madeira-Mamoré Railway Brazil" in the *Engineering News Record* of May 12, 1939, announced,

> Acquisition of the Madeira-Mamoré Railway by the Government of Brazil closes the last chapter of the history of this spectacular enterprise as a private

Survivors of the administrative staff of the Madeira-Mamoré Railroad
gathered on February 22, 1952, in Sarasota, Florida, to renew old acquaintances
and exchange stories about their jungle experiences. The man sitting on the
right side of the table with the four women is Frank Kravigny, and the tall man
standing on the left in the photo is Fernado J. Torras.
Photo by Oscar Pyles from the Gary Neeleman collection.

line. The event calls to mind the romantic enterprise of the construction of
this 250-mile railway in the jungles of the heart of Brazil by American engineers. Its purpose was to bypass a series of rapids on the Amazon River and
connect two of its navigable tributaries, thus extending transportation for
several hundred miles up these rivers. The first survey of the line was made
by a party of American engineers as far back as 1878, but work was abandoned after a few miles had been actually built and operated. In 1907 another
American engineering expedition took up the exploration and surveys, and
the line was completed about 1912.[2]

The railroad did have one more surge of glory during World War II when U.S.
warships sailed up the Amazon and docked at Porto Velho to take on huge rubber

shipments for the United States military machine. The Madeira-Mamoré Railroad delivered the rubber from the depths of the Amazon Basin and once again proved its usefulness.

Although the Madeira-Mamoré continued to operate for many more years, it never fulfilled its expected destiny. Finally, on May 25, 1966, the Brazilian government closed the railroad indefinitely. In 1971 the government gave a demolition order for the railroad, and much of it was destroyed with the exception of some short sections.

In 1991 the government of the state of Rondônia asked all of the descendants of the workers on the Madeira-Mamoré Railroad to unite in an effort to restore the old railroad. An article by Peter Eisner, published in *Newsweek* in 1991, praised the railroad as

> A feat of engineering that winds through jungle canopy and traverses pictur-esque waterfalls on its course into one of the most out-of-reach territories of the hemisphere. The restoration is in part a tourist enterprise, but also re-flects the passion with which the descendants of those who built the railway recall their frontier heritage. "It's just iron and railroad ties, but there is a part of us that has given our lives to this project," said Joao Cirino, a former army sergeant who has been working for years to restore the railway.[3]

The two-hundred-mile trip by road from Porto Velho to Guarajá-Mirim is a journey into the past. Small towns and villages along the way display railroad rel-ics in their town squares, and old-timers living along the route talk warmly of times past when the Madeira-Mamoré passed through their town. About ninety miles from Porto Velho, a family has covered one end of the Jaci Paraná bridge with a thatched roof, an extension to their small wooden house situated close to the bridge.

Other steel bridges along the bumpy highway are silent reminders of the en-gineering genius of the early railroad workers. An old locomotive sits in the center of the little town of Mutum Paraná; it was built in Philadelphia late in the 1800s, and arrived in Porto Velho by steamship. Next to it is an old rail crane used to load rubber and off-load supplies for the workers. In the square on the banks of the Ma-moré River in Guajará-Murim is the engine that was used in the filming of the TV Globo miniseries, *Mad Maria*. Behind the locomotive is the Madeira-Mamoré Mu-seum, which houses more of the remaining bits and pieces of the old railroad. Al-though the little Amazonian railroad could never compare with the impact of the U.S. transcontinental railroad, it has certainly secured an important place in history.

The inauguration train on the Jaci Paraná bridge.
Photo by Dana Merrill from the Gary Neeleman collection.

In recent months, the city government of Porto Velho has made a decisive move to renovate the old rail yard and restore approximately seven kilometers of track through the city to the Santo Antonio dam site. In a meeting, city officials explained that the master plan includes making a park of the old yard. The city has already restored two of the railroad buildings, one to be used as a restaurant and the other for a museum on the banks of the Madeira River. City officials are working to restore at least two of the old locomotives, which will make the seven-kilometer run as a tourist attraction. The city is also in the process of building old-style cobblestone and brick walkways along the boardwalk in front of the restored locomotive buildings.

Although the Friends of the Madeira-Mamoré committee members are pleased with this new city initiative, they still feel more should be done to preserve what is left of the precious patrimony of the old railroad.

In recent years, Brazil's television station, TV Globo, produced a novella (TV miniseries) about the railroad. Known by various names—*The Madeira Mamoré Railroad, The Devil's Railroad, The Ghost Train,* and *Mad Maria*—the novella was a huge success in Brazil as it explored the unusual history and the larger-than-life characters who were involved in the railroad's construction.

The future of the rail yard and the surviving equipment is in question while descendants of the workers and Porto Velho city officials squabble over the best way to preserve what is left of what was, undoubtedly, the most unique and costliest railroad in the world.

In retrospect one wonders why the Brazilian military ordered demolition and carried out the final dismantling of the railroad in 1972. Was it for security reasons? Financial reasons? Or was it simply a lack of appreciation and consideration for one of the great engineering feats of the twentieth century? The descendents of the railroad workers in Porto Velho wistfully ponder why this amazing piece of Brazilian history could not have been converted to one of the most unique tourist attractions in the world.

Now—in a strange twist of fate—the original concept of using the Madeira-Mamoré Railroad as a hydrobyway from the heart of the Amazon has once again become a controversial issue. In 1867, when Colonel George Church optimistically initiated the Madeira-Mamoré Railroad project, the objective was to carry natural rubber from the Bolivian Amazon 1,650 miles down the river to the Atlantic Ocean and world markets. In the last few years, the Brazilian government has announced a massive dam project on the Madeira River. As many as four hydroelectric dams are planned to use the mighty Madeira as a hydrobyway to transport the many new, undiscovered products of the Amazon Basin.

The first two dams scheduled for the Madeira are the Jirau and the Santo Antonio. The Brazilian government is also studying the possibility of a third and maybe a fourth dam. This complex system will have locks that will enable large boats to move upriver to bring down lumber, rubber, minerals, and soybeans. The initial plan is to clear thirteen million acres of trees to plant soybeans. The first dam will be situated just five kilometers upriver from the city of Porto Velho, the origin of the Madeira--Mamoré Railroad.

The Madeira River supports an ecology of more than 750 species of fish, including the world's largest catfish, and more than 800 species of birds. Brazilian scientists claim that building the dams will endanger much of this fauna. Both Bolivia and Peru are fiercely opposed to the dams, but the construction of this huge project is already under way. The estimated cost of the Santo Antonio Dam is 14.2 billion U.S. dollars. The Jirau Dam will be located 136 kilometers upstream from the Santo Antonio and cost an estimated 20 billion U.S. dollars.

Ecologists claim the Madeira is currently considered among the most threatened rivers in the world. Scientists estimate that there are more than twenty-four hundred fishermen who derive their living from fishing the Madeira, and the city of Porto Velho alone consumes between five and six tons of fish every day.

The similarities between the Madeira River dam project of today and the Madeira-Mamoré Railroad project of yesteryear are striking. In both cases, the individuals and groups involved stand to make millions of dollars in profit. The cost of the 366-kilometer Madeira-Mamoré Railroad is estimated to be as much as if the rails were made of solid gold, not to mention the estimated ten thousand lives that were lost in its construction. Although the railroad did have some beneficial results over its history from 1867 to 1946, its usefulness was severely compromised by the Panama Canal. Was it worth the price?

Unlike the transcontinental railroad in the United States, the Devil's Railroad had only a single purpose: make as much money on Bolivian rubber and other Amazon products as possible and then get out. It was a speculator's dream, and it finally came crashing down. Although the financial risks of the Madeira-Mamoré Railroad were small in comparison with those of the current Madeira River dams, the two projects echo each other.

For the past 150 years, landlocked Bolivia has been seeking a more efficient way to reach the markets of the world. The country has always depended upon Chile's

Pacific ports, but when it lost the Pacific War with Chile in 1884, these ports were closed.

Seventeen years earlier, Bolivia had begun negotiations with Brazil to create a waterway down the Madeira and Mamore rivers into the Amazon and onward to the Atlantic Ocean and markets in the United States and Europe. The main obstacle was the nineteen cascades in the Madeira, which made the river impossible to navigate. The answer to this problem was the construction of the Madeira-Mamoré Railroad.

Over the years of its operation, the jungle railroad from Porto Velho to Guajará-Mirim, Brazil, had moments of glory both during the days of the rubber boom at the turn of the century and World War II from 1942 to 1947, when it transported critical rubber from the Amazon to the United States for the war effort. But by 1972, the railroad had been losing money for years and was decommissioned and dismantled by the Brazilian military government. In 2008 the Brazilian government revived the concept of the Amazonia waterway by beginning construction on the series of four dams.

Although the dam is described as using a "run-of-the-river" design, which employs a bulb turbine to generate electricity and therefore covers relatively less surface area, it will still flood 105 square miles and cover fourteen small communities along the Madeira River. These communities are Engenho Velho (currently a collective resettlement), São Domingos, Trata Serio, Cachoeira dos Macacos, Ilha Grande, Jatuarana, Vila Amazonas, Porto Seguro, Padre Eterno, Teotônio, Betel Morrinhos, Joana D'Arc I,II and III, Zeca Gordo, and Jacy, most of which were stops along the Madeira-Mamoré Railroad. The steel bridges in the cities of Jacy and Teotônio will be under an estimated thirty-six feet of water, and the Brazilian government will relocate the inhabitants of the fourteen communities.

The Santo Antonio Dam was scheduled to be completed by December 2011 but has been delayed. With the completion of these huge dams, the last vestiges of the Madeira-Mamoré Railroad will be underwater for all time. The curator of the railroad museum in Porto Velho is making every effort to gather the remaining bits and pieces of the iconic railroad ahead of the rising waters.

The Porto Velho Marconigram

THE PORTO VELHO
Marconigram

"LA VIDA SIN LITERATURA Y QUININA ES MUERTE"

Published at Porto Velho (Rio Madeira), Amazonas, Brazil

| VOLUME 2 | SATURDAY, OCTOTBER 15, 1910 | NUMBER 3 |

NOTES ABOUT TOWN

A. B. Jekyll has gone up-the-line to look after the construction work. J. H. Randolph remains in Porto Velho to take care of affairs here.

Two boats in this week but very little mail, and no men on either of them.

G. E. Cribbs who has been in charge of the Structural Iron Work in Porto Velho and vicinity has been appointed Superintendent at Jacy-Parana, relieving J. H Digby who after about two years' service with the Company, is on a much needed and well earned vacation.

Monday was pay day, and everything went off so smoothly and quietly that one could hardly believe the noise and confusion of the past to be possible.

Paymaster Hudson, and assistant Bell are up the line, having paid Porto Velho, Candelaria and San Antonio the first of the week. However, for those who have not gotten their pay for September, the Paymaster's Office will be open for a few days upon his return to-day.

H. G. Brown is also up the line collecting transportation, and assistant Bryne is in charge of his office.

When to the highest of medical attainments and best skill and attention in nursing is added "that one touch of nature, that makes all the world akin," it makes one feel that it's almost worth while being sick just to realize what Dr Lovelace and his staff of helpers are doing for the men on the job who come under their care.

"Jack" Douglass' many friends will be pleased to learn that he is getting well rapidly as can be expected and may be able to be out in a few weeks

(Continued on Page 4.)

BIG SNAKE KILLED

On Thursday afternoon there was quite a little excitement created around the General Office and the Engineering Department, when four or five hombres were seen coming up the hill bearing the huge folds of a monster reptile.

Evidently his Snakeship intended to investigate what all this noise and hubbub meant and was on his way to Porto Velho. When he was first seen just below the barricones he was near the railroad on the edge of the Igarape. The police force was called out, but a shot from a Winchester did the work. The snake measured a little over 16 feet in length, and 24 inches round. After Sr. Knapp had photographed about twenty men holding the snake up, he was taken by Mr. Wilhelm Vass, (who was in at the death), and his skin will go to increase Mr. Vass' collection of souvenirs of his skill with knife and rifle.

A great many expressions as to what would be cone should a snake of that size be met with, were heard, and it is not a bad suggestion that some of us who have any fear of running into one, should "change the brand" or cut it entirely.

NOTICE TO THOSE UP THE LINE

In making remittance for draft applications to Cashier please give the No. of camp from which you send it so you may receive receipt for same. Also in writing for Second of Exchange please give No. of your application from receipt of Cashier.

LEVEL AND TRANSIT NOTES

G. M. Russell has been transferred from Residency No. 11 to Porto Velho, where he has been assigned as Pile Recorder.

Official Photographer Merrill made a trip up the line as far as Camp 30 during the past week.

MADEIRA-MAMORE A FEW YEARS AGO

In another column will be found an article from "The Rubber World," but we confess the conditions as prevailed at that time are known no more on the Madeira-Mamoré. Since then an up-to-date little City has taken place of the Village; all the improvements, machinery and tools necessary to a First Class Terminus have been installed, and 160 kilometers of road built and a portion of it has been in operation for several months, the second division will be opened in a short time.

THIS IS THE ENGLISH OF IT

Below we give a translation of the poem on page 2. The writer said he wanted to save the boys from a headache trying to translate it:

One year of hard labour donated,
  And the money all laid by at home
I would like very much, I assure you,
  Ma-ali sa-banua acon

My strength and my spirit I've given
  I've railroaded best that I could
You ask if I want to return here?
  Uala, indi aco, matu-ua.

The Wholesale Commissary office will be renovated throughout and when Chief Murphy's men get through, it will be one of the swellest places on the job. "There will be no easy chairs" says Mr. Dahl. Wonder what he meant?

[One of the least inspiring subjects for a poet would seem at first glance to be a railway time-table. But a poet who writes in *McClure's* has found the time-table freighted with "treasures golden" and "hot with passion."]

LINES ON A RAILROAD TIME-TABLE

How very reticent a page it is
To be so hot with passion, and so proud
With treasures golden, guarded, wonderful,
Won in an utter wrath of surging war—
That shrill, terrific war where gray old Time
Went fighting, beaten backward, while the field
Rang with the cries of hammers clamoring !
These leaves are light, but they are whirled before
The very tempest of that Victory.
It is a young, hot, eager wind, of steel
And hissing steam, black coal, and human will,
Bursting from cities, dusk Chicago's breath
And Pittsburg's, panting.
                    What a pageant,
A pomp of strength and moving majesty,
That gale of battle lays upon its path !
A hundred roaring trains go every day
With hasty hands stroking Niagara bridge—
As children stroke a cat November nights
To see the sparks—and leave the long beast purring.
Beyond, out in the Rockies, coupled engines
Stamp smoking up the great moon-flooded grades,
White miles of winter where the old Wind sits
To weave his tapestries in trailing snow,
And all alone he hears the loud train climb.
And morning after morning, when, aflame
And mighty, bent about the sturdy world,
Dawn like a maned sea-breaker rushes down
Off the Atlantic, all those pallid rails
Take heart before it and the brightness runs
To lead the day a three hours' westward chase.
Then farmers wake, and cities, and the land
Stands up, a tall young man in sun-dashed strength,
Son of the world, and turns to search for tasks.
So searched the Colorado when he flung
Away the flimsy bank ten thousand years
Builded and held against him, and peered down
Upon that crisp, embittered Salton land,
And filled himself an ocean for a toy.—*By Joseph Boardman.*

(Many of the men now on the job have worked, sometime, on the Island of Panay in the Philippines, and it is for the benefit of these men that the following polyglot effusion was thrown off the system.)

UALA ACO

Con isa ca tuig trabajo,
  Con madamu nga pilac caron
Maluiag aco madamu
  To return to the land of my home
Ang lauas cag halug nag-hatag
  Pag-buhat ang ferro-carril ;
Maluiag aco ma-oli ?
  No ! I'll be darned if I will
            —*The Black Sheep.*

MONROE DOCTRINE MUST WAIT

The proposition looking to the declaration of adhesion to the Monroe doctrine, which has been discussed among the various delegations to the Pan-American Congress, was not introduced at the sessions, held at Buenos Ayres last two weeks in July, says a report recently received here.

The majority of the committee on the subject of a sanitary convention have accepted in principle the conventions entered into at Washington and at the Costa Rican conference.

THE POKER PLAYER POET

While playing poker the other day,
  A poker player was heard to say
With life I'd be content
  If I only had the money I have spent.

How many cards the dealer said
  Give me two—one to me—three here
I'll play these the poker-poet said,
  Your bet—bet two—check—bet five
I'll raise it five he cried,
  Pass—check—see it—
Another said four ACES here
  Then did our poker-poet realize

That with life he'd be content
  Now his money was all spent
He dreams of what he might have won
  If his hand had not been bum.
            On-looker.

YOU MUST LISTEN

There isn't a man in the lot,
  Who hasn't some deed to confide,
Though whether it happened or not
  I don't think I'd like to decide.

Let them talk, if they have a mind,
  (And a mind where invention prevails.)
It's extremely amusing, you'll find,
  To listen to travellers' tales !
            La Touche Hancock

A ROOF FARM THAT IS A PROPHECY

Here is a prophecy for later in the century. A New York man, Joseph S. Holden, has not only planted a garden on the roof of the building at No. 118 Fifth Avenue, but has all the appointments of a farm, including chickens. He raises small trees and shrubs, vegetables, and his busy hen house is on the basis of the "little farm" so highly praised by Mr. Rockefeller and looking to a solution of the high cost of living. However, Mr. Holden, while he has a "high" farm, is not thinking so much of the high cost of living as of having fun. And he is succeeding in a novel way and having a busy time in his spare hours with the only "farm" on fashionable Fifth avenue.

The Collector (endeavouring to raise funds for a widow and orphans) : "Now Mr. Flanaghan, can I put you down for a small subscription ?"
Flanaghan (a very hard case) : "Shure, it's a very laudable objic, and ye can put me down for three-and-sixpence, and Heaven knows I'd give ye the money if I had it."

THE PORTO VELHO
MARCONIGRAM

Published at

Porto Velho (Rio Madeira) Brazil

Telephone Connection

Post Office Address:
BOX, 304, MANAOS, BRAZIL.

C. L. JONES—*Editor*
D. M. MALONEY—*Publisher*

SATURDAY, OCTOBER 15TH, 1910

NEW AVENUE TO BOLIVIA—THE MADEIRA-MAMORE RAILWAY

In the opening paragraph of the Sixth Letter of a series, the subject being Para, Manaos, and the Amazon, by the Editor of "The India Rubber World" of September 1st, 1910, the writer says that it was not until he got to Manaos that he really appreciated what a great undertaking the Madeira-Mamore Railway was, and how energetically it is being handled. Continuing, the writer says:

"One of the partners in the contracting firm that was putting the road through resided there, and I got to know him well. His official headquarters were at Manaos. But Iticoatiara, at the mouth of the Madeira river, was the place where supplies were stored, and many of the men housed going and coming from the railroad camps.

The Madeira, it will be remembered, is the Amazon's greatest tributary. It comes from Bolivia and furnishes about the only outlet for that landlocked republic. From where it enters the Amazon to San Antonio, nearly 500 miles away, it is navigable by ocean steamers. Then come 250 miles of rapids, in which there are nineteen cataracts. When the water is high the big rubber scows, or *batelaos*, are able to get through by floating part of the way and making portages around the falls, but shooting the rapids. These portages are furnished with narrow gauge tracks. The *batelaos* are unloaded, pulled upon a small truck, and dragged up over the hills, and then eased down on the other side. The return trip involves 25 portages, and three trips a year are all that is possible.

The enormous effort required in moving these heavy boats can hardly be imagined. Every season at low water new roadways must be made by clearing the great boulders out of the river bed, and then laying a corduroy road of green poles, over which the keel of the *batelaos* can slip. Where it is possible they use tackle block to help in the pulling, but sometimes everything must be done by main strength.

There is a loss of 10 to 15 per cent. of the rubber sent down by the upsetting of the scows. Not only that but many men are drowned. The *batelaos*, by the way, are flat bottomed scows 30 feet long and 8 feet wide, and carry about 10 tons of rubber. They are manned by 16 paddlers, or *bateleiros*, and usually make the journey down in 20 days, while it takes 60 to return.

LIFE IN A RAILROAD CAMP

The headquarters of the construction camp was not at San Antonio, but at Porto Velho, where were assembled from 4,000 to 5,000 men. Of these 300 to 400 were Americans. Here were built substantial quarters for the engineers, bunk houses for the men, an up-to-date thorough equipped hospital, an ice plant, and large storehouses. The company had also drilled wells for the water, and was making every effort to keep the men well. In spite of that there were sometimes nearly 300 men in the hospital, and seven to ten doctors and eight male nurses were constantly employed. The experiment of having female nurses were tried, but they were married and carried away so constantly that it was voted a failure.

The camp was under military discipline, and liquor was taboo. In spite of this the native laborers smuggled in more or less "cachaca." The most trouble-some diseases were *beri-beri*, black water fever, and dysentery. Quinine, of course, was the remedy generally used and most potent. It was bought by the ton, and three laboratory men were kept busy from morning until night making it up into pills.

The town was noted as publishing the only English paper on the Amazon, called *The Porto Velho Times*. The first issue appeared on typewritten sheets. Then the company sent in a font of type and a printing press, and the paper appeared with more or less regularity. It was a remarkable looking sheet, typographically. There were no "w's" in the font, and two "v's" placed close together were the alternative.

The paper was full of camp news and genuine fun, and everybody subscribed. Under the general announcements of the paper's scope and policy appeared the subscription price, which was—

Six months nothing.
Three months, half price.

The railroad workers were only in this camp at stated seasons. Some of them were far ahead with the preliminary party of engineers, who were deciding upon the location, or they might be nearer the camp on construction. The company paid the men on the 10th of every month, and five men were in the employ of the pay office to prepare the $175.000 that the paymaster carried in person to the various camps.

All of the men were obliged to sign a contract not to meddle with the Carapuna women, or to sell firearms to the men. If this contract was violated they were discharged without pay. The result of this wise policy was that the Indians were very friendly, and furnished the camps with many turtles and lots of fish. The company shipped in beef on its own steamers from Manaos, and furnished such delicacies as Boston baked beans and rice *ad libitum*.

NEWS BY MARCONI WIRELESS

Courtesy of May, Jekyll & Randolph

October 13, 1910.

London—The striking laborers in Manchester refuse to enter upon the agreement proposed by the factory owners.

Rio—The project to reorganize the sanitary inspection in Manaos has been approved.

A new telegraph line will be built between Pernambuco and Rio, in order to facilitate telegraphic communication with Amazonas.

Kanioff's Party

NOTES FROM JACI-PARANA

The iron is going up pretty lively at Jaci-Parana bridge. That gang certainly knows their business.

Work on the last pier is well under way, and will be completed this month.

Camp Foreman Yale fired the chambermaid and hired four new Chinamen.

How They Didn't Kill the Hog

Great excitement prevailed in this camp on Sunday, October 9th, when Camp Foreman Yale decided on killing a hog for Sunday dinner. The question arose "who would do the killing," whereupon Foreman Doyle and fourth pusher Davis volunteered their services as chief executioners of said porker. Armed with Winchester rifles, loaded to the muzzle, they proceeded to the scene of action. Camp Foreman Yale wished to have hog killed in the pen—Foreman Doyle objected saying, "give him a chance for his life." The hog being turned loose Foreman Doyle raised his deadly rifle to his shoulder and taking deliberate aim at the hog's heart fired, the bullet penetrating the hog just below the tail. The hog becoming enraged at such treatment charged upon his tormentors. Davis hit the trail at a ten second clip, while Doyle took to the tall timbers climbing up a prickle palm so fast that the prickles did not have time to enter his hide. The hog becoming disgusted took to the railroad track, whereupon Doyle came down from his lofty perch and grabbing his trusty rifle yelled "turn him this way, until I get another shot at him." The last seen of the hog he was crossing the railroad track with Doyle and Davis in hot pursuit a safe distance behind. Doyle and Davis returned about 11 p.m., leg weary and heart broken saying they did not like pork anyway and the rest of the camp agreed with them in regards to *Hog Meat*.

Our Publisher, Business Manager and "News Getter" D. M. Maloney, made a short visit to Candelaria the early part of the week, but to the great relief of the Editor is back on the job again, feeling good and looking good.

NOTES ABOUT TOWN

The General Commissary vacated their offices in the Retail Commissary building and moved into their new office last Tuesday.

Work on the concrete pillars and the porch and platform around the Brain house is in full swing and it will not be long before the Brain house presents a new appearance.

E. N. Little, Chief Clerk Transportation Department, who has been visiting the ladies at Candelaria is back on the job again.

The shipping department of the commissary has a new office now, one of the best on the job.

Lots of material being sent to the front every day, keep the cars and train crews on the move.

The clerks of the material department are busy getting an inventory of stock.

A. B. Marshall, one of the new recruits arriving on the last boat, is located in the Transportation Department.

What would the breakfast be if pancakes were no more?

John O'Brien, one of the Old Timers, went down the river on Friday, bound homewards.

The new Mad house is going up rapidly. When Pascoe's on the job there's no chance of any grass growing on it.

Among the last lot of arrivals were a number who had at some time worked on the Isthmus or in the Phillipines and they were surprised to meet so many old acquaintances here. This little sphere, called the World, isn't so big after all.

We are certainly glad to note that the river is rising slowly but surely.

ABOUT YOUR MAIL MATTER

The Post Office will be open from
8 a. m. until 12 noon
1 p. m. until 5.30 p. m.

Distribution of mails will be made two hours after the arrival of the steamer.

The last collection for letters will be made *one hour* before the departure of every boat.

A FEW LAUGHS

"Captain," remarked the nuisance on shipboard who always asks foolish questions, "what is the object in throwing the anchor overboard?"

"Young man," replied the old salt, "do you understand the theory of seismic disturbances? Well, we throw the anchor overboard to keep the ocean from slipping away in the fog.

"We've been having a regular clearance at home," explained Mr. X. at the office, "throwing all sorts of old things away. I put one of my wedding presents on the fire this morning."

"Did you, really?" asked a horrified colleague; "what was it?"

"A copper kettle," replied X.

Willie had tried by various means to interest his father in conversation.

"Can't you see I'm trying to read?" said the exasperated parent. "Now, don't bother me."

Willie was silent for almost a minute. Then, reflectively:—

"Awful accident in the Tube to-day."

Father looked up with interest. "What's that?" he asked. "An accident in the Tube?"

"Yes," replied Willie, edging toward the door; "a woman had her eye on a seat and a man sat on it."

"So Bliggins has written an historical novel?"

"Yes," answered Miss Cayenne.

"Who is the hero of the book?"

"The man who has undertaken to publish it."

A Sunday-school superintendent wanted to "show off" the intelligence of his pupils to a wealthy visitor on the platform, so he smiled at the school and said:—

"Now, children, what kind of people go to heaven. Now, who can tell?"

"I can," said Tommy. "The dead ones."

OCEAN STEAMSHIP SAILINGS

Sailings for New York: Booth Line 7th, 17th and 27th of each month; Lloyd Brazileiro Boats sporadic sailings.

Sailings for Europe: Booth Line, 3rd, 13th, and 23rd of each month; German Line 1st and 15th.

Postal Rates to U.S. and Europe

200 reis per half ounce First Class matter.

100 reis per half ounce Second Class matter.

Please advise your foreign correspondents to put five cent stamp on your letters, so additional postage will not be charged at Manaos.

THE PORTO VELHO
Marconigram
"LA VIDA SIN LITERATURA Y QUININA ES MUERTE"
Published at Porto Velho (Rio Madeira), Amazonas, Brazil

VOLUME 2	SATURDAY, OCTOBER 22, 1910	NUMBER 4

NOTES FROM THE CAMPS

Camp 32 has been established at kilometer 205 with Mr. Bailey in charge.

Right of way clearing is finished to kil. 190, with the exception of a few stations here and there, and clearing is under way to kil. 205, about 200 men on clearing under Mr. Watkins.

The bridge at station 1620 is rapidly nearing completion. This bridge will have about 82 bents when completed. The large bridge at the Mutum Parâna is also well under way and will be completed before the high water can interfere any with the work.

The office building for the construction auditor and his force is being built at the Mutum Parana river and they will move into their new quarters in about fifteen days.

Track is laid to Camp 25 on the Madeira River just below Tres Irmaos falls.

The steel bridge over Jaci Parana is fast nearing completion.

The camps at Mutum Parana make the place look like a city. We now have Craswell's bridge camp on one side and the camps of Landis, Tarver and the engineers on the other side and the construction camp still to move there.

W. B. Horsey, assistant timekeeper at track camp, killed a 10-foot snake early this week. The reptile was making its way across the track when a gang of hombres sighted it and they scampered away. But Horsey picked up a cudgel and made for the animal and with a deft blow broke the snake's neck and put it out of business. He will retain the skin as a trophy.

STRENUOUS TIMES UP THE LINE

The beginning of the rainy season means something more to the men at the front than it does to us in Porto Velho. On the last trip of the Paymaster to camp 24 he saw something of the difficulties they are up against.

Train despatcher Guilfoyle had told him at 18 that it had been raining up at 24 all afternoon, but as no serious difficulty with the track was anticipated the motor started at 8.30 in the evening and drew near 24 about two hours later. The ride over the last five kilometers was like a trip at sea, as the motor swayed and careened over the uneven track, but the rain had ceased. The supply of kerosene had run out at camp 24, so that when they arrived all was dark except for a candle light in a distant barracone. The money box, rolls, blankets and slickers were picked up and a start made to walk to the light. Then the rain came, and came hard. Slipping and sliding down the steep clay embankment in the darkness, stumbling over a little bridge and splashing through unseen puddles of water, they made their way to the barracone. A watchman showed where the cots were prepared for the party, and all night they could hear the steady, soaking downpour on the palm roof overhead. A tent next door became overloaded as the canvas sagged to the growing weight and sometime in the night one side fell in, with a crash and a rushing flood of water that startled the sleepers from their beds.

About four in the morning a locomotive whistled, and a minute later Conductor Higgius came in, dripping, and told how he had worked all night to get through from 18 with the swing train. They

(Continued on Page 4.)

A NIGHT IN THE JUNGLE

At one o'clock Sunday afternoon J. E. James, Chief Timekeeper, and A. L. Marshall, Stenographer, started out on a short hunting trip intending to make a semicircle through the jungle from Porto Velho, coming out at Candelaria. They had made the trip together some time before, but this time they went a little deeper into the jungle—probably 2 kilometers from the river. About four in the afternoon, when they were headed back for Candelaria, Marshall grew suddenly faint and was able to go on only with the greatest difficulty, continually stumbling and falling. James urged him and encouraged him to keep up, but he finally collapsed and then, the fear of spending the night helpless in the jungle overcoming him, he became delirious. James had no *machete* but he built a rough palm bed for the sick man and a palm shack over him, using his bare hands to tear down the necessary vines and palm. There they stayed all night. The matches were wet and he couldn't build a fire. Towards nine o'clock Marshall became violent and tried to tear down the hut, and from then until morning James struggled with him to keep him quiet.

At daylight Marshall was much worse and appeared to be dying. It became necessary for James to choose between staying at his side till help came or leaving him, unconscious and unprotected from the animals of the jungle, while he made his way in to the hospital for a doctor and assistants. Marshall's weight, about 180 pounds, put carrying him out of the question. He decided to make his way in.

There was no sign of a trail but he made good speed, although he had to stop continually and break down branches to leave a trail to mark the way back after he had secured a relief party. At about seven in the morning he reached the railroad a little above Candelaria where he met a gang working for Arthur Decker. Decker carried word to the hospital, and Dr. Garnett and seven laborers with *machetes* and a stretcher cut their way out to the sick man, James leading the way following the trail of bent and broken branches which he had left to mark a trail. They found Marshall in a serious condition. His heart had nearly ceased to beat and Dr. Garnett worked over him half an hour before they were able to carry him in to the hospital on the stretcher. His delirium continued on Monday and Tuesday. He failed to recognize Mr. Jekyll and Mr. Randolph, and even James appeared as a stranger to him

Mr. Marshall had spoken of some slight heart trouble recently and it was probably a partial failure of the heart which caused his collapse. Mr. James was badly scratched and all his clothing torn by thorns and brambles, but otherwise he was none the worse for his harrowing experience.

This morning (Saturday) Dr. Lovelace reports that Marshall is getting along splendidly and that a few more days would find him fully recovered.

PARSON CARRIED SAMPLES

A minister who had been doing missionary work in India recently returned to New York for a visit. He was a guest at a well known hotel where everything pleased him except the torrid sauces and spices to which he had become accustomed in the Far East. Fortunately, he had brought with him a supply of his favourite condiments, and by arranging with the head waiter, these were placed on his table. One day another guest saw the appetizing bottle on his neighbor's table and asked the waiter to give him some of "that sauce."

"I'm sorry, sir," said the waiter, "but it is the private property of this gentleman." The minister, however, overheard the other's request and told the waiter to pass the bottle.

The stranger poured some of the mixture on his meat and took a liberal mouthful. After a moment he turned with tears in his eyes.

"You're a minister of the gospel?"

"Yes, sir."

"And you preach hell and damnation?"

"Yes," admitted the minister.

"Well, you're the first minister I ever met who carried samples."—

THE LORD'S PRAYER

The following beautiful composition was captured during the war at Charleston, S. C. It was printed on heavy satin, July 4, 1823. It was picked up by A. P. Green, of Auburn, Ind., at Corinth, Miss., the morning the Confederate forces evacuated it, May 30, 1862.

* * *

Thou to the mercy-seat our souls doth gather,
To do our duty unto Thee. Our Father,
To whom all praise, all honor should be given;
For thou art the great God Who art in heaven.
Thou by Thy wisdom, rul'st the world's whole frame;
Forever, therefore . . . . Hallowed be thy name;
Let nevermore delay divide us from
Thy glorious grace, but let Thy kingdom come;
Let thy commands opposed be by none;
But Thy good pleasure and Thy will be done,
And let our promptness to obey, be even
The very same On earth as 'tis in heaven.
Then for our souls, O, Lord, we also pray,
Thou would'st be pleased to Give us this day,
The food of life, wherewith our souls are fed
Sufficient rainment and . . . . . . Our daily bread,
With every needful thing do thou relieve us,
And of Thy mercy, pity . . . . And forgive us
All our misdeeds for Him whom Thou did'st please
To make an offering for . . . . Our Trespasses,
And forasmuch, O Lord, as we believe
That thou will pardon us . . . . As we forgive,
Let that love teach, wherewith Thou dost acquaint us, to
Pardon all Those who Trespass against us,
And though sometimes thou find'st we have forgot,
This love for Thee, yet help And lead us not
Through soul or body's want to desperation,
Nor let earth's gain drive us Into Temptation
Let not the soul of any true believer
Fail in the time of trial. But deliver,
Yea, save them from the malice of the devil,
And both in life and death, keep Us from evil
Thus pray we, Lord, for that of Thee, from whom
This may be had . . . . . . For thine is the Kingdom,
This world is of Thy work, its wondrous story,
To thee belongs. . . . . . . The power and the glory,
And all thy wondrous works have ended never,
But will remain forever and Forever,
Thus we poor creatures would confess again,
And thus would say eternally Amen.

(This rare poem is reproduced by permission of H. M. Crouse, of the Henneberry Company, of Chicago, Ill.)

THIS IS WHAT THE BOY WROTE ABOUT THE DACHSHUND

"The dockshund is a dorg notwithstandin' appeerencis. He has fore legs, two in front an' two behind, and they ain't on speakin' terms. I wunst made a dockshund out of a cowcumber an four matchis, an' it lookt as nacheral as life. Dochshinds is farely intelligent, considerin' thare shaip. Thare brains bein' so far away from thare tales it bothers them sum to wag the lattur. I wunst noo a dockshund who wuz too impashunt to wate til he cood signal the hole length of his boddy when he wanted to wag his tale, so he maid it up with his tale thet when he wanted it to wag he would shake his rite ear, an' when the tale seen it shake would wag. But as for me, gimme a bull pup with a peddygree."

Time to send Christmas presents home.

NOTES ABOUT TOWN

G. E. (Kid) Moore, of Construction Auditor's Office was in town on business early this week.

Where, oh, where are those Mosquito Bars for the New hotel ?

Mr. J. H. Nunn handed in an inventory of the Material Stores last Saturday which gives evidence of a great amount of work and care. The inventory covers over 500 contos worth of material and enumerates about 2,000 different articles.

On behalf of the Stationery clerk we wish to state that the envelopes have not yet arrived. But they're on their way.

W. G. Cooper was down from the Hospital Wednesday. His arm is now in good shape and he expected to be on the work again in a few days.

Foreman Arthur Loebsack will sail on the *Madeira* for Manaos and the Land of the Free.

The *Victoria* is expected to arrive on Tuesday next with Master Mechanic MacMillan and fourteen others and 37 hombres.

The General Office staff lined up for their photograph on Friday a.m. We hope the plates are good and strong to stand the strain.

The men as they go to and from their meals look with longing eyes on the four turkeys that make their feeding grounds outside the dining room. Turkeys and November are synonymous to all Americans.

November 24th will be Thanksgiving day in the States.

With the completion of the Round house another of the group of buildings will be finished which is to make Porto Velho a model Railroad terminus.

Foreman Frank Pascoe was at Candelaria for a few days early this week. Couldn't resist, eh ?

In last week's issue in noting the change in G. E. Cribb's posi-

tion we should have said "In charge of Masonry and Construction between Camp 16 and Porto Velho."

Engineer Lindsey is at Candelaria suffering with rheumatism.

In writing of the big forest fires a Western (U.S.) contemporary says : "Beer is being used at Wallace, Idaho, for drinking purposes." A reader wishes to know what beer should be used for if not for drinking purposes.

The *Madeira* which was to have sailed from Santo Antonio on Tuesday could not get away on Saturday, owing to the delay of a battalao in getting in with a load of rubber.

Friday morning word was received by cable that Mr. W. G. Cooper's father had died. We extend our sincere sympathy.

Mr. E. C. Pickett of the Live Stock and Timber Department, who came down from Camp 24 1/2 last Saturday, spent almost a week in Porto Velho, ere he departed for Candelaria. Wonder if the fellows at Camp 25 are surprised ?

R. G. Jenckes, our Electrical Engineer spent a few days at Candelaria the past week.

Work on the dock at Candelaria is being rushed right along.

Cutting the weeds and grass has certainly improved the looks of things round town.

OH! HOW SHOCKING

"The engineers find Gatun Dam safe," read Mr. Jones from his newspaper headlines to grandma.

"Well," she said, looking up over her glasses in pained surprise. "I don't know anything about the safety of Gatun, but I think a family newspaper oughtn't to use such language in print."—*Emporia Gazette.*

STEAMER PASSENGER RATES

First Class to Manaos	.	165$000
Third Class "	.	55 000
First Class to Para	.	267 000
Third Class to Para	.	89 000
Manaos to New York		
First class	.	$140.00 gold
Manaos to Liverpool		
First Class	.	£30

LEVEL AND TRANSIT NOTES

J. O. Wanzer came down from the Abuná the other day, loaded down with Indian arrows and other curios. He leaves for the States by next boat.

G. A. Knapp is visiting at Candelaria for a few days.

C. W. Hillers leaves on the *Madeira*—whenever that may be.

Principal Assistant Engineer Bayliss is up the line.

E. L. Ford expects to leave for the States on the next boat.

Mr. J. M. Robinson, assistant Chief Engineer, returned from Porto Velho this week, accompanied by Messrs. A. B. Jekyll, Marion Hills, and D. P. Bailey. Before returning to Tres Irmaos, they made a trip in the launch to Abuna, Bolivia.

From one of the engineers now near Abuna we have received the following :

"After locating the 45 k lometer tangent through the Catinga, from *kilometer* 177-216, with experiences which will doubtless never be duplicated on the Madeira-Mamore, we pitched camp on the banks of the Madeira River, where we have plenty of fish, game, fruits, etc.; for example, one day last week, we had six pigs, six bunches of bananas, and other fruits, together with a case (24lb. cans) of assorted pound cakes, picked up in the middle of the river, undoubtedly from some batalao going over the falls at Araras."

Word received from Bob Reed, of the Engineering department, at his home, Michigan City, says that J. O. Wanzer's monkey was much admired and created a great interest among the people as to just which species he (the monkey) belonged.

OCEAN STEAMSHIP SAILINGS

Sailings for New York : Booth Line 7th, 17th, and 27th of each month ; Lloyd Brazileiro Boats sporadic sailings.

Sailings for Europe : Booth Line, 3rd, 13th, and 23rd of each month ; German Line 1st and 15th.

STRENUOUS TIMES UP THE LINE

(Continued from 1st page)

had stopped eight times with different cars off the track. and he had finally climbed on the engine and come on to 24 for help, leaving the train stuck in the mud near camp 23.

Daylight opened on a dreary and forlorn looking camp. The large open space before the barracones was flooded except for here and there an island of mud. The gray, gloomy sky seemed to rest on the tops of the giant trees and though the hard rain had stopped, there was still a dismal drizzle coming down. Things were a little better on the side track in the woods where McIver, Provo, Thorne, Fallaise, Horsey and the other *chefes* slept. In their dry, comfortable box cars with windows and doors all fitted with screens they could laugh at the weather, as well as at the mosquitos and flies But they couldn't stay there long. A big gang of laborers was loaded on flat cars at daylight and Engineer Stipp and Conductor Higgins hauled them back toward the abandoned swing train. This train, loaded with supplies, was due the night before; it did not get in until four the following afternoon.

Another gang, under Provo, was taken by Conductor Thorne and Engineer Nat Fraser over the newly laid rails toward 25, to continue track laying, but every hundred yards or so they had to stop and "pick up the track." An ambitious but inexperienced youth who had been sent out a few nights before to "pick up the track," took his mission very seriously and not only picked up the track, but brought it bodily *back into camp!* No wonder one of his laborers exclaimed " Boss, you sure do know Railroadin' !"

This little operation is carried on slightly differently under Mr Provo's supervision. The train of flat cars loaded with rails and ties is backed up slowly over the yielding track, the ties sinking one by one out of sight in the mud as the weight presses them, until a point is reached where the fill is softer than usual There the train is

stopped, the black laborers tumble off the cars and bring up poles from the piles of brush and logs left at the edge of the right of way by the clearing gangs. Fifteen or twenty men take the largest of these and, using it as a lever, pry up one side of the track and hold it about a foot above the ground while other men roll smaller poles under the projecting ends of the ties, laying them parallel to the rails. After a hundred feet or so of track has been so picked up, the train comes creeping over the bolstered rails and the gang rides on to the next soft spot. The end of track was about eight kilometers away. After working all the morning the track gang had only advanced two kilometers from camp As most of the men were sent down the line in the afternoon to help rescue the stranded swing train, which finally got in at 4.30, the end of track was not reached at all that day.

McIver, limping around camp with a lame foot, was not able to get into all this He had a chance to use up some of his repressed energy, however, when in the afternoon one of the tents by the track, where some laborers lived, took fire and burned up like a pile of hay. When the Paymaster left, McIver was threatening to arrest every man loafing in the camp, tear down all the tents and put every workman on the job in the barracone.

Taylor, Lawton, Lindsay and some more very tired train men were at Camp 22 that night Some of them had worked twenty hours through the rain and mud, without a bite to eat. And they didn't belly ache about it. Theirs is a man's job, and they all took hold and stuck to it, as Americans have a way of doing. And they got the train through.

ABOUT YOUR MAIL MATTER

The Post Office will be open from
8 a m. until 12 noon
1 p. m. until 5 30 p m
Distribution of mails will be made two hours after the arrival of the steamer
The last collection for letters will be made *one hour* before the departure of every boat.

NOTES FROM JACI-PARANA

Senator Freeman, of Camp 18, is complaining about the dynamite that is being sent him. He says it is all left-handed as it explodes the wrong way and blows the rock on the track, thereby stopping traffic for some time after each shot.

A certain bridgeman while acting as engineer of the derrick car was told by the pusher to slack on his load, the engineer looked at the pusher, and said "which way do you want me to slack, up or down." What was he ?

The wounded hog came back to visit his family on Saturday, but made a very brief stay on learning that the sharpshooters were in camp as he did not wish to make a target of himself.

The through span on Jaci-Parana bridge was swung on Wednesday night, that's going some.

The last concrete pier will be finished this week.

There was weeping and wailing and gnashing of teeth on Saturday last on account of firing the nigger cook. The chinese cooks are an improvement. I don't think !

HE'S LOOKING FOR YOU (?)

Jimmie James is out with a stuffed club looking for the man who packed his clothes in the suit case which was sent to him at the hospital from Porto Velho.

RISING TIDE

A Kansan sat on the beach at Atlantic City watching a fair and very fat bather disporting herself in the surf. He knew nothing of tides, and he did not notice that each succeeding wave came a little closer to his feet. At last an extra big wave washed over his shoe tops.

" Hey there ! " he yelled at the fair fat bather. " Quit yer jumpin' up and down ! D'ye want t' drown me ? "

All items that are likely to prove of interest are requested by the Editor. Be brief ; write on one side of paper.

Mr Pyles

THE PORTO VELHO
Marconigram

"LA VIDA SIN LITERATURA Y QUININA ES MUERTE"

Published at Porto Velho (Rio Madeira), Amazonas, Brazil

VOLUME 2	SATURDAY, NOVEMBER 19, 1910	NUMBER 8

OBITUARY

The announcement of the death of Mr F. C Englesing, former Assistant Chief Engineer of the Madeira-Mamore Railway, will be received with deep regret by his friends here, especially the old engineers who worked under him and knew him best. After Mr. Englesing left Porto Velho last May he was very ill in Paris and the physician there who attended him did not think he could live to reach the United States. His wife was called to Paris by cable and later it was reported here that he eventually reached New York and had gone to his home in Mississipi. The sad news of his death arrived here by mail on the S. S. *Humaytha*.

Through the *Marconigram* we, his friends here, wish to extend to his family our sincere sympathy in their bereavement and to express our sense of personal sorrow and loss in his death.

NOTES ABOUT TOWN

The plumbers have been busy for a week past refitting the Mad House with baths, etc.

Al Wasserbaur has got back on the job again. He is at his old place in the Machine Shop.

The *M-M* sailed from Manaos on Friday, the 18th instant, bound for Itacoatiara and Porto Velho.

A letter received from W. P. Heyl, at Madeira, on board the *Lan Franc*, stated that he was steadily improving. He wished to be remembered to all.

On page 2 we publish an article on "Progress on the Madeira" which is worth reading. We thank the editors of the *India Rubber World* (N. Y.) for their appreciation of our modest efforts in the journalistic field

Late arrivals here report seeing Geo. C. Taulbee and Verne Hendrickson in Barbados. They only saw them for a moment, as our informant said he was "broke" and Verne and George were "riding in a carriage." Well he is not the first man who has been in Barbados without "cabfare."

New Hotel II will not be finished any too soon In fact it looked as if the boys would soon be compelled to get down to the Booth standard of four in a room.

GIANTS DEFEAT HIGHLANDERS

In the contest for the Baseball supremacy of the Metropolis the Giants have succeeded in winning two of the first three games of the series of seven. They won the first by Christy Mathewson's superb pitching. The second was won by the Highlanders and then the Giants, by putting Mathewson in the box in the seventh inning of the third game secured another victory. The scores are not at hand.

In the item about baseball on page 3 we were led into an error, our informant getting the World's Championship Series confused with others.

PERILOUS ENCOUNTER WITH AN ANT BEAR

While making the return trip from Camp 16 to Porto Velho, on a hand car, on November 17, Road Doctor Garnett and Timekeeper Hirst were attacked by a vicious ant bear, who, being tired of walking in the heat of the day, decided to take possession of the car. At the first onslaught of the beast the crew on the hand car took to "the shade of the sheltering palms" and left the doctor and timekeeper to defend themselves as best they could. After a short decisive struggle the brute was defeated and put to rout and started to climb a tree, with the doctor, who was by this time thoroughly aroused, in hot pursuit.

Seeing that there was no hope of escape in this way the bear again took to the ground and started up the track, only to be headed off by Mr. Hirst. With Hirst in front and the doctor behind the animal became nonplussed; not so the doctor, seizing the opportunity and the bear's tail he had the enemy in his possession; however, after capturing the animal the doctor was at loss what to do with him and the captive was all the while battling for his freedom with renewed vigor; he grappled with his captor and with one sweep of his mighty paw tore away part of the doctor's boot, inflicting a slight wound on his leg.

Seeing that it was useless to attempt to take the brute alive, Mr. Hirst uprooted a nearby tree and with a few sharp blows on the head quickly dispatched him and the danger was over, but it is unlikely that either of the men will ever forget this thrilling encounter.

LEVEL AND TRANSIT NOTES

Among the passengers on board the *Humaytha*, which arrived on Wednesday were G. L. Judson, D. B. Cutler, and M. Aguirre for the Engineering department.

Principal Assistant Engineer Bayliss has returned from a trip to Tres Irmaos.

A. S. Karsner has been transferred to Residency No. 11.

F. C. Kyte and Axel Carlsson have been transferred to Porto Velho, for duty at that point.

Paul Kennedy and R. B. Mantor left Camp 25 yesterday on a batelao for the front.

S. C. Mullen is now located at Camp 16.

We understand that Geo. L. Judson was tendered a reception by his friends upon his arrival at Porto Velho. Incidently, the "Hamburg Show" has a new "Orchestra."

PERSONAL MENTION

Dr. Walsh has been transferred to Candelaria. Dr. Marsteller, who has been stationed at Track Camp for the past few months, relieving him in Porto Velho.

Mr. Jekyll, who in looking after things generally up at the front, was in town the first of the week. He reports work progressing rapidly at his end of the line.

J. E. Boykin, who has been on the job sixteen months, left on the *Madeira-Mamore*, for a vacation. Mr. Boykin was among the first to land in Porto Velho, and is now taking his second vacation, having put in over 3 years on the work here.

P. O'Neil is back at work after a short visit to Candelaria.

We are glad to report Mr. E. C. Pickett is improving rapidly now, and will soon be out again.

L. Klienpaul, who has been stationed at San Antonio has been relieved by Mr. Orr, at that place, and will be in Porto Velho for the time being.

Our announcement about the arrival of the envelopes was a trifle premature. They'll get here some day and Oh, let it be soon.

THE PORTO VELHO
MARCONIGRAM

Published at
Porto Velho (Rio Madeira, Brazil

C. L. JONES—*Editors*---C. R. HUDSON
D. M. MALONEY—*Publisher*

SATURDAY, NOVEMBER 19TH, 1910

A FITTING COMPARISON

NoLe but the initiated know the accuracy required in a printing office. The average reader who detects a mispelled word or letter upside down feels that his mission on earth is not accomplished until he has called the attention of the overworked editor to the glaring defect. He does not notice the thousands and tens of thousands, of letters that are in place or the multitude of words correctly spelled, but his eagle eye is glued on the one that is out of place.

So it is with our deeds. Man does a thousand good deeds and no attention is paid to them, but if he makes one mistake it is flashed all over the world. A life-time may be spent in building up a reputation that may be wrecked in a moment. The world is a harsh critic, exacting to a fault.

Moral—Avoid that one mistake.

PROGRESS ON THE MADEIRA

The readers of *The India Rubber World* have been kept informed of indications of commercial progress of the Madeira river, which is destined to become an outlet to the world's richest natural rubber field—Bolivia. Not the least important of these indications is the regular publication, at the headquarters of the engineering corps at work on the Madeira-Mamore Railway, by some of the bright young American employees temporarily exiled there of a newspaper—The Porto Velho *Marconigram*.

This remotely published little sheet is not as yet impressive in appearance, but it happens to be of the same size and general appearance as the earlier numbers of the *Sun*, which long has been one of the principal newspapers of New York. As indicating the up-to-dateness of the Madeira river newspaper, it may be mentioned that the latest issue received in New York mentions the new prices for automobile tires quoted by some of the leading American manufacturers.

But what is of very much more importance is the fact that a large part of the contents of the *Marconigram* is devoted to the work in progress for improvement in the sanitation of the Madeira Valley. It is evident that definite results are being attained in this work, and this is one of the most promising facts in connection with the great enterprise now developing for opening the Bolivian rubber field to the world.

It is not unreasonable to suppose that ultimately the Madeira region will become as habitable as the now populous Mississippi Valley in the United States, a region which Charles Dickens, in his "Martin Chuzzlewit," not longer than 65 years ago, felt called upon to warn the world against.

DOPE

If only the dreams that we like to dream
　　Were the only dreams to come true;
I wonder what boys on the line would
　　dream—
　　Just listen, I'll dope it to you;

They dream of a land with hills of
　　crack'd ice
　　And huge geysers of scotch high-balls;
Of rivers of bourbon, and corn and such
　　And flunkies awaiting their calls.

Of valleys of bright green creme de
　　men he,
　　Where the cows give absinthe frappes;
Of parks with fountains of sparkling
　　gin-fizz
　　And pools of pousse cafes.

Of mint julep marshes, fringed round
　　with green,
　　Near oceans of champagne clear;
Where rainstorms are naught but heavy
　　downpours
　　Of amber-like cold German beer.

They'd dream such a dream—and enjoy
　　it too,
　　As you would; and, so too, would I;
But, alas! the heart aches when the
　　sleeper awakes,—
Far better to dream on and die.

　　　　　　　　　—*The Black Sheep.*

SEEING CIVILIZATION

The other day a score of "tame" Bolivian Indians stopped their batelão at Camp 25 and all filed solemnly up the river bank to see the locomotive and train come in. A box car was off the track and the train stood a hundred yards away from the camp, the air brake pump coughing away cheerfully and black smoke pouring from the stack. While the crew was working on the distant car the Indians stood in a silent, stolid group for a full ten minutes and then, being convinced that the thing couldn't move, after all, they all turned and marched in single file back toward the river. Just then the engine gave three shrill toots of its whistles. It was worth an admission fee to see that bunch whirl round and gaze in excited expectation toward the train. The engine backed up a few feet, the car evidently refused to go back on the rails and the train stopped. Still the Bolivians stood and waited. Minute after minute passed by and nothing moved. At last they all turned, as if at a secret signal, filed down the bank to their batelão and, now thoroughly assured that the train was a humbug, paddled silently away.

NOTES FROM JACI-PARANA

The Hon Mayor of the Mad House at Jaci resigned his office on Sunday in favor of sharpshooter Davis, a prominent member of the bridge gang, who immediately took the chair and a farewell reception was given the parting Mayor.

The camp at Jaci is practically deserted as there is nothing left but the bridge gang, two Chinamen and a yellow dog.

Nigger Richie and Eagle Eye Bill, two prominent members of the bridge gang are recuperating at Candelaria.

The rattling of the air guns at Jaci is a sure sign that the bridge is drawing near to completion.

All items that are likely to prove of interest are requested by the Editor Be brief: write on one side of paper.

ARRIVALS ON RIVER BOAT

The *Humytha* arrived on Wednesday bringing eight passengers: They are James Street, G. L. Judson and Geo. H Smith who are returning from vacation and D. B. Cutler, S. Wellwood, L F. Maughn, Harry Street and Matias Aguirre new men. There was also mail aboard.

BASE BALL IN THE U.S.

At this writing the latest news from the baseball fans who arrived on the last boat was that Chicago and Philadelphia had each won one game in the World's championship series.

B-U-G-S

Have you seen Dick?
Dick who?
Cidic.

Skinny gent, ain't he?
What gent?
Nugent.

Looks like a rag doll, don't it?
What doll?
Kendall.

Goin' to have a lot of geese here soon.
Wild geese or tame geese?
No, Portugese.

Hark! Did you hear that heart-rending cry on the river?
No, what was it?
Oh, I guess it was only the gunwale on one of the new batalãos.

It is the current rumor that a bed-bug was found in the clock in the general office. The office boy said he supposed it crawled in between the ticks.

Query: Don't you suppose there is a chance for me to get invalided down the river as a psucopathic patient? I am the author of the foregoing. —*Black Sheep.*

Well, one more emanation like the above, would we think, justify the Doctors in placing you under observation.

Postal Rates to U.S. and Europe

200 reis per half ounce First Class matter.

100 reis per half ounce Second Class matter.

Please advise your foreign correspondents to put five cent stamp on your letters, so additional postage will not be charged at Manaos.

OUR TRADE WITH BRAZIL

Sewing Machines Part of Cargo to River Plate Countries

Brooklyn, N.Y., Daily Eagle October 7th, 1910.

Both the inward and outward trade with Brazil and the River Plate countries continues to be excellent, with good rates to Brazil. Lamport & Holt's steamship *Tennyson* sailed this forenoon from Pier 9, Roberts Stores, for Bahia, Rio de Janeiro and Santos. She takes out 63 cabin and 75 steerage passengers and had to refuse others for want of accommodations. She takes out a full cargo of sewing machines, electrical appliances, plain and barbed wire, cable reels, case oil, lubricating oil, fish and general merchandise. A rather unusual shipment is 2,000 barrels of apples, packed in two of the tanks; another shipment of similar size will go on the *Byron* of the same line.

Soon after the *Tennyson* had sailed the *Verdi*, also a Lamport & Holt liner, arrived at Pier 12, Pierepont's Stores, from Montevideo, Buenos Ayres, Rio de Janeiro, Santos and Barbados. She brought 85 cabin and 90 steerage passengers, 33,000 bags of linseed, 20,000 bags of quebracho wood extract, 9,000 bags of coffee, 1,400 packages of caseien and 2,000 bales of hide clipping, hair and glue stock.

The steamship *Boniface* of the Booth line arrived at Martin's Stores, Brooklyn, N.Y. on October 7th from Manaos, Para and Barbados. She brought twenty-five passengers, two hundred and fifty tons of rubber, fifty tons of Brazil nuts and some general merchandise. Although two hundred and fifty tons of rubber looks small, rubber is still, in spite of the big drop from the high-water mark of $3 per pound, worth $1.65 per pound, this item of the *Boniface's* cargo is worth about $3,300 per ton.

ANSWERS TO CORRESPDEONNTS

Reader, Porto Velho: No, it is not on account of a hole in the pocket, nor fear of the light fingered gentry, neither is it on account of a weak wrist, nor for eccentricity's sake, nor yet for convenience or for the looks of the thing, but to tell the time by, that Mr. Armitage wears his alarm clock on his wrist.

Gardening seems to do very well in this century. It is said that they raise currents with an electric plant in Porto Velho. People on the line are not supposed to requisition these by the quart, as these currents are disposed of only by the shock.

CONTENTMENT

It's blitherin' cold outside,
And blowin' to beat the band,
And snow and sleet is a flyin' wide
Over the whole broad land.
The icicles hang from the eaves,
And the pond and the brooks is froze ;
The frost has withered the autumn leaves,
And bit up the farmer's nose—
But me an' mine
Is feelin' fine,
So wnat do we care for snows?

There isn't a bird in sight,
And even the cat stays in,
Desertin' the joys of night
And the call of her kith and kin.
The days they are short and chill,
The nights are a decade long;
And out on the bleak and distant hill
The blizzard is goin' strong—
But me an' mine
Is feelin' fine,
For our hearts is full o' song.

Her heart is singin' of me,
And mine is singin' of her!
No thinkin' of what's to be,
No thinkin' of things that were,
But just of the joys that is,
Not worried 'bout things that's not;
So let the hoary blizzards blizz,
And Boreas go it hot—
For me an' mine
Is feelin' fine,
And thankful for what we've got!
John Kendrick Bangs, Munsey's.

OCEAN STEAMSHIP SAILINGS

Sailings for New York : Booth Line 7th, 17th, and 27th of each month ; Lloyd Brazileiro Boats sporadic sailings.

Sailings for Europe : Booth Line 3rd, 13th, and 23rd of each month ; German Line 1st and 15th.

EXPERIMENTS ON CONVEYING CONCRETE THROUGH PIPES UNDER AIR PRESSURE

The various kinds of machines and devices for measuring, feeding and mixing concrete ingredients are too well known and numerous to require description. Such machines are too be found on all works of any size or importance and have served to reduce the cost of the various operations to a point which makes possible the use of concrete for all classes of construction.

Notwithstanding the wonderful strides made in the reduction of cost and time by the use of machinery for these various operations, mixed concrete is still conveyed into place by the same crude, slow and expensive methods that existed from the first, namely, wheelbarrows, carts, cars, buckets, chutes, etc , requiring enormous proportional outlays for runs, trestles, railways, engines, derricks, and other plant as well as cost of operation and maintenance of same. These crude methods have other marked disadvantages. Concrete handled by wheelbarrows, carts, buckets, etc., is subject to considerable waste and tends to set in transit, particularly where transported considerable distances as is frequently the case. Concrete construction is often from necessity carried on in cold weather subjecting the concrete to the danger of chilling; therefore, any apparatus that conveys the mixed concrete instantly from the mixer into place is particularly desirable

With the idea of devising some method by which the transportation of the concrete mixture might be simplified the writers of this article some years ago started experiments on forcing the wet mixture through pipes by means of compressed air. The writers were then engaged in the construction of a difficult piece of concrete work where it became necessary to place the concrete by causing it to flow through a long length of pipe placed in an approximately vertical position. It was thought at the time that if the force of gravity would cause the concrete to flow downward through the pipe, there was reason to believe that concrete could be made to flow through a pipe in any position when acted upon by some force other than gravity, such as steam or air pressure.

This conclusion was not arrived at until considerable experimenting along other lines had been done. The first trials were made by attaching the suction end of a large centrifugal pump to the discharge end of a concrete mixer which scheme proved to be a failure, due to the fact that the stone separated from the sand and cement and discharged separately. The first encouraging results were brought about by attaching a large steam pipe to the pump casing, thereby introducing a pressure into the body of the pump which acted upon the mass of concrete in it, causing it to discharge in a more satisfactory manner These experiments led to the design and trial of a cylindrical receptacle provided with a sealable opening at the top for the admission of mixed concrete, a discharge pipe and valve at the lower end and means for introducing pressure at the top. The discharge pipe at the lower end led to the place where the concrete was to be deposited Upon applying pressure the concrete was instantly forced through the pipe and deposited in the same condition as when introduced into the receptacle. Many minor difficulties were encountered during the experiments, which, however, were overcome and patents were secured on the process and apparatus.

In order to obtain necessary engineering data, other more elaborate experiments were conducted using the same type of apparatus, and covering a period of several months.

The device used in the experiments consisted of an iron tank provided at the top with an air-tight gate, on the side with a pipe entrance for the compressed air and at the conical bottom with an exit pipe for the concrete. Concrete was first mixed on a board at the top of the hopper and poured into the tank through the upper gate which was then battened tight Simultaneously, then, valves on the intake air pipe and the outlet concrete pipe were opened and the compressed air forced the concrete out of the tank through a 4-in. pipe, to the point of exit. The 4-in. pipe used to transmit the concrete was about 400 ft. long and contained several 90 degrees bends and one 180 degrees bend around a 4-ft radius There seemed to be no obstacle to the use of a much longer pipe had it been convenient at the time and place

Tests were carried on with air pressures up to 100 lbs per sq in., but it was found that 50 lbs. was the most efficient. Under this pressure the concrete mixture was forced out of the end of the pipe in a well-mixed mass, but at a velocity too great for practical work. To reduce this velocity a nozzle was devised. This is simply a plank box with a curved upper cover which diverts the fast-moving stream of concrete and drops it, thoroughly mixed, on the ground or, on actual work, within the forms.

The concrete was hand mixed, of 1:3:5 proportions, and was made with stone up to 2-in. diameter. About as much water was used as in ordinary reinforced-concrete work, that is, it was a fairly wet mixture.

The main object of these experiments was to determine the amount of power necessary to convey concrete through pipes of different sizes and lengths; and the coefficient of friction between the concrete and the pipe so as to make possible the use of Bernoulli's Theorem in the design of other apparatus.

Inasmuch as during experiments concrete was deposited without difficulty at a height of about 100 ft. above the mixer through a vertical pipe line, it is reasonable to assume that it can be conveyed by this means to any height that would be encountered in ordinary construction.

The process of making concrete resolves itself naturally into several separate and distinct divisions, namely: manufacture of cement, the handling of cement, sand and stone, measuring, feeding and mixing the aggregates, conveying and placing the concrete. The invention of the rotary kiln, and numerous devices for measuring, feeding and mixing the aggregates, has reduced the cost of concrete to a point where it is now used on all classes of construction. It is a fact, however, that concrete is still conveyed and placed by the same crude and expensive means that were in use from the beginning. Inasmuch as the greatest factor in the present cost lies in the conveying and placing of the concrete it would seem that these experiments in pneumatic conveying offer a solution of the problem of still further reduction in cost, as statistics obtained during these experiments show that on works of even moderate magnitude concrete can be conveyed by pneumatic means for less than 10 cts per cu. yd.—*Engineering News.*

STILL ANOTHER JOB FOR VICTOR

Construction Paymaster Cooper and Transportation Clerk Hazard need have no fear from the bold bad bandits on this month's trip. They are accompanied from camp to camp by an armed guard. Some guard, too, you will admit when you see who it is. Can't guess? Why its our old friend Vic Meyer. Yep! regular guard.

The *Vincent* is expected to arrive soon with a general cargo for this port.

THE PORTO VELHO
Marconigram

"LA VIDA SIN LITERATURA Y QUININA ES MUERTE"

Published at Porto Velho (Rio Madeira), Amazonas, Brazil

VOLUME 2	SATURDAY, DECEMBER 17, 1910	NUMBER 12

SENHOR LIMA'S VIEWS ON THE REPUBLIC OF PORTUGAL

Paris, October 14 —Senhor Lima, one of the leaders of the Portuguese Republican party, who is now in Paris, looks upon the revolution in his country as the beginning of a revival among the Latin peoples of far-reaching results

"If would not be an isolated event, it would have world-wide consequences, and first of all there would be an immediate re-percussion in Spain. There would be an alliance with Brazil and an alliance between Republican Spain and the South American States. A federation o the Iberian peninsula would be the first step toward the federation of the Latin peoples; that would mean, without doubt, the political transformation of Europe, and who knows that this Latin federation would not be a step toward that still distant ideal, the federation of mankind?"

Senhor Lima dealt at some length with the relations between England and Portugal.

"The Republicans," he said, "are the first to proclaim the necessity for a solid alliance with England, rendered so desirable by the commercial interests of the two countries and their close Colonial relations Alliances are to peoples what associations are to individuals—an element of strength and power Dynastic alliances may have had their reason d'être four or five hundred years ago, but to-day they are not admitted, not even tolerated; the only lasting alliances are those between peoples.

"It is a mistake to think that there is ill-feeling toward England on the part of the Portuguese people; what there always has been is ill-will toward the Braganza dynasty; this dynasty has been fatal to us. It It is to it that we owe the loss of Brazil, of Tangier, of Bombay, and other places. It is not possible for a nation to forget such souvenirs." —N.Y. *Times*.

WHERE BAGMEN PAY HIGH

The Amazon country is a fine market for Americans to develop, but it will cost them good money to send commercial travelers there. Special Agent Turner gives some prices in a recent consular report: "No self-respecting salesman," he says "can cover the northern Brazil trade at a less expense than $12 a day. Hotel service will cost him not less than $6. Ginger ale costs $1 25 for two drinks. Linen-coated paper collars cost $1.50 per dozen. Linen collars of old style, ordinary 3-ply English make, cost $6 per dozen. If a salesman attempts to entertain at dinner he will be fortunate to get up from table with a bill less than $25." To get his luggage from steamer to hotel will cost him at least $5 and may cost him $10 —*N.Y. Mail Express*.

BIG NEW TUNNEL TO BE BUILT

The 5 1-2-mile Arthur Pass tunnel on the New Zealand Government Railways (3 1-2 ft.-gage) will be one of the largest tunnels in the world It is on a line crossing the South Island east and west, between Christchurch and Greymouth. Work was commenced in 1908, and the contract allows five years for completion. It is of horseshoe section, 14 ft. wide at rail level. with sides of 15 ft radius and a roof arch of 7ft 3. ins. radius In soft ground it has an invert with a radius of 15 ft. at the center and 4 ft. 6 ins. at the sides. The height above rail level is about 15 1-2 ft. The ordinary section has a 12-in. lining and a rectangular side draw (below the level of the floor) covered by concrete slab. The invert section has a 24-in. lining, and a center drain of concrete blocks and slabs The lining is of concrete, faced with concrete blocks. Compressed-air drills are used and the explosive is gelignite. The compressors at each end of the tunnel are driven by Pelton wheels operating under 700 ft. head. A bottom heading about 8 ft wide and 7 ft. high is driven first, and behind this is a smaller top heading. The rate of progress is said to average 12 ft. per day at each end of the tunnel. —*Engineering News*.

LEVEL AND TRANSIT NOTES

Mr. Editor :—

Why is the Rio Madeira like the N.Y. Stock Market ?

'Cause its always rising and falling.

The Chief Engineer's Residence has received an attractive coat of paint, adding considerably to its appearances.

Albert Kopp, of the Accounting Department, is visiting friends at Candelaria

The Sounding Squad continue taking elevations in North Porto Velho.

W. J. Hanna, who has been visiting Candelaria, has returned to Porto Velho.

E. B. Karnopp and party, who left Porto Velho, Oct. 4th, arrived at Guajara-mirim on Nov. 7th and advises that all are well.

D. B. Cutler has been sent out to join Bolton's party at the extreme front.

———

Mr. D. D. Colvin, Assoc M. Am. Soc. C. E., formerly Chief Engineer of the Pan-American R. R at Gamboa, Oaxaca, Mex., has been made Assistant Chief Engineer of the Combined Pan-American R. R and the Veracruz & Isthmus R. R., both of which have been merged with The National Rys of Mexico and are under the general jurisdiction of Mr. J. M. Reid, Chief Engineer of The National Rys. of Mexico. Mr. Colvin's headquarters will be at Tierra Blanca, Ver., Mex

LEVEL AND TRANSIT NOTES

Chief Engineer Dose returned to Porto Velho on the *Vincent* from Manaos.

Among the passengers on the last trip of the *M-M* were the following for the Engineering department: W. H. Bennett, R. A. Bennett, W. E. Lord and C. F. Cartwright.

R. C. S. Watson, formerly rodman with Miller's party, left on the *Madeira-Mamore* for Manaos, en route to his home in England.

Photographer Merrill left for a trip up the line on Wednesday.

J. Y. Bayliss, Principal Assistant Engineer, was one of the passengers on the last trip of the *Madeira-Mamore* for Manaos.

J. M. Robinson, Assistant Chief Engineer, arrived in Porto Velho Friday morning. He reports that Marion Hill is now locating camp sites for camps 34 and 35. He also says there is only one falls now between camp 25 and Araras that cannot be passed in a launch.

C. J. Kalbfell has been transferred from Miller's party to Bolton's party, which is now located at Riberao. They expect to be at Villa Bella about the first of the year.

Mr. Robinson reports that clearing will be finished up to camp 33 by the first of the year, and the location will be about kilometer 250—about to Araras.

OCEAN STEAMSHIP SAILINGS

Sailings for New York: Booth Line 7th, 17th, and 27th of each month; Lloyd Brazileiro Boats sporadic sailings.

Sailings for Europe: Booth Line, 3rd, 13th, and 23rd of each month; German Line 1st and 15th.

New Publication

Rubberhide Co., Boston, Mass Paper; 3 1-2 x 6 ins.: pp. 16; illustrated.

This little pamphlet describes a patented water-proof footwear for use of engineers, contractors laborers and others who have to work in wet places.

THE LATE MR. E. C. PICKETT

The death of Mr. E. C. Pickett of typhoid at Candelaria Hospital last Sunday, December 11th, was a severe blow to his many friends here. He had been sick for over six weeks but owing to the splendid fight he was putting up, his good physic and the expert medical attention he was receiving, all had hopes of his recovery.

He came to Brazil in April 1908 after having spent three months in Cuba securing laborers for work here. Previous to that time he had been with the firm of May & Jekyll in Cuba and was one of their oldest employees. His record with the firm is of the best, showing him as honest and straight dealing, intelligent, and a hard worker. His rapid advancement was a tribute to his many sterling qualities.

As a friend he was perfect. Always obliging and unselfish. His lovable character gained him the friendship of all, the enmity of none.

He was a good son as many of us know. His devotion to his family being well known to his intimate friends.

Honest, upright; true to family, friends and duty. No man can do more.

We extend our heartfelt sympathies to his family in their sad bereavement.

THEY WENT TO CHURCH

The Editor of the *Marconigram* received a post card from our old friend J. O. Wanzer, of the Engineering department who is on vacation. The post card was written from Barbados, and brought the information that they were all well and in fine spirits. What was the hardest part of it all to believe is that he and our once erstwhile Poet Laurete, had grasped the first opportunity offered and attended church. Now that sounded funny to us, but we bet if it were true, and they did go, their prayers were "Lord forgive us for what we are about to do."

NOTES ABOUT TOWN

Just a week until Christmas, and the *Marconigram* wishes to extend a gentle hint to its readers to be good, or Santa Claus won't bring you a thing.

Paymaster C. R. Hudson, went up the line the early part of this week to pay off; he was accompanied by Mr. H. G. Brown who looks after the transportation. Mr. D. B. Merrill whose photographs are about the only view that the most of us in Porto Velho get of the "Way up front" was with them.

Dr. A. A. Marsteller who has been in Porto Velho for the past several weeks, took the trip down to Manaos on the *M-M* this week. Dr. A. C. Fitch, who made the last trip with the boat taking his place here. It goes without saying that the sick ones around Porto Volho will get all that is coming to them, as will also those who happen to need medical attention on the boat. Dr. Fitch took hold of the dispensary like an experienced druggist, and even knows a good prescription when concocted by another.

W. B. Horsey, who has been at Track Camp for the past few months is again located at Porto Velho, being in the General Office with Chief Clerk, J. H. Nunn.

Albert DeBaer who has recently returned to Porto Velho has been appointed Agent at Kil. 152, and Mr. H B. Walling, Traffic Clerk, went up yesterday to install Mr. DeBaer in his new position.

The first class passengers arriving on December 13 on the *M-M* were as follows:—Ed Lehman, river transportation E. C. Pike, assistant camp foreman C. G. Allen, packer. A. V. Hunt, ice plant. Wm A. Whelan, foreman water service. Harry Brenner, boiler maker. Clyde M Kenyon, motor car.

ACROSS SOUTH AMERICA BY WATER

Daring Trip by a London Doctor and His Friend

2,000 MILES JOURNEY

White Traders who Hold the Natives in Veiled Slavery

"You will never make the journey. If you try you will be drowned in the rapids. If you escape drowning you will be killed by the Indians; and if you escape both the rapids and the Indians, you will die of the fever."

Such a threefold prophecy of disaster might have scared the pluckiest of adventurers But an Englishman and a Scotsman decided to risk all, and for love of adventure made a two thousand miles journey on the Amazon and its tributaries. Both of them—Dr C. J. Wilson. M.R.C.S., and L R.C.P. of London, and Mr. J. C. McLean—have been employed in connection with the new Trans-Andean Railway tunnel in South America.

They could have come home in the ordinary way to Southampton in about three weeks they told a *Lloyd's News* representative on Wednesday; but they were told that no one had ever made the trip across the continent by river, so they decided to try it. With the various delays, it took them about five months

"We started from Antofagasta, in Chile," said Dr. Wilson, "running up to La Paz by train, and then taking to the mules and the water, on one of the tributaries of the Mamore, I suppose. Thence we got on to the Mamore itself, and so to the Amazon, which we joined east of Manaos

In the Land of Rubber

"From Riberalta to San Antonio is about two hundred miles. Then it is about eight hundred from San Antonio to Manaos, and another nine hundred from there to Para, the great rubber centre. So that, with the preliminary trip from La Paz to Riberalta, we probably did considerably over two thousand miles.

"There were dangerous bits, but we never discovered the killing Indians, and the only difficulty we had with human beings arose from the disinclination of the white employers of labor, chiefly Germans and descendants of the Spanish, to assist us with the necessary 'boys' to navigate the craft on which we had to travel; and the 'boys' themselves are so tied to the employers that they dare not move without permission

"At one point some of them asked us to take them down the river with us. They said they could earn a lot more money in the rubber plantations than they were getting, but were in debt to their employers and could not get permission to leave. Under the system of signed agreement at so many dollars a month, and obligation to buy all goods from stores owned by their employers, who charge what they like, a debt of $1,000 may be built up easily, and if a 'boy' clears out while in debt he is brought back by the police. If another man desires his services, he pays the first employer what is owing by the 'boy' and then the debt and the 'boy' are transferred.

"There is no slavery, but it is very much like it in effect. The unfortunate laborer is never out of debt, and so he is always a bondman. He is charged 14s. or 16s. a bottle for whisky or brandy, and about the same amount for a bottle of German beer. At Riberalta, the whole population, with very exceptions, make Sunday a day of drinking."

The Scourge of Fever

On the subject of rubber cultivation Dr Wilson said: "There are thousands of miles of rubber trees, and the supply appears to be almost unlimited. But labor is still so scarce, and the distance so great and difficult, that you cannot get the stuff into the market except at a big price, and therefore there will be a good price for years to come "

As soon as they got into the rapids the explorers found the dangers foreshadowed for them. The water ran two or three miles in the open, and fifteen or sixteen miles an hour in the rapids To navigate these they had only flimsy rafts, a few inches above the water surface. So that, with the heat of the sun and standing in the water, when they had done a few weeks of it their feet were swollen and their agony almost unbearable.

Of danger from Indians they saw no trace. Dr. Wilson describes them as all thoroughly civilised, and very willing and obliging. But the fever was terribly real, and there were grim jests in connection with it that showed how familiar the natives and traders had become with death It was no rare thing for one-half of those making a trip in the fever area to be stricken and die in the course of a few weeks. In one case a party of forty started, and twenty-seven died during the journey.

In another case the question of anchorage for the night was being discussed. Some of the crew were known to be dying. "No; don't stop here," one trader responded to a suggestion. "There is a good piece of soft ground a bit higher up, and we can plant these fellows (the dying 'boys') more easily." They did so, and the graves were marked by a simple little wooden cross, replicas of which can be found all over the district, which has claimed so many victims In that area Dr. Wilson found practically everyone suffering from a mild form of ague or fever, but he and his companion both came through without contracting the sickness

AUSTRALIA ADOPTS METRIC SYSTEM

A step toward the metric system was taken in Australia on August 4. The House of Representatives of Australia on that date adopted, by a vote of 35 to 2, a resolution pledging the Government to seek the approval of the next Imperial Conference to a common decimal system of metric weights and measures throughout the British Empire. The resolution further provides that in case this proposition is not adopted, the Government will proceed with the consideration of such a reform in Australia and invite the cooperation of New Zealand

London's Chamber of Commerce has announced the preparation of a scheme by the Russian Government for introducing metric weights and measures in Russia, and that legislation looking to that end will shortly be laid before the Duma.

LAUGH and the World Laughs with you

Read these and Join the Ha ha ha's!

FROM EVERYBODY'S MAGAZINE

The dinner had not gone at all well. The waiter was slow, the food was cold, and the cooking was bad. The guest in the German restaurant was of a naturally peevish disposition anyhow, and he complained vigorously to the head waiter, and especially complained of the waiter at his table. As he was leaving, the waiter said humbly,

"If you only knew vat a hardt time us vaiters hat, you would nicht be so hardt."

"But," said the guest, "why be a waiter?"

"Vot else couldt I do?" asked the waiter.

"Well," said the guest, "up at the Metropolitan Opera House they pay a man five dollars a night to play the oboe. You might try that."

"Budt" said the waiter, "I don't know how to blay dot oboe."

"What is the difference?" observed the guest as he turned away leaving a much mystified waiter. "You dont know how to wait, either; you might scatter your incompetence."

There lives an editor in interior Pennsylvania, "Jim" Sweeney by name, who has a keen sense of humour. Seeking to increase his fortune, Sweeny once wrote to a prospective advertiser, setting forth in attractive fashion the value of his paper as a medium of publicity.

The advertiser was captivated by Sweeney's letter, but, desirous of more specific assurances before he invested his money, he wrote to Sweeney, saying that he hadn't heard of the *Trumptown Sentinel*. "Where does it circulate?" he asked.

And, in his illuminating way, Sweeney wrote back,

"The *Trumptown Sentinel* circulates in Europe, Asia, Africa, North and South America, and it's just about all I can do to keep it from going to hell."

EQUAL FOR HIM

A certain American naval officer brought a Chinese servant named Quong home with him from the Far East. One day the Oriental asked permission to attend a funeral.

"Go ahead, Quong," consented the officer. Then he supplemented, "I suppose you will place different kinds of food on your dead friend's grave, as they do in your native country."

"Samee as in China," said Quong.

"Now, Quong," continued the officer, good naturedly, "when do you think your friend will come up to eat what you leave on his grave?"

"Allee samee time that 'Melican man comes up to smellee flowers you put on his," retorted Quong in the same spirit.— *E. Mack's National Monthly.*

Making a Vacancy

"Perhaps," remarked the college oarsman, who really wasn't fit to be on the crew, "perhaps I might improve if I should try a faster stroke."

"If you should get a lightning stroke," replied the disgusted trainer, "it certainly would improve the crew.—*Catholic Standard and Times.*

Preparation

"John," said the politician's wife, "what do you mean by standing in front of the looking glass? I never knew you to be so vain!"

"I'm not vain. I'm going to call on a great statesman and afterward I shall meet the interviewers. I am practising my smile."—*Washington Star.*

HOMEOPATHS AND ALLOPATHS

If on the doctor's you should be a caller,
You will find there's not much in a name;
Though the dose of the one is much
   smaller,
The size of their bills is the same.
   —*Lippincott's.*

Placing the Blame

Mr. Penman—Poets are born, not made. Mrs. Penman—Of course; go and blame it on the poor stork!—*Yonkers Statesman.*

No Tobacco There

"Why don't you try one of those tobacco cures on your son?" asked Gaddie.

"That wouldn't have any effect on him" replied Popley.

"Oh! yes; they simply kill all appetite for tobacco."

But he smokes cigarettes."—*The Catholic Standard and Times.*

Two of a Kind

"What makes you think it is such a suitable match?"

"Well, she is light-headed and he is lantern-jawed."—*The Widow.*

A citizen of Memphis, Tennessee, lost a valuable scarab which he had been wearing on a watch-fob. He advertised his loss in the daily papers and offered a generous reward for the return of the trinket.

Early the next morning he received a call from a colored boy leading a miserable yellow cur. "Say, boss," said the boy, "I seen yo' ad in de papeh. Am dis yo' scarab?"—*Everybody's Magazine.*

THE PORTO VELHO

Marconigram

"LA VIDA SIN LITERATURA Y QUININA ES MUERTE"

Published at Porto Velho (Rio Madeira), Amazonas, Brazil

VOLUME 2   SATURDAY, DECEMBER 24, 1910   NUMBER 13

SOUTH AMERICA'S FIRST TRANS-CONTINENTAL

A Journey Over the Line of the First Railroad to Pierce the Andes—Buenos Aires to Valparaiso by Air-Line Instead of by the Dangerous Straits of Magellan

(Charles Wellington Furlong in "The World's Work.")

Since pre-dawn of history, before the first Abel bore sheep on his shoulders or a Cain garnered his primal harvest, one of man's principal considerations has been how to best slide, roll, push, drag, sail, or propel his possessions in the quickest, quietest, safest manner by the shortest or most feasible route.

Thus transportation has developed from the hand-paddled log to the *Lusitania;* from the thong backpack to the modern Mallet compound locomotive; from hardbeaten forest trails to systematic railroad extension until to-day man has built enough steel track to girdle the world at the equator twenty-five times. A fifteenth of this track (40,000 miles) stretches across South America, placing it fourth (including Australasia) among the world's continents in point of mileage.

Two natural systems of railroad routes suggest themselves as one looks over the great kite-shaped continent of South America—the longitudinal from Panama to Magellan Strait and the transcontinental routes from ocean to ocean. Already more than half of the longitudinal mileage is in operation in Chile and Peru and three-tenths in Argentine.

The history of South American railroad development is preëminently a tribute to American engineers and captains of industry.

William H. Aspinwall in 1850 turned his attention to the building of the Panama Railroad — a desperate and dramatic undertaking. Five years later the last rail was laid and the forerunner of the Panama Canal completed. His contemporary, William Wheelright, "rounded the Horn" about this time and left his name indelibly engraved in the engineering annals of Chile: so great was his record that Chileans have linked it with that of Magellan.

To Henry Meiggs can be attributed forty-two miles of road between Valparaiso and Santiago, Chile—the first lap of the transcontinental line On the other side of the continent George E. Church surveyed and located the Great Northern Railway of Buenos Aires. Other Americans were doing much to forward railroad projects in South America, and Benjamin F. Bates had no less than fifteen routes surveyed across the northern Andes at his own expense.

Meiggs turned his attention to Peru. Six important roads were actually constructed, and practically the whole railroad system of that country is an outcome of his indomitable perseverance. His greatest work, however, is the famous Pacific and Transandean Callao, Lima, and Oroyo Railway. This remarkable engineering feat, known as "the railroad among the clouds," culminates in a tunnel 3,848 feet long and 15,645 feet above sea-level—less than a stone's throw lower than Mont Blanc—and is the highest railroad in the world

Colonel Church meantime, at the request of South American governments, surveyed railroads through the upper Amazon, finally resulting in the Madeira and Mamoré Railway, now nearly completed.

Another American whose name will stand in the forefront in the annals of South American industry is that of William R. Grace It was under the "Grace contract" that

(Continued on Page 3)

PRESERVATIVES FOR R.R. TIES AND TELEGRAPH POLES

Treated ties and poles in Denmark and western Europe are dealt with in a pamphlet prepared by Mr. A. Collstrop, of Kjobenhaven, Denmark, who is interested in plants which use the Rueping system of creosoting. The Danish State Railways have all ties treated by a preservative process, and their renewals are estimated at 2.7 per cent. in 10 years, 13 per cent in 15 years and 28 per cent. in 20 years. Of 41 private railways, the majority use treated ties in renewals. Since 1905, the Rueping process has been employed by all the State and private railways. One private railway with 49,000 treated ties and not one of these ties replaced during 12 years; another line with 22,344 treated ties had only 10 renewed in 10 years, and these were renewed on account of mechanical wear. The same process is used in a number of other European countries, including parts of Russia where it is possible to obtain Russian creosote oil. Experiments made with crude oil in Russia have given satisfactory results, but it is said that this can compete with creosote oil only within a limited distance from Baku (in the oil district) and at low freight rates. The Rueping process is said to have been applied to about 50,000,000 ties (including those used in America).

Telegraph and telephone poles in western Europe are treated with copper sulphate (Boucherie process), mercury chloride (Kyanising), and creosote oil. For the last, both the full and limited absorption processes are used, but Mr. Collstrop states that the use of the Rueping limited-absorption process is increasing, while that of the three other processes is decreasing. The average life (kind of wood not stated) is given as follows: untreated, 7 7, years; with copper sulphate, 11 7; with mercury chloride 13 7; with creosote 20.6 years About half of the poles in Denmark are stated to be treated by the Rueping process. The Prussian telegraph department had used the same process to treat 433,000 poles from 1892 to the end of 1909, and expects to have an additional 394,000 treated by the end of 1911.

NOTES ABOUT TOWN

Notice

The Wholesale and Retail Departments of the Commissary at Porto Velho will be closed December 31st and January 1st, in order to take annual inventory. All departments are advised, in order that they may draw necessary supplies to run them over the two days.

J. H. Byrne has been appointed acting Accountant at Porto Velho effective January 1st, 1911. The position of Accountant at Porto Velho has been vacant since Mr. Hayes left.

D. C Bell, has been appointed acting Accountant at the Construction Office effective January 1st, 1911, vice O. L. Niggli, resigned.

Frank Pascoe, foreman carpenter, and Chris. Thompson, assistant, expect to sail down the river on the next trip of the *M-M*.

Robert Craswell, who has been foreman at the Mutum Parana bridge stopped in town waiting to go down river on his vacation.

James Hynes, who has been up-the-line in charge of a gang of carpenters came into town Friday evening.

Our good-natured young friend "Red" Anderson departed northward on the *Humaytha* on Monday.

Love often makes a wise man feel like a fool, and sometimes it makes a fool act like a wise man.

Steamer *Oteri* arrived on Friday afternoon having on board three first class passengers : W. E. Shanahan, locomotive engineer; F. Ralf, conductor; Antonio Miranda, track foreman. Also 265 third class of which about 130 were Spaniards and the balance West Indian negroes.

New Hotel II has been screened in and now presents an almost habitable appearance. 'Tis rumoured this Hotel is for the use of the Mechanical Department.

Another rumour says that the men are going to be treated to—hush, don't give it away—turkeys and "fixings" to-morrow at dinner, also something to wash it down with.

To the Editor: When, and by whom was work on the Panama Canal begun? *Ans.*—In 1883, by a company of Frenchmen They carried on the work for six years. Then the company failed, and gave place to another. This second French company worked on the canal on a smaller scale for ten years, ending with 1904. In that year it sold its rights to the United States Government

One evening when Irving was playing Macbeth he worked his audience into an unusually high pitch of excitement. He was in his best mood and had just reached the point where Macbeth orders Banquo's ghost to leave the table.

"Hence, horrible shadow! Unreal mockery, hence!" declaimed Irving in his most tragic manner, as with convulsive shudder he sank to the ground and drew his robe over his face.

On the withdrawal of Banquo, a high-pitched, sympathetic voice shouted from the top gallery,

"It's all right now, 'Enery; e's gone!"

An American tourist hailing from the West was recently out sightseeing in London. They took him aboard the old battleship *Victory*, which was Lord Nelson's flagship in several of his most famous naval triumphs. An English sailor escorted the American over the vessel, and coming to a raised brass tablet he said, as he reverently removed his hat,

"Ere, sir, is the spot where Lord Nelson fell."

"Oh, is it?" replied the American blankly. "Well, that ain't nothing. I nearly tripped on the blame thing myself." —*Everybody's Magazine.*

The Foreman's Mess moves to-day into the adjacent room.

THE CARIPUNA MAIDENS

(*Rio Madeira, Brazil, S.A.*)

An image of living bronze is she,
The Caripuna maiden.
She roams amid the forest wild
With nature's garb her rainment.

'Tis said, that in the long ago
These maids were large and handsome,
But times have changed since then,
'twould seem
And so have the Indian maidens.

Those far famed maids of the Amazon
We read about in fiction
Are, so it seems, but idle dreams
Of some misguided mortal.
—*Onlooker.*

SAULT STE. MARIE LOCK

The new lock at Sault Ste. Marie is progressing, and it is expected that the excavation for the lock pit will be completed early in 1911 The contract for the concrete will be let about January 1st, and work on this will be commenced in the spring. The MacArthur Brothers Co. has the contract for the western section of the approach canal and John Marsch is the contractor for the lock excavation. The work is under the direction of Col C. McD. Townsend, M Am. Soc. C.E, U S. Engineers, and Mr. L. C. Sabin, M. Am. Soc. C. E., is Assistant Engineer. This new lock (known as the Davis lock) will be 1,350 ft. long between the gates, 80 ft wide, and 24 1-2 ft deep below the level of extreme low water. It will be parallel with and adjacent to the two existing locks: the Weitzel lock (1881), 515 x 80 ft., with a depth of 16 ft., and the Poe lock (1895), 800 x 100 ft., with a depth of 21 ft —*Eng. News*

It has been beautifully said by a great writer that the veil which hides the future from our mortal eyes has been woven by the Hand of Mercy.

THE "MARCONIGRAM" WISHES ALL A MERRY CHRISTMAS

(Continued from 1st Page)

SOUTH AMERICA'S FIRST TRANS-CONTINENTAL

the Oroya road was finished; and now, under a second "Grace contract," another section of the great transcontinental railroad (the Transandine Railway) is finished.

Through my port-hole as I write, I look away toward that largest South American country — Brazil, with the most wonderful navigable river system in the world. From the Pacific coast, cutting across Peru and northern Chile, a number of railroads run inland toward its head. Some of these spurs of line cross the Andes and enter Bolivia and will soon connect with a number of the navigable tributaries of the Amazon.

The great northern, central, and southern region is devoid of roads; Buenos Aires, Rio de Janeiro, Sao Paulo, Santiago, and Lima stand out as radiating centres, but in Argentina is found fully half of the mileage of all the rest of South America combined. Thirty-five degrees south of the equator, where the yellow, muddy waters of the Uruguay and Parana broaden into the Rio de la Plata to meet the sea, Argentina has called the peoples of the nations, and modern Buenos Aires has been born. This "City of Good Airs" has woven about it, like a colossal web of a meadow spider, the greatest network of railroads in South America. It sends its antennæ of steel north into Paraguay and to the Bolivian frontier, and south to the Rio Negro; and by the time this article is in print the most important line of all will find its other terminus at Valparaiso, Chile—connecting the two great oceans by rail for the first time.

The 888 miles of this big transcontinental railroad run across three topographically different natural divisions: over level pampas from Buenos Aires to Mendoza is 650 miles; through mountain regions from Mendoza to Los Andes, 160 miles; and the remaining 78 from Los Andes through the Valle Central region of Chile to Valparaiso. The line is also divided into three management divisions: the Buenos Aires

and Pacific, the Transandine, and the Chilean State.

Across Argentine, a gradually rising plain shunts back from the Atlantic to the Andean chain—that great barrier which runs the length of the continent, which has made peoples, changed customs and languages, set natural and political boundaries, and lastly has made historical the building of the first South American transcontinental railroad.

Toward that great barrier some months ago I found myself speeding. A few hours away from the color-tinted, stucco houses and flower gardens of Buenos Aires one enters the great cattle and wheat country. Brown or green stretches away in level monotony to the horizon, broken only by the little dark copses of trees which indicate the *estancia* (ranch) buildings. From lagoons great vermilion-colored flamingoes startle in confusion; ostriches feed and nest near the railroad among the giant thistles whose tufted stalks, now dry and brown, are seen on either hand. Long-tailed hawks sit like silent sentinels on the fence-posts, and swarms of locusts rise in showers of silver flecks until against the sun they transform into dark, low-spreading clouds. Occasionally rough, dark-visaged *gauchos* (cowboys) pass with droves of cattle or sheep along the roadway following the tracks.

From Junin (159 miles from Buenos Aires) for about 200 miles to Mt. Kenua, the train rolls along an absolutely straight track; but clear to Mendoza—almost across Argentine—wire fencing follows every mile of the way on either side of the track and only darkness or storm shuts out the sight of cattle or sheep.

The sun pours down fiercely on the car roofs in the heat of the day, and the fine dust sifts its gray coating over everything. Wealthy *estancieros* in ponchos and silver spurs, *gauchos* and half-breed Indians in broad trousers, high boots, and with long knives thrust through their belts, gather at the stations (eight of which lie between Buenos Aires and Mendoza) offering interesting studies of pampas types. From this great central region comes

the bulk of Argentina's enormous wheat, wool, and hide exports. As the sun in gorgeous splendor drops below the long, level line of prairie and under the glistening chalices of the Pleiades and the Southern Cross, we rumble steadily on toward the great wall which forbiddingly raises its massive peaks against the intrusion of man.

In 1860 William Wheelwright, of Massachusetts, was first to present a feasible plan for a transcontinental road from ocean to ocean across Argentina and Chile. This he submitted to the Argentine Government. From Rosario, then the principal port of Argentina, the line was to run by way of San Francisco Pass to Caldera, on the Chilean coast ten degrees (600 miles) north of Valparaiso.

"IN THE HOLE HE GOES"

A little Atlantic City girl was an awe-struck but attentive witness at the baptism of her baby brother. Not long afterward there was another birth in the house. Her big maltese cat was the proud mamma of a kitten. So little Ethel thought if the latest arrival was to have a name it ought to be given officially and with all due ceremony.

Without consulting the rest of the family Ethel carried the kitten to the beach one sunny afternoon and, holding it under one arm, scooped up a hole in the sand which soon filled with water. Ethel poised the kitten solemnly over the little pool. "Your name's Fuzzy," she pronounced slowly "The Father, the Son, and in the hole he goes."

And in the hole he went.—*Philadelphia Times.*

GOLD PAVED ROAD

London streets are not paved with gold, but some Australian ones are. At Daylesford, the town which has grown up around the "Jim Crow diggings," a man the other day noticed the gleam of gold as he was walking along a road.

He picked up a piece of the quartz rock with which the road was metalled and extracted $25 worth of gold from it. A further search was rewarded with $150 more of gold used in the making of the roadway.—*Westminster Gazette.*

PAVING THE ROAD TO HELL

A Tale of Good Intentions

From the Docket.

Getting married is about the most risky thing a man can do, unless it is being born. The chances taken by a gambler or a north pole explorer are not to be mentioned in the same breath. When the natural hazards of the act are complicated by legal entanglements, the situation really becomes serious. With these few preliminary remarks, to indicate that the tale we are about to tell is a hard-luck story of law and marriage, we will proceed to relate the chapter in the life of Henry Stowell, which made him a felon in spite of himself.

Stowell was a good man, up to his lights. In fact, he was one of those abnormally conscientious men whose reports to the tax assessor correspond exactly with their insurance schedules. He voluntarily paid his street-car fare when the conductor overlooked him, and he would wake a neighbor up in the middle of the night to correct an unintentional misstatement which he might inadvertently have made. You would not think that a man of that sort would give the law courts much occupation. What with the thieves and embezzlers, the insurance presidents and the mob leaders, the porch climbers and the confidence men, you would naturally suppose that the department of justice would be sufficiently occupied without meddling with people of Henry's sort; but as George Bernard Shaw says: "You never can tell." Henry was not content with his state of civic and single blessedness; he wanted to be married. That's where his troubles began.

When Henry was 27 years old he married Bertha Haynes. Just why, it might be difficult to say; but then it always is difficult to say. Probably he fell in love with her by force of contrast. Perhaps he thought that he could reform her. Good women are always marrying men who are not so good with the expectation of reforming them; so it is not to be wondered at if a man occasionally falls into the same sentimental quagmire. At any rate, Bertha was not of the abnormally conscientious variety. She had been brought up that way. Perhaps that was why she thought it would be useful to have a man like Henry in the family. He could supply the virtue, while she furnished the good times. It did not take more than a few months, however, for her to reach the conclusion that, after all, she really could not stand it. She departed somewhat hastily, for another state. She went in the company of another man, whose conscience and standards of conduct were more in harmony with her own than Henry's were.

Henry did not attempt to follow her, but after a short time one of her sisters went to look her up, and shortly afterwards this sister wrote back to the remaining members of the family, who were

Henry's neighbors, a circumstantial account of Bertha's death. This happened to be an imaginative sketch, for Bertha was not really dead at all; but it was very well done. It possessed verisimilitude in a high degree. It is not customary for a sister to attach a formal affidavit to a family letter containing a touching account of the last hours of her deceased relative, so the omission of that technicality did not excite particular comment. Bertha's brother sewed a black band on his coat sleeve, and showed the letter to Henry. Whether Henry was grieved or secretly relieved does not appear from the evidence, and it is not necessary for us to inquire. He was a decent fellow, and if he did draw a sigh of relief he said nothing. The chapter had been a miserable one, but it was ended—so he thought.

Time went on, and after five years or so Henry's bitter experience had faded far enough into the distance to enable him to think of marriage without shivering. This was when he met Mary Blake. His experiences had made him a wiser man and he was able to appreciate the fact that Mary was a different sort of woman from Bertha. They were married and people wished them joy, with less of the cynical doubt that accompanies that wish than usual. They had no doubt themselves, whatsoever. Henry's only regret was that he had not waited for Mary in the first place. It is just possible that he allowed this regret to become too manifest, and that the Haynes family were provoked by his cheerful aspect to prick his bubble of satisfaction. Or perhaps their moral sensibilities (which being long unused, must have been uncommonly sensitive) were shocked by the moral aspect —or rather by the immoral aspect—of the present situation. At any rate, they began by nods and shrugs and lifted eyebrows to suggest a disquieting rumor that Henry Stowell's first wife was still living, and that for all his high and mighty airs he was no better than he should be, or than the rest of us are.

The report, after the fashion of its kind, had gone the rounds of the town a good many times before it reached Henry's ears, and when it did come to his notice he at first thought it too absurd to answer. It persisted, however, and grew more annoying, so finally, he decided to put his lacerated pride in his pocket and give the public the facts of his bitter experience. He went to Bertha's sister to get the details of the record of her death. He found, instead, that her record was very lively, and that she herself was very much alive.

There was only one thing for him to do, and he did it promptly. He obtained a divorce from Bertha and remarried Mary. He began to hope that things were at last settled but he still had the public conscience to reckon with. Harlan County was a moral county, and its grand jury brought in an indictment charging Henry Stowell with being a bigamist, inasmuch as, while his first wife was still living he

did unlawfully marry Mary Blake, against the peace and dignity of the commonwealth. He was convicted in the circuit court and branded as a bigamist.

Henry was not a lawyer, so he found it difficult to understand wherein his guilt lay. He insisted that he really did not not belong to the chain gang, and he did not believe that the legal machinery of the state could force him into that class. He, therefore, prosecuted an appeal to the supreme court. There he learned more about the law. The law deals with facts, and if the facts do not balance with justice, who is to blame? Henry had married Mary while Bertha, his wife, was still living and undivorced. That was the fact which eclipsed all others. The statute of the state provided the penalty for bigamy to be imprisonment for a term not less than three years, and not more than nine. That was the second fact to be faced. The facts that Henry had believed his wife dead, that he had formed this opinion upon the written and spoken testimony of members of her own family, that he had married Mary in good faith, and that, upon his discovery that Bertha was still skulking about in the land of the living, he had divorced her and married Mary again, were all considered "irrelevant, immaterial and inconsequential" facts. He was a bigamist and the law must have its pound of flesh. His only chance of escaping the penitentiary was held to be through an appeal to the executive clemency; in other words, he must sue, as a criminal, for pardon. Justice, with bandaged eyes, could not see through the act to the motive. Such is the law, as declared in Cornett vs. Commonwealth, 121 Southwestern Reporter, 424.

OCEAN STEAMSHIP SAILINGS

Sailings for New York: Booth Line 7th, 17th, and 27th of each month; Lloyd Brazileiro Boats sporadic sailings.

Sailings for Europe: Booth Line, 3rd, 13th, and 23rd of each month; German Line 1st and 15th.

STEAMER PASSENGER RATES

First Class to Manaos	165$000
Third Class "	55$000
First Class to Para	267$000
Third Class to Para	89$000
Manaos to New York	
First class	$110.00 gold
Manaos to Liverpool	
First class	£30-

Postal Rates to U.S. and Europe

200 reis per half ounce First Class matter.

100 reis per half ounce Second Class matter.

Please advise your foreign correspondents to put five cent stamp on your letters, so additional postage will not be charged at Manaos.

THE PORTO VELHO
Marconigram

"LA VIDA SIN LITERATURA Y QUININA ES MUERTE"

Published at Porto Velho (Rio Madeira), Amazonas, Brazil

VOLUME 2   SATURDAY, DECEMBER 31, 1910   NUMBER 14

A LITTLE VEST TO VEST TALK WITH THE CHILDREN

Xmas has come and went—all except a few sore heads. Isn't it funny the effect this damp weather has on hat bands? Ours has tightened up so it won't fit. Thought at first it was due to the poor quality of hat, but so many of the fellows are complaining of the same trouble that we are convinced it is the dampness.

Well, what did old Santa Claus bring you? We hung up our stockings alright, alright, but Xmas morning it was not there At first we thought a rat had probably eaten it but on second consideration a queer brown taste in our mouth caused us to allow that maybe it wasn't a rat. No telling what a fellow will do when he walks in his sleep.

Did you hear the quartette at the Mad House? They started practising Xmas Eve but got stuck on one particular "barber shop chord" and up to noon of the 27th were still unsuccessful. As their practising was interfering with the work, a squad was sent over with fire extinguishers and the thing stopped. Latest reports shows 'em still sizzling.

The Marconi boys went up to Santo Antonio Xmas day on an "Irish Special" that the boss kindly loaned them. Barron is still raving about the scenery. We've never looked at it through the bottom of a bottle. It probably is grand that way.

They had a blow-out at the Hospital Xmas. Great times. One of the Porto Velhians attended. About 11 o'clock he remembered that he had failed to put out his light and being unable to secure a hand car, according to his story, he footed it. Owing to the unequal spacing of the ties and the slippery state of the mud that particular evening, he experienced considerable trouble. He fell through the ties at one place—says it was a ditch—we think it was the bridge. Anyhow, when he had climbed out his lantern had gone out, he had no matches and had lost his hat. When he finally loomed up 'neath the arc lights at Porto Velho the police naturally held him up. Who wouldn't Think of a supposed respectable member of a respectable colony blowing in home at midnight minus a hat or lantern and plus bunches of mud and several sore ribs. And all because he forgot to put out his light before starting for Candelaria

We wish to apologize for our Society Editor. He attended several of the social events Xmas Eve and Xmas day but after one or two drinks thought that he was as good as anyone else and forgot what he had been sent for. This will explain the poor description of some of the events as we do not claim to be Society Editors and had depended entirely on him. That's always the trouble with the reporters that handle this end of the news. One or two drinks and they become ordinary guests.

NOTES FROM THE CAMPS

Reports from Camp 18 indicate that Christmas was well celebrated there. Chicken with Oyster Sauce and Plum Pudding were among the delicacies served, and the occasion was by no means a dry one either. We might be in Brazil, but it was Christmas just the same anyway.

James Street who left Porto Velho to assume the position of Timekeeper at Camp 23 is reported following his duties in his usual calm and serene fashion. Also that he celebrated Christmas in a manner befitting an exponent of the simple life.

PEACE THROUGH COMMERCE IN SOUTH AMERICA

A review of the political and diplomatic relations of the various republics in South America shows that, in the main, they have worked out vexatious disputes and controversies fully as satisfactorily as have European nations In a pamphlet recently published by the American Association for International Conciliation, Mr Charles M. Pepper gives such a review In the first place the record of boundary disputes in South America which have been settled by arbitration is a long one In every case it has been noted that the development of domestic industry and neighborhood and foreign commerce follows such settlement. Argentina's $700,000,000 foreign commerce to-day makes strongly for peace. Food is becoming so precious that the world cannot well afford to have Argentina's wheat lands and pastures interfered with. The enormous sums of European capital invested in the Argentine railways are a potent argument for maintaining peace Adjustment of the boundary between Argentine and Chile in 1898 was one of the most effective means of securing South American tranquility at a critical period and "back of the agencies which secured tranquility was the legitimate influence of capital invested in commerce." The result is the trans-Andine tunnel which has recently been opened.— *Review of Reviews.*

A LITTLE NONSENSE NOW AND THEN

Barber: Have something on your face when I get through, Sir?
Customer: Yes, please. Some skin and a nose, I hope. (From Boston).

"How often does your road kill a man," asked a passenger on the Southern recently of the conductor.
"Just once," answered Mr. C., sourly.— *Wireless Reporter.*

THE PORTO VELHO
MARCONIGRAM

Published at
Porto Velho (Rio Madeira) Brazil

C. L. JONES—*Editors*---C. R. HUDSON
S. WELLWOOD—*Publisher*

SATURDAY, DECEMBER 31ST, 1910.

NOTES ABOUT TOWN

Little drops of water
Little gobs of clay
Make the hills so slippery,
We're ashamed of what we say.

Mr. Daly was asked to send some fire extinguishers to the General Office for use on the clerks the morning after Christmas. But it is understood, Mr. D. replied "Naw, I know that bunch; they'd drink 'em dry."

It seemed sure enough Christmas when Chef Martin brought in his Christmas spread. Roast Pork and Apple Sauce. Um, Um! And that wasn't all either There was something else Something that came in bottles. It was Christmas alright.

Some people say it was Christmas up the line as well as in Porto Velho, but from the silence of the line boys we are led to believe this was a mistake—still, maybe they haven't recovered yet, no?

Messrs. Kendall and Foley have opened a class in bridge. Messrs. Bell and Nugent are the pupils. Tuition seems to be rather high.

It is said that the W.C.T.U is petitioning the Insterstate Commerce Commission for a certain railway ruling It seems the ladies are disturbed over the fact that conductors are in the habit of giving the engineers "highballs" when they wish to proceed. For shame!

Young Lady: "My! that Madeira-Mamore Railway bunch must be a gay, sporty crowd. Hardly a ship goes up that river but takes up a consignment of 'ties.'"

Mr Chas W. Frederick, with the Electrical department since September 19th, was transferred and is now located at Camp 26, he having left Porto Velho on December 28th.

"Spring is here" said Pascoe as he opened a bundle of door springs. Then he let it Fall and seriously remarked "Summer springs and some are not." He was favored with a Wintry glare from all within earshot, for his remarks were entirely out of season.

Joseph B. Fordyce, for the Timekeeping department was the only first-class passenger to arrive on the steamer *Chamie.*

Mr. Hills has just made the record trip over the line of the Madeira-Mamore, having come from Araras to Porto Velho in two days.

A. J. Calegari, who has been in charge of the steam laundry was a passenger on the *Aymore* when she sailed for Manaos on the 25th. He was accompanied by Mrs Calegari and their little girl.

George Dahl, Commissary storekeeper, complains of the potatoes received from Portugal. He don't like the color of their eyes.

Geographical Definition—Christmas Dinner: A piece of Turkey entirely surrounded by Scotch.

Oh! see the man!
No, child, it is not a man.
What is it?
It is a stenographer.
What is a stenographer?
A stenographer, my child, is one who makes little marks which no one can decipher, so he can prove he did not make a mistake in writing the letter
Why has it such a distressed look?
Because Christmas is only one week past.
Do stenographers have names?
Yes, dear, but I do not know this one's name. The first letter of his last name is McCarney, however.

Nunn: What is the principal industry of the Scotch?
Byrne: Making high-balls

What was the most appropriate song sung Christmas in Porto Velho? Coming through the "Rye."

Christmas comes but once a year— Hum! What's that the Governor of North Carolina said to the Governor of South Carolina?

MARINE INTELLIGENCE

December 23-29
River Gauge (Meters)

	1910	1909
23rd	89.90	87.27
24th	89.71	87.21
25th	89.65	87.10
26th	89.40	87.00
27th	89.33	86.71
28th	89.27	86.73
29th	89.20	86.62

ARRIVALS

River steamer *Chamie.* Manaos and Madeira River landings, December 26th. Company mail, passengers and mixed cargo.

River steamer *Rio Jamary.* Newspaper mail and freight, Manaos and Madeira River landings. December 31st.

SAILING

River steamer *Chamie,* for Santo Antonio, December 29th.

LEVEL AND TRANSIT NOTES

25th—Mr. S. G. Mullen, Resident Engineer at Camp 16, Residency No. 8, together with Messrs. W. H. Bennet and W. F. Lord, stationed with Mr. Mullen, came to Porto Velho on the afternoon train Sunday to spend Christmas. The party left on the morning train Monday, after having spent an enjoyable day.

Although Christmas was without Turkey, his absence was not felt, owing to the generosity of Mr. Randolph, who kindly furnished a pig. A few dozen bottles of liquid cheer, the decorations in the dining room, the songs and high-spirits and friendly chaff of the whole Engineer Corps in Porto Velho, clearly showed the day was a holiday and being enjoyed. A special feature of the evening was the well known song, "I'm Going to the Hamburg Show" rendered very feelingly by Mr. Judson, the whole audience gathering in the 'Lion's Roar.' Everybody enjoyed themselves.

27th—Mr. H. F. Dose, Chief Engineer, went up the line on this morning's train.

26th—Mr. A. S. Pitcher, Chief bookkeeper, received a fruit cake from home through one of the passengers on the *Chamie.* "A day late," said he, "but fruit cake improves with age." And he expects to leave Porto Velho on the next down-river trip of the *M-M.* Lucky Pitcher.

29th—Mr. H. F. Dose, Chief Engineer, returned to Porto Velho this afternoon from a trip up the line.

30th—Mr. F. C. Kyte, engaged in the work to the north of Porto Velho, and his corp of engineers had to send into Porto Velho for 'munitions of war' in the shape of smoke-making implements, an army of wasps blocking progress. Sr. Kyte has had his and isn't taking chances. Can you blame him?

The calendar for 1911, turned out under the supervision of 'Frau' Voss, of the Drafting Room is a neat and useful article. Copies for the Residencies will be forwarded as early as possible.

Mr. F. J. Torras, of the Drafting department, left to-day for a visit to Candelaria.

Mr. Axel Carlsson, the 'Terrible Swede' in charge of the contracted test-boring gang, reports good progress, despite the moist weather.

HERE'S HOPING ALL A VERY PROSPEROUS NEW YEAR!
The Virginian.

THE WEATHER

December 23-29, 1910

	Temperature High	Low	Rainfall (Inches)
Fri.	85 deg.	78 deg.	0.05
Sat.	86 "	78 "	0.08
Sun.	83 "	78 "	0.40
Mon.	90 "	77 "	0.00
Tues.	90 "	78 "	0.40
Wed.	86 "	76 "	0.22
Thurs.	88 "	75 "	1.41

CHRISTMAS IN BRAZIL

One of the most enjoyable events of the Christmas holidays at Porto Velho was the Christmas Eve dinner given by Mr. and Mrs. J. H. Randolph at their home "Villa Hill Top."

The house was beautifully decorated with palms and other tropical plants which with numerous flags and electric lights caused the guests to forget for the time that they were several thousand miles from home and family.

The heavy rain did not interfere with the arrival of all guests. The host, a past master in the art of dispensing joy and hospitality, opened the festivities by proceeding to balance the dampness, which up to that time was mostly *outside* Due to this wise precaution no sickness has resulted from the exposure to rain

The dinner was perfection personified; the toasts numerous and appropriate. The Victor Orchestra, hidden by a screen of palms rendered several selections, the Star Spangled Banner and Dixie bringing everyone to their feet.

After dinner the party adjourned to the spacious veranda where the hours were spent in dancing and story telling. The Victor Orchestra supplied splendid dance music with songs between, dances ranging from operatic selections by Caruso to "Has Anybody Here Seen Kelly?"

In the wee sma' hours o' the morn, the guests, wishing the host and hostess a Merry Christmas and Happy New Year, departed to that very appropriate song of Harry Lauder's "For I've Something in the Bottle for the Mor-r-r-r-ning."

These present were:

Mr. and Mrs. J. H. Randolph	
Miss Siders	Frank Pascoe
A. B. Jekyll	T. H. Yale
H. F. Dose	J. H. Byrne
C. J. Nixon	J. H. Nunn
A. S. Pitcher	D. C. Bell
D. B. Merrill	C. L. Jones

HEARD AT THE POST OFFICE

When a laborer comes to the wicket to get a receipt for his transportation up the river:

What boat did you come on?

Yes suh

I say what boat did you come on?

No suh.

You black sud I say, can't you understand what boat did you come on?

I did'nt comes suh.

Blast your eyes, strike me blind, blame me you fool, you idiot, you lunatic, can't you understand. I say what boat did you come up the river to Porto Velho in?

I comes from Bolivia suh.

AT THE CLERKS' MESS

History! Redpath, Gibbons, and Caesar, all those old codgers wrote it and improved on it and rewrote it until they handed it out in allopathic doses at the end, but even then it was a dry affair. But there's history and history. And this is a history of Christmas Eve at the Clerks' Mess, Porto Velho, and is not (or at least *was* not) a dry affair,

Dinner was eaten in good time—in fact all the evening was a good time—and then it was discovered that there were only eight bottles of beer on ice. The rest was locked up and the key was gone. But in a bunch of tropical clerks it is not a hard matter to find an expert at picking locks. Suffice it to say that soon only the empty bottles were locked up in that little storeroom.

Next, after various speeches, songs toasts, etc., some guardian angel fluttered his wings and descended upon us with a case of Scotch and—yea; even so—a case of Champagne, bubbles, joy, thinks, thrills, headaches, and all. He, the rather muldy looking guardian angel, was hailed with loud acclaim.

What need we continue? All of you have been there on various occasions But this one was successful, accomplished, polished, rare, indeed a work of art. It was too good to be wasted on the desert air. McCarney told of experiences on the Isthmus of Panama, and held his listeners spell-bound. J A. Byrne rendered several ditties, sentimental and otherwise, being ably assisted by Messrs. Bresnahan and Abeling. Brown and Hudson sailed o'er stormy seas in old time wind-jammers for the edification of those with nautical aspirations, while Walling discoursed at length of railway traffic and auditing. Keeler seemed to spend most of his time looking down the necks of empty bottles, "searching" as he said, "for that Demon Rum." Brandon and Herrick paid strict attention to the business at hand In fact everyone enjoyed himself Further than that they kept on enjoying themselves. It was the longest evening ever experienced in the tropics, It was like one of those polar evenings. It lasted for thirty hours straight, from 8 p.m Saturday. The audience was increased from time to time—one of the most worthy additions being Mr 'Bob' Craswell, who nobly assisted Mr. J. A. Byrne and others in accompanying the vocal efforts of the assembled chorus upon the new Byrne - Craswell pianolo. This instrument in itself deserves especial mention, being of home manufacture and consisting of one galvanized iron bucket filled with broken bottles. The method of playing consisted in grasping the

CHRISTMAS AT CANDELARIA

To realize one was five thousand miles from home was a hard task for those that sat down to dinner at Candelaria last Saturday evening.

To his reputation for the curing of physical ills his guests unanimously presented all honors for the curing of the mental ailments as well.

The evening was inaugurated by fourteen hungry but happy guests of Dr. Lovelace, and it wasn't many moments before all forgot their hunger through their happiness,

Tribute must be paid to " Mamma's fair haired boy " who did his best to live up to his reputation, and succeeded, to the silent (?) members of "the cave" and last, but second only to our host, "The Ladies,"

After dinner, which all survived most beautifully, the balance of the evening was devoten to dancing and the celebration of the passing of another mile stone—(number 22) of one of the party.

About 9 30, the dancing was interrupted by a serenade to Dr. Lovelace by the Spanish and Barbadian laborers of the hospital, followed by the " not to be outdone " Chinese contingent, a trifle small in quantity but equal to all in quality and sincerity.

The dawn of Christmas, 1910, will long be remembered by the fifteen, who heartily agreed that life in Brazil is far from being as black as it is painted. The table:

Dr. Lovelace	
Miss Hardy	Dr. Forsythe
Mr. Garnett	Mr. Smith
Dr. Fitch	Dr. Walsh
Mr. Foley	Mr. Heflin
Miss M. Hardy	Dr. Garnett
Dr. Whittaker	Mr. Putland
Mrs. Farrell	Miss Irwin

ELECTION RESULTS

Democratic Governors elected for State of New York, Ohio, New Jersey, Connecticut and Massachusetts, Republican majorities being greatly reduced in other States. Milwaukee elected Socialist to Congress for first time.

English election results:

Unionists	272
Liberals	270
Nationalists	72
Labor	43
Independent Nationalists	9

bucket firmly with one hand and beating it sharply on the floor in 2-4 time, accentuating the flats by sharply kicking the bucket (literally, not figuratively).

The crowd departed by ones and twos in plenty of time to reach the offices by seven a.m Monday, all quite sure there had been nothing overlooked in the matter of enjoying a quiet, homelike Christmas Eve.

SOUTH AMERICA'S FIRST TRANS-CONTINENTAL

A Journey Over the Line of the First Railroad to Pierce the Andes---Buenos Aires to Valparaiso by Air-Line Instead of by the Dangerous Straits of Magellan

(Charles Wellington Furlong in "The World's Work.")

PART II.

The year 1869 found John and Matthew Clark, brothers, connecting Chile and Argentina by telegraph, and while thus climbing over rock and ridge in that desolate mountain wilderness, thousands of feet above the Pacific, they perceived the possibility of a transandine route through the heart of those Cordillera.

In 1873 these hardy engineers were again in the Cordillera, surveying the railroad. Argentina was the first to respond to the project with a concession in satisfactory form, Chile following the succeeding y. ar. The Clark plan was adopted in preference to either that of Wheelwright or of certain others providing routes over passes to the south. Although involving heavier engineering, it connected Buenos Aires and Valparaiso by almost an air-line.

The dividing line of Chile and Argentina here follows the watershed of the Andes, and these two governments were expected to cooperate in the construction of the railroad from either side to the boundary line culminating in the heart of a mountain 10,500 feet above the sea in the *Cumbre* or Crest Tunnel. This arranged, the first section (known as the Argentine Great Western) was built in 1880 by the Argentine Government from Villa Mercedes to Mendoza. The Clarks, three years later, connected Villa Mercedes and Buenos Aires; thus 650 of the 888 miles were accounted for.

Work progressed slowly on the Chilean side, but railhead had been extended as far inland from the Pacific as Los Andes All but 160 of the 888 miles had been constructed, but the great problem—the passing of the Andes—had hardly been touched.

In 1886 the Argentine Government granted a concession to the Buenos

Aires and Valparaiso Transandine Railway Corporation of London (capitalized at $2,500,000 and with an annual subsidy of $416,850), authorizing it to carry railhead from Mendoza through the Andes to the Chilean frontier. In 1887 the new corporation, after obtaining control of the Clark interests in the Argentine Great Western, began work at once; by the end of 1893 trains were run as near the Chilian frontier as Punta de las Vacas and within twenty miles of Las Cuevas, the point on the Argentine side of the Cumbre Tunnel entrance. Ten years later (1903) work on the Argentine side had crept up the valley to Puente del Inca; but it had not progressed so rapidly on the Chilean side, having reached a point called Salto del Soldado, seventeen miles beyond Los Andes.

From Mendoza to Los Andes (about 160 miles) up to 1903, 115 miles of road had been laid and were in operation, but in the intervening forty-five miles the heaviest engineering was still to be done.

The old Chilean concession, never satisfactory, was modified in 1887. The Clark brothers on their own limited resources superintended this work until 1893, when they secured some assistance from the Chilean Congress.

In August, 1901, the Transandine Construction Company, Ltd., of London, bought up the portion of line already built, and the work took a fresh start.

In February, 1903, the Chilean Congress authorized the President of the Republic to contract, by means of public tenders, for a one-metre-guage (nearly 3 1-2 feet) railroad from Los Andes to the Cordilleran summit, to unite with a railroad of the same guage then under construction from Mendoza, Argentina, to the summit boundary-line.

The state agreed to guarantee for twenty years the interest of 5 per cent annually on an amount not exceeding $7,500,000.

The Transandine Construction Company tender, which had been submitted on the following terms, was accepted in June, 1904.

The company undertook to build a one-metre-gauge railroad, starting

from the city of Los Andes and making connection in the Cordillera with the railroad of the same gauge from Mendoza.

The company solicited a guaranty, for the term of twenty years, of the interest at 5 per cent. per annum on a capital of $6,750,000, specifying that each month saved in the period allowed for the construction should entitle the contractors to a bonus of 1 per cent. of the total sum, the total bonus, however, in no case to exceed 10 per cent. of the amount of the tender. The portion of the line already constructed had, through the want of funds, much deteriorated; and before the section from Los Andes to Juncal was accepted, a great deal of work had to be done as far as Salto del Soldado to bring it up to the new government standard.

Banks and cuttings had to be widened, fencing put up, telegraph service introduced, a short extension made connecting the State Line station with the Transandine station, a crossing and water station, waybridge and side lines constructed, workshops, buildings, sheds, sidings, new offices, staff headquarters, and permanent gang quarters erected and various works of a minor nature carried out. The first section of the line, Los Andes to Juncal (32 miles), was inaugurated for public traffic by the President on February 12, 1906.

The December following the purchase of the road by the Transandine Construction Company, Ltd., the contract was awarded to W. R. Grace & Co., of New York and London, the Chilean Government granting a guaranty of 5 per cent. annually on $6,569,775 for a term of twenty years.

Old Lady: I want you to take back that parrot you sold me. It swears awfully.

Bird Dealer: Well, Madam, he is a young bird. It'll learn to swear better when a little older.

Two colored brakesmen, one in the employ of the Southern Railway and the other with the Seaboard Air Line, recently had an argument as to the number of passengers their respective roads hauled. As the words waxed warm and the noise interfered with other patrons of the salo n who objected to it, some one shouted "Shut up." To close the argument with a decided majority of opinion in his favor, the Southern Railway darkey answered back loudly, "Oh! We'uns *kils* more peoples than de Seaboard hauls!"—*Wireless Reporter.*

THE PORTO VELHO
Marconigram

"LA VIDA SIN LITERATURA Y QUININA ES MUERTE"

Published at Porto Velho (Rio Madeira), Amazonas, Brazil

VOLUME 3	SATURDAY, JANUARY 7, 1911	NUMBER 1

FOOD AND AMAZON RUBBER

The following article taken from *The India Rubber World* published in New York City is an illustration of the progress we are making in Journalism as well as Railroad Building.

When we see our Porto Velho *Marconigram* quoted in a paper published in what will soon be the largest city in the world, we feel that the efforts we have made in this line, in the jungles of Brazil have not been in vain.

The building of the Madeira-Mamoré railway, to reach the rich rubber fields of Bolivia, is in itself a most important undertaking, but what may prove of even more concern to the world is the influence which the sanitation work installed in connection with it may have in tropical America as a whole. Not only this, but the whole rubber trade of the world may in the end benefit from the work now centred in the Madeira-Mamoré construction camps, which camps, by the way, have lately been described in some detail in *The India Rubber World.*

It is no secret that the high cost of rubber from the Amazon has been due largely to the sparse population of that region, and the fact that conditions of life there have been most unattractive to European laborers. Not the least unfavourable condition has been the difficulty of acquiring food of a suitable character and at reasonable prices.

A recent issue of the Porto Velho *Marconigram* devotes most of its space to the question of food supplies in the railway construction camps, where more than 4,000 men are employed, most of whom are from other countries and a number of them professional engineers. It is pointed out in this paper that satisfactory food conditions prevail already, and that there is a continued improvement in this respect. Fresh beef is served to all the camps, being slaughtered and dressed at Porto Velho. An ice making plant is operated successfully. While the vegetables used have been derived in canned shape from the United States, the *Marconigram* mentions: "Lately we have been getting fresh vegetables from a farm about a day's sail down the river and from present indications this farm will probably be able to supply quite a quantity of fresh vegetables. Eggs are brought in by the natives."

It must be taken into account that the successful sanitation and satisfactory food supply at Porto Velho have been due to the work in progress there being on a large scale and under capable scientific and financial control. If each engineer and dirt digger had to look out for himself probably the enterprise would have ended long ago in disaster. The lesson for the rubber interest in South America is the reorganization of rubber camps on a large scale instead of the work being conducted by *seringuieros* singly or in small groups. This change, by the way, is already in progress, and it is reasonable to suppose from indications already apparent that ultimately the food supplies on the better *seringues* in the Amazon basin will compare favorably with those on farms in the United States. When this new régime becomes better established it is not to be doubted that rubber supplies will be increased, and the cost to consumers materially lessened, while still yielding an adequate profit to the producers.

A ROUSING WELCOME

Porto Velho certainly gave a royal welcome to the New Year of 1911 and a hearty send off to the Old Year of 1910. The population of Porto Velho doesn't amount to much in numbers but when it comes to general all around enthusiasm and celebrating, Porto Velhians go the limit.

We have been in large cities where on New Year's Eve they hurrah around the gilded cafes with their little tin horns, but that kind of demonstration and the Porto Velho kind are not to be mentioned in the same breath.

Promptly on the stroke of twelve, the ice-plant, machine shop and engine whistles began screeching forth their welcome, and a second later began a fusilade of firearms, lasting about twenty minutes, that would have made a revolution in a Central American Republic look like thirty cents Mex. If there is any man on this job that came to Porto Velho with any less than two Gatling guns he has got to do the Missouri stunt and show us before we will believe him, and by the amount of noise some must have brought at least six. Since he found this out the Editor's New Year's resolution is to be mighty careful of the opinions he expresses through the columns of his paper.

Once more we remark that for all around celebrating we hand over the laurel wreath to Porto Velho and Porto Velhians.

By the way, there was a little refreshment, too—on the side of course.

HUNTING NOTES

Reports from up the line show that the sportsmen are shooting off a goodly number of leaves.

"I'm rather a poor hunter," said the man who likes outdoor life. "I miss everything I shot at."

"That's all right," replied the guide, who has a proper regard for his personal safety. "But do you miss everything you aren't shooting at?"—*Washington Star.*

THE PORTO VELHO
MARCONIGRAM

Published at
Porto Velho (Rio Madeira) Brazil

C. L. JONES—*Editor*
S. WELLWOOD—*Publisher*

SATURDAY, JANUARY 7TH. 1911

Notice

Employees sending Company drafts home are requested to inform their families that the Seconds of Exchange are for record only and are not to be presented for collection unless the First of Exchange fails to arrive.

We are in receipt of advice from the Company's foreign offices that in two or three instances both Firsts and Seconds have been presented for collection, causing a great deal of trouble. This has no doubt been due to the women folks not understanding the nature of these documents.

LEVEL AND TRANSIT NOTES

December 31st—New Year was ushered in by a large proportion of the Porto Velho engineers and received a welcome from many 38s, 41s, and 44s, the variety of noises reminding us of "Home, Sweet Home." As everything moved smoothly the next day, Sunday, all must have begun the New Year with a clean sheet. Nathaniel and Lynch had charge of this and must have performed their duty well. Carlsson, that ter-ree-ble Swede, was the only complainant but, fortunately, there was some left and his trouble was adjusted without damage. Some class to him. Deep in the stilly night Messrs. Weiss, Weston and Pitcher crept down stairs and "got theirs," waking Messrs. Bolton, Bennett, Woodward and Cartwright, with their banging the doors, who, too, went to see what kind of water made such funny noises. Sr. Kyte, though asleep, only turning over when the whistles were blowing at midnight, awoke as Mr. Weston passed his window with a "Pabst"

and had a "look in." Taking all in all, most everybody was happy and wished for more New Years.

Monday, Tuesday and Wednesday drew blanks, especially for Messrs. Pitcher and Ramirez. Hopes died fast when the *M-M* arrived, but, after her ozone excursion down the river Wednesday afternoon, both "spruced" up in the assurance of a beginning of their homeward trip Thursday. All's well that ends well, so off they go towards G's C.

5th—Poor old "Teddy," Ramy gone and who is to look after you. You should see him looking around as if inquiring his friend's whereabouts. Expect a vote is necessary to locate his future sleeping chamber. Who is in favor of upstairs?

Mr. A. S. Pitcher, Accounting Department, loaded with—now not "that"—but injun spears, bid all a fair farewell as he boarded the *M-M* on his way to New York to spend his vacation. He assures us that every effort will be made to make up for lost time and that he will 'take one' about 'so' high at the first opportunity. We believe he prefers "Budweiser" but expect most any brand will do. Here's Godspeed, old pal, and a pleasant time.

Mr. J. C. Rameriz, (Ramy) of the Drafting Room force, was also a passenger on the *M-M* on his leave of absence. Sr. Rameriz expects to go to his home Peru, via Bridgetown and Panama.

Messrs Kyte, Howser and Aguirre report good progress on their work in North Porto Velho. The bush here is particularly close and the work hard.

Messrs Jenkins, Bennett and Cartwright continue on their location work south of Porto Velho, along the igarape.

Why don't some of you young men at the Residencies send in some new notes occasionally? A line or two from this one, and another from that will help materially in keeping the *Marconigram* up to its high standard. Send in some news. The Postmaster knows us.

Sr. Gomez, Official Interpreter, was among the passengers on the *M-M.* At present he is spending a few days with friends on the island but is expected in the office next week.—*The Virginian.*

DOES THE WIRELESS WORK?

On December 11th the old Gardener at Porto Velho reported to the General Office that he had been robbed the night before of nearly two contos of reis. He stated that he suspected his room mate who was missing that morning. As the S.S. *Campos Salles* had sailed late the night of the robbery the Manaos office was advised by wireless giving the man's description.

On arrival of the *Campos Salles* at Manaos Mr. Chambers, our genial Purchasing Agent was on the job and discovered a man that answered the description. He (the man—not Chambers) was turned over to the police and Porto Velho received the following wireless message:

"Refer to your telegram of the 12th. Spaniard with cut above nose and pox marked was arrested on arrival of *Campos Salles.* Gave name Joaquim Lagos, 23 years. Found on him 1,540$000 and 85 pesos. Also a hospital ticket bearing name of Manoel Rodriguez. Have you any evidence against him, otherwise will be liberated to-day."

In the meantime the Gardener had left for Manaos on S.S. *Madeira-Mamore*, not doubting the effectiveness of our force at Manaos and the eagle eye of that Chambers, Manaos was informed that evidence was on the way and Mr. Pox Marked was held.

On the arrival of S.S. *Madeira-Mamore* at Manaos, Emilio Perez, the victim, was met by Mr Chambers and taken around to the police station where he identified the robber. The man confessed and Perez recovered his loss.

That must have been a surprised Spaniard. He had no doubt spent his entire time on the way down river figuring out what he could do with that bunch of wealth back in Spain and instead of his dreams he has been urgently requested to remain as a guest of the police at Manaos for 12 months.

We hope this will serve as a warning to all other would-be-get-aways, tin-horn sports and Get Rich Quick Wallings that may be on the job.

Oh you Wireless. Oh you Chambers.

FROM UP THE LINE

Camp 28,
December 28, 1910.

My Dear Sir,—Owing to the difficulty the boys up here are continually experiencing in keeping their laundry separate, won't you please send up a small bottle of India Ink and a few Marking Pens, such as are used by the Porto Velho Steam Laundry that they may mark their "stuff" and thus be able *should they ever receive it back from our Barbadian "Button-Buster,"* to identify their own.

So far as I am concerned personally this is a matter that causes me but little worry for I only possess Ein Sox and a pair of Ear Tabs, and as I never have the Ein washed and no one cares for the Ear Tabs, I'm safe; but poor Vic and Oscar ! ! ! It's really pathetic to witness the heart-rending troubles they have to keep their hard-earned (?) possessions intact. Really something should be done to alleviate their discomfort. Vic is surely losing his rotundity, whilst O. L. on the other hand, if he keeps it up, will have a being in the States by the name of Taft "backed off the boards." While the doctor refrains from expressing an opinion or even diagnosing the case, Vic unhesitatingly declares it is simply a clear and unquestioned matter of "clotheserites;" that it takes O. L. two hours and eight minutes to undress before retiring on account of the many and varied uniforms he carries around with him.

Therefore, be it resolved and enacted that each and every one here mark his (or her) linen, cotton, cheese cloth, or whatsoever kind and description of clothing they possess or may become possessed of, hence the above would be appreciated.

Yours sincerely,
"SNOOKUMS."

The above letter is self-explanatory in a way. We can understand why Niggli would wear all the clothes he has with the surroundings he has. As to Victor, well he has very taking ways when it comes to raiment, and "Snookums" explains his shortage by saying his trunk was left behind. He can't be positive if the "Boarding House Lady" forgot to send it to the pier, or whether he forgot to pay his board bill. So we think it a safe bet, to wear all you have, or some one else will wear it for you

ARRIVALS

January 2nd — Madeira-Mamore tug. *Uncle Tom*, with barge *Jaci-Parana*. Iticoatiara—Construction materials.

January 3rd—Madeira-Mamore steamer *Madeira-Mamore*. Manaos and Iticoatiara—Passengers, mail, provisions and Construction materials.

January 6th—River steamer *Rio Jamary*. From Santo Antonio.

SAILINGS

December 31st—River steamer *Chamie*. Madeira River Landings and Manaos—Passengers and freight.

January 5th—Madeira-Mamore steamer *Madeira-Mamore*. Iticoatiara and Manaos —Mail and passengers.

January 7th—River steamer *Rio Jamary*. Madeira River Landings and Manaos—Mail, passengers and freight.

NOTES ABOUT TOWN

Pay day, cash in hand,
Country no good, foreign land,
Man as cunning as a fox,
Little milreis behind the locks.

Mr. R. T. Patton, of Camp 18, spent Thursday in Porto Velho on business. He is looking well, copying the Porto Velho style of beard. Come again, always glad to see you

D. M Maloney, first publisher of the Porto Velho *Marconigram*, was among the passengers on the " 3 - M " on her downward trip Mr Maloney published the first volume and all but one number of the second volume. He is leaving us to seek a broader field for his prinitorial and journalistic talents and no doubt he will be successful.

Harry Street who has been in charge of the Store House at the Commissary is now holding down the position of Freight Agent at Candelaria.

The *Marc nigram* suffered a loss in the departure of C. R. Hudson, one of its editors. Mr Hudson was one of our most regular contributors, and his articles were of a bright and entertaining nature.

Newspaper reports (November 20-22nd) mention some revolutionary trouble in Mexico.

Frank Pascoe who has been in charge of the Carpentry Construction in Porto Velho was also a passenger on the "M-M" last Thursday. Frank has been with us for fourteen months and we will miss his smiling countenance and cheery word.

The following first-class passengers arrived on the " A -M" last Wednesday : — O. Hoyer, Timekeeper; C. H. Carr, Engineer; D. Wilder, Conductor; A. E. Hill, Timekeeper; T. W. Finney, Officeman; J. E. Behrens, Car Inspector; Oscar Gomez, Engineer; Manoel Ignacio Mendez, Commissary ; Daniel Kelly, Camp Foreman; W. Tillman, Construction; John King, Saw Mill; G. G. Kitchen, Conductor; and J. W. Lord; Trackman.

Following is a list of those who went away with the " M-M " on her trip down the river

F. Pascoe, C. R. Hudson, H. G. Brown, A. S. Pitcher, H W. Kelly, E. F. McGlone, W. McClellan, H. Berman, jr, F Kiperos, C, Thompson, P. O'Neill, Chas. Green, A. Hemming, D Maloney, R McGovern, H S Cahill, J. Murphy, Lee Freeman, R. Craswell, F. Cross, G. B Johnson, H. Bergman, H J. Emerson, I F. Hill, P. A Lindsay, J Connell, M. Varella, H F. Burns, G. Sutherland, J. C. Ramerez, E. Martinez and G. A. Fitzgerall.

MILLER'S PARTY HEARD FROM

The following letter from a member of Miller's Party is a cheerful example of the difficulties experienced by our frontier men.

Miller's Party,
December 25, 1910.

Dear Mr. Editor,—Mr. Jekyll and Mr. Hills paid a visit to our camp lately and incidentally Mr. Jekyll got our duck or one mightily like the one we have been feeding for a long time. It was so big and fat that it experienced difficulty in flying. Every time it passed our camp our appetites was whetted and we swore anew to kill it. If Mr. Jekyll had shot it on his way up we should have applauded the deed, but the opposite was the case.

Numerous incidents illustrate the uncertainty of the Madeira River. Just the other day one of the line physicians who would rather shoot rapids than eat was indulging in his favorite diversion when his canoe upset. As a result he remained perched in an exceedingly friendly rock for a good many hours, until finally he was rescued by a Good Samaritan who happened along.

Some ten days ago one of our long time machete men started in a canoe to see a friend down the river. He has not returned and it is quite certain that he ran afoul of a whirl-pool. Recently one of Bolton's laborers fell out of a batelão and was drowned.

Let me record one more cheering incident one of our laborers, a Spanish lad, lost the trail the other day and spent forty-eight hours in the woods without food and during an almost continuous rain. A happy thought struck him to follow a small stream to the river. Was he happy when he found himself in familiar territory? He was. He looked very gaunt and "skeered" even after he had got back.

Mr A. B. Jekyll left on the *M-M* for vacation.

RIVER GAUGE

December 30-January 5
River Gauge (Meters)

	1910	1909
30th	89.2o	87.05
31st	89.01	87.42
	1911	1910
1st	88.93	87.71
2nd	88.8o	87.97
3rd	88.67	88.26
4th	88.59	88.53
5th	88.55	88.49

THE WEATHER

December 30-January 5

	Temperature		Rainfall
	High	Low	(Inches)
Fri.	85 deg.	78 deg.	0.00
Sat.	83 "	76 "	0.80
Sun.	9o "	75 "	0.08
Mon.	86 "	79 "	1.76
Tues.	84 "	77 "	0.05
Wed.	85 "	76 "	0.32
Thurs.	83 "	78 "	0.56

Total Rainfall for Dec '1o, —9.12 inches

SOUTH AMERICA'S FIRST TRANS-CONTINENTAL

A Journey Over the Line of the First Railroad to Pierce the Andes— Buenos Aires to Valparaiso by Air-Line Instead of by the Dangerous Straits of Magellan

(Charles Wellington Furlong in " The World's Work.")

PART III.

On my first visit to the Pass in May, 1908, I found trains in operation as far as Juncal in Chile and Las Vacas in Argentina; on my third visit in March of this year, trains were above Portillo, and railhead was within a hundred yards of the tunnel at Caracoles, and at Las Cuevas in Argentina.

Gradually for six hundred miles westerly from Buenos Aires our train had been climbing up the continent or a day and a night, until, just above La Paz, the grain-fields and pasture-lands merged into the orchards and vineyards of Mendoza province. Early morning found us in the heart of this region of green leaves and purple fruit at Mendoza City, 2,359 feet above the level of the sea and 650 miles from the Atlantic.

Here passengers and luggage were shifted to the narrow-gauge train of the Transandine road. Twelve miles ahead the beautiful Valley of Mendoza stretches toward its background — the supernal Andes, at whose foothills the fruit trees and vines gradually give way to the low shrubs and stunted trees of the lower mountain slopes and a steeper grade.

The panting engine stops in an arid section and, like a mighty monster preparing for a final struggle, drinks long at a well-constructed water-tank, while its feed of wood and coal is loaded into the tender. Then begins the long struggle to the foot of the Cumbre.

Nearer, higher, the looming barrier thrusts up towering, impassable peaks—but where is the pass into the mountains? Ahead is no visible sign of an opening, but the deep-cut bed of the Mendoza is the clue. A reverse curve, and suddenly the train, like a colossal black snake, glides into a crevice of the mountains. The pass, which from Argentine follows up over the Cumbre down into Chile, is a trail over which countless hordes of primitive aborigines have passed for unknown centuries, whose feet have hard-packed the path which showed the Spaniard the way. "*Camino de los Andes*" (the Andean Trail) he named it, and a-mule or a-foot he scuffed his way for three centuries more. Meantime the man of the North came, and now the railroad—following more or less this same old pack-trail, save at the Cumbre Pass, 12,605 feet above the oceans. Here, nearly 2,500 feet below it, the engineers have left the old trail and burrowed through the mountain to meet it on the other side in Chile.

Up the entering crevice the train turns, and crosses and recrosses the muddy Rio Mendoza, which is helping to carry away the mountains. Ever upward, seven tunnels are passed through; Chacheutta is left behind, and again a stop for water at the little stone station of Uspallata, hemmed in by rugged peaks save to the west, where the broad open plateau of Uspallata stretches away as far as the eye can reach, a prairie in the heart of the mountains. Here the railroad meets *El Antiguo Camino à Mendoza*, the trail to the east, wriggling into the mountain from the plain.

Ever upward twists the railroad to Punta de las Vacas (7,709 feet), which, like many names hereabouts, tells a story of the old pack-trail and cattle drives. All along, elaborate work through gravel and rock-cuttings and extensive flood defenses shows the construction to be of a heavy nature. A sudden jerk a few miles before Punta de las Vacas is reached shows you that the grade has increased and that the powerful triplicate sets of teeth of the engine have clinched the third or rack-rail, for wherever the grade exceeds 2 1-2 per cent. the "Abt system" of cogs and racks is used to safeguard and expedite the running of the trains.

Westward and upward puffs the straining engine; down the towering slopes shunt avalanches of weathered rock spreading out valley-ward like great fans. Forty-three miles southward the hoary, extinct volcanic peak of Tupungato shows itself and is lost to view; then the promontories of the cathedral-like ridge of Los Penitentes in seared dignity stand out in this impressive desolation, To the north, if you are quick, Aconcagua can be glimpsed.

After entering the mountains all is one vast desolation of rock and water, and far up on the peaks is snow. From Punta de las Vacas we have been heading straight up a wonderland of color, the Valle de las Cuevas. Along this valley, if one looks sharply, can be seen evidences of man—little red pegs at intervals and a "spotted" trail. Dig below and you could take hold of a wire rope, the other end of which is in United States—the cable *via* Colon and Galveston.

The distance between railhead in the early days of the railroad construction was traveled on foot or in the saddle; then, later, the broad-gauged, white-covered, four-horse coaches were introduced, which for years have been the regular means of transporting passengers between railhead. With them go outriders, baggage wagons, and the mule pack-train carrying mail, baggage, fodder, or supplies for the tunnel work. This whole outfit which connects with the train is known as "the Combination" or "the Transport." Little by little the gap of 160 miles between Mendoza and Los Andes has been shortened and we found only a little more than the two miles of the Cumbre Tunnel separated railhead, and the time of crossing of "the Transport" had been reduced to two hours. Four times the air-line distance over the Cumbre must be covered along the zigzagging road up, over, and down the Cumbre Pass.

As the afternoon shadows began to creep into the valleys, the train drew up before some little corrugated-iron-roofed buildings — near a few corrals—Las Cuevas, the Argentine end of the railroad. Between the buildings and the train was a living mass of horses, mules, and men, through which a long line of the white-covered, broad-gauged coaches stretched on up the road.

THE PORTO VELHO
Marconigram

"LA VIDA SIN LITERATURA Y QUININA ES MUERTE"

Published at Porto Velho (Rio Madeira), Amazonas, Brazil

VOLUME 3	SATURDAY, JANUARY 14, 1911	NUMBER 2

ENORMOUS GATES FOR PANAMA CANAL

Being Made in Pittsburg at Cost of $5,500,000

Mischievous boys, dreaming to-night of gates they will seize as Hallowe'en trophies, would not in the wildest nightmares imagine such enormous gates as are being made in Pittsburg for the Panama canal.

They will be the largest gates in the world. Any one of the ninety-two of them, for there are to be forty-six pairs in all, will be about as high as a six-story building, as wide (65 feet) as many city buildings are, and 7 feet deep or thick. The structural steel that will go to make them will weigh 60,000 tons, or more than eight times as much as was used to build the Eiffel tower in Paris.

The mighty portals, designed to admit a world's commerce from one ocean to another, must withstand a tide of criticism as well as a tremendous pressure of water and possible convulsions of earth. For years the controversy over gates or no gates, locks or sea level, has been the dividing issue of the canal problem. In the face of fear in some quarters that the foundations on the isthmus are not sure enough for locks, that earthquakes or water pressure would dislodge them, and that an enemy's mines or accidental explosions might easily destroy them, the government has begun to bu'ld the gates

Gates to Cost $5,500,000.

The cost will be $5,500,000. The builders are the McClintic Marshall Steel Construction Company, a half of whose independent plant here has been given over entirely to the gate contract. Of the 60,000 tons of steel required, the heaviest single piece will weigh 18 tons. These will be the base girders, which are 7 feet wide, and which will be placed much like the first-floor girders of a skyscraper. The series of girders above them will range from 3.8 feet apart near the bottom to 5 feet apart at the top, and over the skeleton structure thus formed a sheathing of water-tight armor plate will be bolted much after the fashion of clapboards on a house. The thickness of the plates will range from an inch at the base to 7-16 of an inch at the top. The weight of a single gate will be about 600 tons, and the dimensions are 77 to 32 feet high, 60 to 65 feet wide and 7 feet thick

The thousands of individual pieces, numbered and fitted to go together as easily as children's blocks, will be shipped by steamer via Baltimore, and with them will go more than four hundred skilled structural steel builders from Pittsburg to set them. The advance guard of experts left here in December, and the first work probably will begin early in 1911. It will take three years to complete the job.

Where Gates Will Be Placed.

The location of the forty-six pairs of gates will be twenty at the Gatun dam on the Pacific side, twelve at Pedro Miguel and fourteen at Miraflores near the Atlantic entrance. The gates are designed to hold back water 47.4 feet deep in a channel 110 feet w'de, which means a pressure of a million pounds Engineers, in reply to alarmists, point out that, even if a tremendous explosion or earthquake should damage or destroy one or more sets of gates, no great disaster would ensue, for all locks are to be made in duplicate to accomodate traffic in both directions at once, and the wreckage of one set of locks would only necessitate the diversion of commerce into another set. But, really violent earthquakes have not occurred in the Panama region for more than two centuries, and it would require a mighty siege for an enemy to destroy the locks.

Each lock will be ample for a ship 50 per cent. larger than any vessel now afloat, and it has been estimated that as many as a hundred ocean ships may be handled in a single day. There are no locks approaching these in size. The famous Suez canal is a sea-level affair, and the few great lock canals would have to combine their gates to equal the size and strength of the great doors of Panama.

RUBBER FACTORY FOR BRAZIL

The *Gummi Zeitung* learns that a rubber goods factory is to be established in Jundiahy, near Sao Paulo, Brazil, with an initial capital of 300 contos [= about $100,000]. The city government supports the enterprise, by the remission, for a term of ten years, of all municipal charges and by the contribution of 10 contos towards the purchase of a factory site.

RAILROADS EARNED $308 PER MILE

Washington, November 11 —The total net revenue of the steam railroads in the United States last July was $75,477,590, or $308.51 per mile of line, against $78,139,043 or $335.06 per mile of line in July of last year, according to the revenue and expenses report issued by the Interstate Commerce Commission to-day. The report gives these figures for July. Total operating revenues, $230,615,776; total operating expenses, $157,458,228; outside operations, net revenue, $320,042; operating income, $64,746,569. There was a total of 238,168 miles reported.—*N Y. Press.*

LEVEL AND TRANSIT NOTES

Tuesday, with its sack of registered mail from 'Home,' brought afresh, thoughts of Christmas. Many were the smiling faces and happy expressions among the Engineers. Though we are Soldiers of Fortune, the little remembrances from home kindle the smouldering spark of 'what use I to, be' and create renewed strength and courage, adding to our pride in the work and the desire to do things better than someone else could. Several late novels were among the packages and these will be a source of recreation to the whole headquarters staff.

Messrs. Maseeger and Weiss made a flying trip to Candelaria Wednesday, on business. The report is current that Mr. Weiss forgot what he went for—or to that effect. Possibly Dr. Lovelace could enlighten any that are interested. Sr. Weiss declares that he didn't forget but that it was the fault of someone else. Probably it was Mr. Maseeger's fault, as he went up again Thursday and expects to spend a few days. There is some secret about this but time will tell. "Here's waiting."

The splendid weather for the last few days reminds us of:—
The roses nowhere bloom so white
  As down in Old Virginia.
The sunshine nowhere seems so bright
  As down in Old Virginia.
The birds sing nowhere quite so sweet
And nowhere hearts so lightly beat,
For Heaven and earth both seem to meet
  Down in Old Virginia.

Splendid headway is being made by the corp engaged in the work to the north of Porto Velho, as is also, with the work along the igarape,

Mr. R. T. McCann, Resident Engineer at Residency No. 11, Camp 25, came down to Porto Velho Wednesday afternoon, reporting a quiet Christmas but a pleasant one. Mr. McCann expects to leave shortly on his vacation.

Mr. H. A. Attrill, of Mr. E. B. Karnopp's party, engaged in the work at Guajara-Merin, arrived here Thursday afternoon, having been 18 days on the trip down. He says all in the party are in good health.

Mr. J. Leahy, engineer of the kerosene launch at Araras is in town, having come in Thursday afternoon. As soon as some repairs are made to the launch's machinery Mr. Leahy will accompany it back to service at the old stand.

A specimen of the 'bird-catching spider,' measuring over 8 inches in length through the the body, 10 1-2 inches from tip to tip and, in its natural posture, occupying an area 9 1-2 inches by 7 inches, was on display in the room of Mr Armitage Monday evening. This specimen is in a fine state of preservation, a giant among the family and held immense interest among those who saw it. The 'varmint' was caught up the line and sent to Porto Velho. If you see a live one, try hard to see it first.— *The Virginian.*

NOTES ABOUT TOWN

Willie smote his little sister
  With a poker made of steel ;
Mamma cried : "Suppose you'd missed her—
  Then how sorry you would feel!"

The following notice was posted this week :

No person residing in Porto Velho will be admitted into Candelaria Hospital without a written order from the Resident Physician of Porto Velho.

We can recommend Dr. Fitch as being a sympathetic person who won't turn away would-be patients in a case of necessity.

There was something doing along the line Sunday alright when Horsey and Keeler, two of our efficient G.O. staff were the proud escort of 100 contos as far as the Track Camp. Gee, what pipe dreams they must have had about it Even if you don't own it, it makes a fellow swell his chest a little to have this much in his possession.

Aaron King and George Fredericks, laborers, rooming together and keeping their money in a bag in the room, were robbed of 475$000 last Sunday night. The bag was taken from the room and later found empty on the railroad track. There is a chance for detective work here

Madeira-Mamore left Manaos, Thursday for Itacoatiara and Porto Velho. She has two first-class passengers on board for Porto Velho.

Charles Falaise who has been acting as Payroll Clerk has been appointed Paymaster, taking C. R Hudson's place Alright Charlie we would just as soon take money from you as anybody we know of.

The arrivals on the *Victoria* were: Harry Sievers, Timekeeper, returning; and F. N. Posson, Conductor.

The *Justo Chermont* arrived on the 10th bringing one first-class passenger, A Hodgson, Electrical Engineer, and 400 registered packages. These Christmas presents are a little late but are acceptible just the same.

"Judge" Cidic, Timekeeper, Porto Velho, has been appointed Transportation Clerk.

J. A. Byrne, formerly Transportation Clerk is now performing the duties of Stationagent at San Antonio.

Notice

Inquiries have been received at the General Office concerning the whereabouts of the following men :

Antonio Rossi, Brazilian
Heinrich Behm, German

Anyone having information relative to either of these men will please communicate with the Acting Accountant, Porto Velho.

NOTES FROM THE CAMPS

The Construction Office moved Friday from Camp 28 to Camp 33. Bell, Meyers and Klienpaul were the advance guard, going by launch to Camp 31. From 31 to 32 the trip is made by mule, and from 32 to 33 on foot, in mud about waist deep. We would like to have extracts from their conversation during the last part of the journey though we wouldn't dare print it. Niggli and Johnson are expected to follow "Snookums," is the wise guy of the bunch, he is going by river. He dopes it out that the "longest way round is the shortest way home." It certainly does look bad though We hope he is well provided with good warm foot gear.

Patton says there is no game within 8 kilometers of Camp 18 on account of the blasting at the quarry just below there.

J. M. Roberts who has been at the front, visited his friends at the General Office, Friday.

The hunter at Camp 23 was bringing in a wild pig as train No. 3 passed through there last Sunday.

The Track Camp expects to move soon to Camp 28. The track is now laid up to between Camp 28 and 29.

MARINE INTELLIGENCE

January 6-13
River Gauge (Meters)

	1911	1910
6th	88.63	88.39
7th	88.92	88.28
8th	89.41	88.09
9th	90.07	88.00
10th	90.70	88.29
11th	90.80	88.64
12th	90.54	88.84
13th	90.29	88.90

THE WEATHER

January 6-12

	Temperature High	Low	Rainfall (Inches)
Fri.	85 deg.	76 deg.	0.18
Sat.	85 "	76 "	0.00
Sun.	86 "	79 "	0.32
Mon.	90 "	78 "	0.03
Tues.	87 "	77 "	0.00
Wed.	92 "	78 "	0.00
Thurs.	88 "	77 "	0.10

ARRIVALS

January 10th—River steamer *Victoria*, Manaos and Madeira River landings. Passengers, mail and freight.

River steamer *Justo Chermont*, Manaos and Madeira River landings. Passengers, mail and freight.

OCEAN STEAMSHIP SAILINGS

Sailings for New York:

Christopher	January 17th
Polycaro (two passengers)	" 27th
Clement	February 7th
Steinhen	" 17th

Sailings for Europe:

Lanfranc	January 22nd
Jerome	February 3rd
Anthony	" 12th
Ambrose	" 22nd
Augustino	March 3rd

The Woman Who Understands

Somewhere she waits to make you win,
Your soul in her firm white hands—
Somewhere the gods have made for you
The woman who understands.

As the tide went out she found him
Lashed to the spar of despair---
The wreck of his ship, around him,
The wreck of his dreams in the air---
Found him, and loved him, and gathered
The soul of him to her breast;
The soul that had sailed on uncharted sea---
The soul that had sought to win and be free---
The soul of which she was part;
And there in the dusk she cried to the man,
"Win your battle---you can---you can."

Helping and loving and guiding---
Urging when that was best---
Holding her fears in hiding
Deep in her quiet breast---
This is the woman who kept him
True to his standards lost---
When tossed in the storm and stress and strife,
He thought himself through with the game of life
And ready to pay the cost---
Watching and guarding---whisperings still,
"Win---you can---and I know you will."

This is the story of the ages---
This is the woman's way---
Wiser than seers or sages,
Lifting us day by day---
Facing all things with a courage
Nothing can daunt or dim;
Treading life's path wherever it leads---
Lined with flowers or choked with weeds,
But ever with him---with him;
Guardian, comrade, and golden spur,
The men who win are helped by her.

Somewhere she waits, strong in belief,
Your soul in her firm white hands;
Thank well the gods when she comes to you---
The woman who understands.

A LARGE FISH CAUGHT

Much has been written of the many strange specimens contained in Brazilian Rivers. The whole world knows of the alligator but pays little attention to the other strange denizens that infest these inland waters.

The rivers of Brazil fairly teem with fish life, particularly so the Amazon and Madeira Rivers. Occasionally one of these strange specimens is seen or caught and attention is momentarily attracted.

At Candelaria this week a monster fish of the Pirihyba species, was caught on a hook and line, that measured seven feet and weighed two hundred and seventy pounds. Shades of Isaac Whalton, what a whopper! His disciples may well gather around and wonder. Several specimens over six feet long have been taken at different times, but this is the biggest on record.

This is no fish story and doubting Thomas's may be convinced by a photograph which was taken by a member of the Medical staff and is on exhibition. It is to be turned over to Mr. Merrill, the photographer, for reproduction.

FROM THE OUTER WORLD

The following clipping was taken from the November issue of the *Monthly Bulletin of the International Bureau of American Republics*, published at Washington, D.C. Last week we published an article taken from the *India Rubber World*, New York City, which quoted the *Marconigram*. When papers like those above mentioned begin to take notice of our little paper it shows that our efforts have not been in vain and we feel justly proud of our success

"**The inauguration of train service on the M-M,**" the leading article of the *Marconigram* of July 2, 1910, published at Porto Velho, Rio Madeira, Amazonas, Brazil, tells of the first trip of any train over any section of the railroad being built on the upper branches of the Amazon. The *Marconigram* is the "official organ" of the American engineers engaged in construction work in this section of the country, full of humor of the pioneer, and all together worthy of the little colony of ex-patriots that are making world railway history in the heart of South America.

MOVING DAY IN PORTO VELHO

Sunday was moving day in Porto Velho. Most everybody shouldered their trunk, bag, or whatever other means they had for carrying their possessions and changed to new quarters.

Bags, boxes, trunks, etc., kept flying through the air all day long with men clinging on to the other end of them in barnacle like fashion.

Bunkies of long standing were rudely torn apart and separated, and young men who had received a father's care from older roommates were to know that fatherly affection no more.

The cause of it all was for the purpose of classifying the men in buildings and the placing of their respective Department Heads in charge of such buildings.

Following is a list of the buildings with their old and new names and the Head of Department in charge:

Brain House, Quarters No. 1, Terminal Superintendent; Mad House Annex, Quarters No. 2, Accountant; New Hotel No. 1, Quarters No. 3, Master Mechanic; New Hotel No. 2, (just finished) Quarters No. 4, Terminal Superintendent; Quarters on the Hill, Quarters No. 5, Terminal Superintendent. The Bull Pen and Mad House retain their old names, but are to be torn down soon. They are under the supervision of the Terminal Superintendent and Master Mechanic, respectively.

The Bull Pen and the Mad House were among the first buildings to rear above the ground in Porto Velho as the first marks of civilization and stare defiance at the sombre jungle.

So do old names and land-marks pass into oblivion and become but a memory and also so are railroads built.

'Way up in the jungle
Where the Madeira River flows,
Where tarantulas by the thousand
And the Palm and Rubber tree grows;
There's a gang of railroad builders
Working just as hard as can be,
To complete a railroad
To take the rubber to the sea;
They are working in the morning,
They are working still at noon,
And some nights you'll find them working
By the light of the bloomin' moon;
They're over in the tropics
In a country far away
But they're here to build a railroad
Called the *Madeira-Mamoré*.

SOUTH AMERICA'S FIRST TRANS-CONTINENTAL

A Journey Over the Line of the First Railroad to Pierce the Andes--- Buenos Aires to Valparaiso by Air-Line Instead of by the Dangerous Straits of Magellan

(Charles Wellington Furlong in "The World's Work.")

PART IV.

The scene was a fascinating one— a bit of Chile dropped over the border into Argentine; the flapping, varicolored ponchos, jingling six-inch spurs, and small, high-pointed saddle and saddle-gear bespoke the Chilean, for such were the dark, swarthy-visaged men who rode and drove.

"Get in, please!" came a warning request, "When we go, we go with a jump."

There was no mistaking the nationality of the speaker—a tall, keen-eyed man in a broad Stetson hat and long vicuña poncho— MacMillen from Kentucky, chief of "the Transport Service." A command, and like a flash "the Combination" was off at a gallop—only ten minutes after the train had arrived with one hundred passengers and twice as many pieces of baggage. Along the mile-stretch of level road, with the pack-train in the rear, went the long string of coaches followed by the two baggage wagons; behind and scattered along the sides of the narrow coach-route were mounted Chileans and some constabulary, for good reason, as will shortly be seen. A sharp turn and the zigzag climb began. Shifting to little side-trails, which almost imperceptibly left the road, the pack-train and many of the mounted men suddenly disintegrated from "the Combination" scrambling, turning, twisting, but ever carefully choosing each his own path— up, over edges of the steep slope, and disappearing to come again suddenly into sight farther up the mountain in a wholly unexpected quarter.

The riders, including the *postilliones*, each with his hitch-rope and hook for helping up the baggage teams, were distributed at intervals along the line of coaches, with MacMillen's lieutenants at certain points of vantage. MacMillen himself was everywhere.

A coach horse suddenly bucks, lies down, kicks, balks, and an out-rider's lasso jerks him into horse sense; the steep ascent at places is too great for the tired little animals of the heavy baggage-wagons, for "the Transport" has already made the trip over earlier in the day—so watch that *postillione*. Swinging by on the run, he dips from his saddle, deftly links in the hitch-hook—and now, five horses abreast, they spring afresh to their work.

Higher and higher winds the serpentine road. The intervening shadows between us and the west gently spread their purple mantle over the head of the Vale de las Cuevas, where far below dwindled a tin-toy group of corrugated-iron buildings at the Argentine tunnel entrance, less than three miles above Las Cuevas station, where we had left the train The shadow of night sent a colder chill down the mountains, and those travelers who had failed to bring heavy coats shivered in the freezing temperature.

We reached 12,000 feet, and I was glad to pass my head through the hole in the centre of the driver's extra poncho and to wrap myself in its warming folds.

THE VALLE DE LAS CUEVAS

Beyond the great purple shadows the big headlands thrust into the valley and caught the sunlight in warm gold in one great galaxy of color. Each mountain point in distant color stenciled into the valley— rose against delicate tourmaline green, pure blue against light yellow, dark blue-violet protruding from orange-yellow — like great colossal rubies, emeralds, sapphires, turquoises, amethysts, and all manner of precious stones; then far away the massive profile of Puenta de Inca rose, stenciling itself as the final bulwark of rock, frowning dark and sinister in a deep violet cloud-shadow. Tones merged and counter-merged as though nature had set between them and the sun some great ever-turning kaleidoscope through whose transparent particles she flooded the valley with color.

But the coaches have stopped; the steepest haul is just above, now. Down jump the drivers to inspect the harness and shorten the collar-strap traces for the descent on the other side; now comes the Cumbre. Behind, across the valley and intervening mountains, the huge volcanic mass of mighty Aconcagua could be glimpsed for a minute, and we saw the snow-capped heights before the winds drew a veil across the peak.

"*El Cristo*," remarked Antonio as we rounded a huge ledge—and there the lone, bronze figure of the Nazarene stood out dark under the purple shadow of a cloud against a darker shadow beyond. To me, in location and significance the greatest statue in the world is this "Christ of the Andes," the great Peace statue of Chile and Argentina. A glint of sunlight caught on the thorn-crowned head, and the whole figure glowed in the sunlight of Chile, into which we suddenly emerged from the western slope.

A Little Nonsense Now and Then

Apropos of the queer interpretation frequently placed by children upon remarks made to them, a Western professor related at a recent dinner some examination stories.

"Once, in a Bible lesson," he said, "I repeated the text, 'Arise and take the young child and his mother and flee into Egypt.' Then I showed the children a large picture in bright colors that illustrated the text. The children studied this picture eagerly. Then they all frowned; all looked rather disappointed. Finally a little girl said;

"'Teacher, where is the flea?'"

A well known Senator was asked why some politicians were always making such a howl about the preservation of our forests. "Oh," he replied, "they probably never know just when they may have to take to the woods."—*Success Magazine.*

An Atlanta man not long ago met a darkey who was driving a horse so thin that it staggered as it walked.

"Why don't you put more flesh on that nag?" indignantly demanded the Atlantan.

"'Scuse me, boss," replied the driver, "but I's doin' de best I kin. Cain't you see, boss, dat po' hoss kin hardly carry what little flesh h's got on him now?"— *St. Paul's Dispatch.*

When you'd grow powerful or rich,
Remember as you stray
Someone may write his memoirs which
Will give you dead away.
— *Washington Star.*

THE PORTO VELHO

Marconigram

"LA VIDA SIN LITERATURA Y QUININA ES MUERTE"

Published at Porto Velho (Rio Madeira), Amazonas, Brazil

VOLUME 3	SATURDAY, JANUARY 21, 1911	NUMBER 3

POINTS EMPHASIZED IN THE PRESIDENT'S MESSAGE

I believe it to be in the interest of the people of the country that for the time being the activities of the government, in addition to enforcing the existing law, be directed toward the economy of administration and the enlargement of opportunities for foreign trade, the conservation and improvement of our agricultural lands, the building up of home industries and the strengthening of confidence of capital in domestic investment.

The policy of broader and closer trade relations with the Dominion of Canada * * * has proved mutually beneficial. It justifies further efforts for the readjustment of the commercial relations of the two countries.

The policy of this government has been directed by a desire to make use of American capital in China an instrument in the promotion of China's welfare and material prosperity, without prejudice to her legitimate rights as an independent political Power.

Whether or not the protective policy is to be continued, * * * it is clear that the necessary legislation should be based on an impartial, thorough and continuous study of the facts.

No man ought to have as a matter of right a review of his case by the Supreme Court. He should be satisfied by one hearing before a court of first instance and one review by a court of appeals.

As an income-producing measure the existing tariff bill has never been exceeded by any customs bill in the history of the country.

Everything which tends to send immigrants West and South into rural life helps the country.

*   *   *   *   *

At the instance of Colonel Goethals, the army engineer officer in charge of the work on the Panama Canal, I have just made a visit to the Isthmus to inspect the work done and consult with him on the ground as to certain problems which are likely to arise in the near future. The progress of the work is most satisfactory. If no unexpected obstacle presents itself, the canal will be completed well within the time fixed by Colonel Goethals, to wit, January 1, 1915, and within the estimate of cost, $375,000,000.

Among questions arising for present solution is the decision whether the Canal shall be fortified. I have already stated to the Congress that I strongly favor fortification and I now reiterate this opinion and ask your consideration of the subject in the light of the report already before you made by a competent board.

One great crying need in the United States is cheapening the cost of litigation by simplifying judicial procedure and expediting final judgment. Under present conditions the poor man is at a woeful disadvantage in a legal contest with a corporation or a rich opponent. The necessity for the reform exists both in United States courts and in all State courts. In order to bring it about, however, it naturally falls to the general government by its example to furnish a model to all States. A legislative commission appointed by joint resolution of Congress to revise the procedure in the United States courts has as yet made no report.

*   *   *   *   *

The Republic of Honduras has for many years been burdened with a heavy bonded debt held in Europe, the interest on which long ago fell in arrears. Finally conditions were such that it became imperative to refund the debt and place the finances of the Republic upon a sound basis. Last year a group of American bankers undertook to do this and to advance funds for railway and other improvements contributing directly to the country's prosperity and commerce—an arrangement which has long been desired by this government.

Negotiations to this end have been under way for more than a year and it is now confidently believed that a short time will suffice to conclude an arrangement which will be satisfactory to the foreign creditors, eminently advantageous to Honduras and highly creditable to the judgment and foresight of the Honduranean government. This is much to be desired since, as recognized by the Washington conventions, a strong Honduras would tend immensely to the progress and prosperity of Central America.

Wages of South African Natives

In South Africa natives working on the farms can earn from $2 to $3 a month. There is a cost of living problem for them, all right!

RECENT CENSUS RETURNS

| | POPULATION | | Per cent. Increase |
	1910	1900	
Birmingham, Ala.	132,685	38,415	245.4
Butte, Mont.	39,165	30,470	28.5
Chattanooga, Tenn.	44,604	30,154	47.9
Delaware. . .	202,322	184,735	9.5
Harrisburg Pa.	64,186	50,167	27.9
Jacksonville, Fla.	57,699	28,429	103.0
Kansas City, Kan.	82,331	51,418	60.1
Lincoln, Neb.	43,973	40,169	9.5
Medford, Mass.	28,150	18,244	3.7
Melrose, Mass.	15,715	12,962	4.7
Missouri. . . .	3,293,335	3,106,665	6.0
New Mexico .	327,896	195,310	67.6
Newport, Ky.	30,309	28,301	7.1
Pasadena, Cal.	30,291	9,117	232.2
St. Joseph, Mo.	102,979	77,403	-24.8
San Jose, Cal.	28,946	21,500	34.6
Shawnee City, Mo.	12,474	16,955	7.2
Topeka, Kan.	43,684	33,608	30.0
Woburn, Mass.	15,308	14,254	13.5
Worcester, Mass.	145,986	118,421	23.3

THE PORTO VELHO
MARCONIGRAM

Published at
Porto Velho (Rio Madeira Brazil

C. L. JONES—*Editor*
S. WELLWOOD—*Publisher*

SATURDAY, JANUARY 21ST, 1911.

SOME RECENT LETTERS

Chief Mogul of the Office,
Porto Velho.

Dear Sir:---I do not know that you will be able to remedy the matter in any way, but I would like to bring to your attention some errors appearing on Manaos waybills.

It is very difficult to translate "Gatnol" into "Oatmeal" and "Gataup" does not look much like "Catsup;" "Lobetern" is more easily twisted into "Lobster." I was in doubt for some time as to what a "Cluts nhifter" was, but have arrived at the conclusion that it is a "clutch shifter." "Stell Enuckles" was easily translated into "Steel Knuckles," but when a waybill shows "white paper" I naturally expect it instead of "white pepper," and I am not sure yet if "flurs" is meant for "flues." "Hage" became "sage" without any trouble but "craushers" for "crackers" was more difficult. "Tobacco sause" was switched into "Tobasco sauce" and such things as "staruch," "gyrup" "clearsideen," "shriam," "glass chowder," "beff" "tinion backs" and many other similar ones were easy.

Nevertheless it is embarrassing when one is asked in a hurry for the Porto Velho name of some of the forgoing

Yours truly,
A. CHECKER.

Manaos Office: Please Note—Absolutely no excuse—these little errors are not limited to your Xmas waybills. Maybe someone switched the keys on your typewriter.

A W(H)AIL FROM CANDELARIA

Everyone in the hospital
Gets some old kind of "dope,"
Morphine, cocaine, strychnine—
For, while there's life there's hope.
Number five gets "poco" whisky,
And so does number nine,
It makes no difference what you've got,
They "shoot you" with quinine.

I have just returned from there,
At meals I stand in line,
Why don't I sit? well, truth to tell,
Well,---er---well I got mine.

---*Hypo Dermic.*

SENATOR GEORGE G. VEST'S EULOGY TO MAN'S BEST FRIEND—HIS DOG

GENTLEMEN OF THE JURY :—The best friend a man has in this world may turn against him and become his enemy. His son or his daughter, that he has reared with loving care, may prove ungrateful. Those who are nearest and dearest to us, those whom we trust with our happiness and our good name, may become traitors to their faith. The money that a man has he may lose. It flies away from him perhaps when he needs it most. A man's reputation may be sacrificed in a moment of ill-considered action. The people who are prone to fall on their knees to do us honor when success is with us may be the first to throw stones of malice when failure settles its clouds upon our heads. The one absolutely unselfish friend that a man can have in this selfish world, the one that never deserts him, the one that never proves ungrateful or treacherous, is his dog. GENTLEMEN OF THE JURY :—A man's dog stands by him in prosperity and in poverty, in health and in sickness. He will sleep on the cold ground where the wintry winds blow and the snow drives fiercely, if only he may be near his master's side. He will kiss the hand that has no food to offer, he will lick the wounds and sores that come in encounter with the roughness of the world. He guards the sleep of his pauper master as if he were a Prince. When all other friends desert, he remains. When riches take wings and reputation falls to pieces, he is as constant in his love as the sun in its journey through the heavens. If fortune drives the master forth an outcast in the world, friendless, and homeless, the faithful dog asks no higher privilege than that of accompanying him to guard against danger, to fight against his enemies. And, when the last scene of all comes, and death takes the master in its embrace, and his body is laid away in the cold ground, no matter if all other friends pursue their way, there by his graves'de will the noble dog be found, his head between his paws, his eyes sad but open in alert watchfulness, faithful and true even to death.

The above was an address to the jury made by Senator Vest of Missouri in the course of the trial of a man who had shot a fine dog belonging to a neighbor.

Roslyn, Md.,
March 7th, 1906.

FOR SALE—One Heavy Bed Blanket. New. Inquire *Marconigram* Office.

NOTES ABOUT TOWN

I was sitting down to dinner
And before me I did see,
A large bottle of quinina,
And I says: "have one with me."

The Accountant's staff moved from Quarters No. 5 to Quarters No. 2 Sunday. This brings them closer to the scene of their daily labors and no doubt we will hear the gentle buzz of the typewriter early and often in the future.

The *M-M* left Itacoatiara last Sunday for Porto Velho, having on board 14 first-class passengers and 240 laborers. Besides a general cargo, she brings 42 head of cattle.

R. B. Tarver of Camp 25, is in town for a day or two.

D. B. Merrill, the photographer, will start up the line to-morrow looking for new views of the work.

A barracão occupied by Philip Savory and George McKenzie, (colored) printers, was entered Thursday morning and 60$000 taken. For the benefit of those who took the money we will state that if they had looked a little closer they would have found a much larger sum.

The Madeira-Mamoré Railway Co. have marketed recently in Europe a bond issue of 450,000 at 6 per cent. at 50 years.

The passengers on the last *M-M*, who were held in quarantine, were released last Sunday.

The *Oteri* is expected to arrive at Itacoatiara on January 23rd, sailing immediately for Porto Velho She has 310 laborers on board.

H. B. Walling, who has been recuperating at Candelaria for the last week is back at his desk at the General Office and looking as well as ever.

S. T. Kendall, who has been Chief Timekeeper, is now performing the duties of Payroll Clerk.

O. Hoyer, Timekeeper, just returned from vacation, has been assigned to Camp 25

A. E. Hill has been appointed Chief Timekeeper.

T. N Finney has been assigned to the General Office.

LEVEL AND TRANSIT NOTES

Mr. L. T. McCann, Resident Engineer at Camp 25, returned to his residency on the morning train, Sunday, after spending a few days in Porto Velho on business.

Mr. H. A. Attrill, left on No. 3 Sunday for Camp

Sr. O. Gomez, Official Interpreter, reported for duty Monday morning.

The sessions of that far-famed and worthy institution, the Windy Point Club, are now being held nightly and are receiving the great attention that is its due Initiation varies, according to Hoyle, from sole leather to the star-lit skies. At present a rumor is making the rounds of club circles that this club is to change its name to the "Porto Velho Clearing House." But more anon.

Our poet-er sends the following, asking us to use our "pull" with the editor to have it inserted. He must be proud of his work. To us, it sounds like Longfellow—in disgust. Here it is:

Beyond, below the Coal Pile,
The engines nightly stand,
All night the stoker shovels coal,
He sure do beat the band,
All night we toss and tumble,
In our little trundle beds,
And long and wish and hope for—
But it's a shame to do it

The location work just to the north of Porto Velho is about completed and Mr. E. C. Kyte, who has been in charge of the Party expects to make a visit to Matta Virgem in a few days With him are expected to go Messrs, Aguirre and Howser. The jolly crowd will be missed by all.

Thursday evening, at about half past seven, Mr. Axel Carlsson, who has been supervising the test-borings on the Location work north of Porto Velho, had the misfortune to accidentally shoot himself in the leg. It seems that he was in the act of removing some papers from the top of a suit case and, while doing so, knocked the revolver, a 38 calibre, to the floor and striking on the hammer, one cartridge was discharged. The bullet entering the right leg on the inner side, ploughed its way upward and outward, from a point about half way between the knee and hip to a point just beyond the hip, leaving the body a little to the rear of the hip joint and making a very painful and nasty wound, almost fifteen inches long clear through the leg. As soon as the report, followed by Mr. Carlsson's cry was heard, many men rushed to his assistance and he was quickly removed to Dr. Fitch, who dressed the wound and had him hurried to the Porto Velho station, placed aboard a locomotive and rushed

RAINS IN PANAMA CRIPPLE RAILROAD

Panama, Panama, via Galveston, Texas.—Heavy rains continue unabated on both sides of the canal zone, and fears are entertained that if the Charges River rises as on former occasions it may cause serious interruption to railroad service and canal work.

No freight trains are being run and passenger trains are irregular.

The Black Swamp track is still submerged and for some distance is not considered safe for trains. Most of the track between Gatun and San Pablo is still under water.

Owing partly to the fact that new locations are not yet available, several stations between San Pablo and Gatun are out of communication. Efforts are being made by railroad and canal employes to repair the line and run trains as regularly as possible,

BEAUTIFUL BUENOS AYRES

In ten years miracles have been wrought in beautifying the great city of Buenos Ayres down in the Argentine Republic. More than 142,000 trees have been planted. By the side of the waving tropic palm rears the stately pine. More than eighty small parks of exquisite beauty have been opened in various parts of the city. This work has been under the direction of Senor Carlos Thays, who will live in the hearts of future generations of his lovely city long after the military heros and financial chieftains of his country are forgotten. The masterpiece of Senor Thays is the Plaza del Congreso, in the heart of the metropolis. Anybody who wants to see an American park system as it ought to be should board a steamer for the Argentines.

to Candelaria. Mr Carlsson has the sympathy of the entire headquarters corp, who wish him a speedy recovery.

Thursday, January 19th, (General R. E. Lee's birthday) was quietly celebrated and observed by the few "Johnny Rebs" among the outfit.
—*The Virginian.*

ANSWERS TO CORRESPONDENTS

AGNES:—Yes, Horsey is his real name, and not a nick-name, just because he is so c It sh.

W. C. T. U. HDGRS:—Our statistics show that there are 387 white residents of Porto Velho, and a census taken on the morning of January 2nd showed 386 of them to be strenuously in favor of temperance.
P.S.—We are not at liberty to state the name of the 387th person.

CHIEF RAIN-IN-THE-FACE, CARIPUNA HDGRS:—No, chief, Tom Greenwood is harmless in spite of his large supply of bows and arrows. He couldn't shoot you with them, for the only thing he can shoot is dice.

ENGINEERING MAN:—Our limited space will not allow us to enumerate all the powers in existence other than water-powers and steam-powers. All powers are valuable to mankind with the possible exception of Powers at the transportation camp.

MARINE INTELLIGENCE

January 14-20
River Gauge (Meters)

	1911	1910
14th	9o.1o	88.81
15th	89.98	88.68
16th	9o.28	88.58
17th	9o.78	88.49
18th	9o.9o	88.42
19th	9o.94	88.39
2oth	9o.82	88.74

THE WEATHER

January 13-19

	Temperature		Rainfall
	High	Low	(Inches)
Fri.	80 deg.	77 deg.	0.20
Sat.	86 "	77 "	0.53
Sun.	88 "	77 "	0.46
Mon.	86 "	77 "	0.90
Tues.	84 "	76 "	0.00
Wed.	84 "	76 "	0.00
Thurs.	86 "	86 "	0.42

ARRIVALS

January 16th – Madeira-Mamore tugs *Parbosa* and *Cecelia* arrived, with mail and construction materials.

SAILINGS

January 13th—River steamer *Victoria*, Manaos and Madeira River landings. Passengers, mail and freight.

January 19th—River steamer *Justo Chermont*, Manaos and Madeira River landings. Passengers, mail and freight.

OCEAN STEAMSHIP SAILINGS

Sailings for New York :

Polycaro (no passengers)	"	27th
Clement	.	February 7th
Steinhen	"	17th

Sailings for Europe:

Lanfranc	.	January 22nd
Jerome	.	February 3rd
Anthony	.	" 12th
Ambrose	.	" 22nd
Augustino	.	March 3rd

SOUTH AMERICA'S FIRST TRANS-CONTINENTAL

A Journey Over the Line of the First Railroad to Pierce the Andes— Buenos Aires to Valparaiso by Air-Line Instead of by the Dangerous Straits of Magellan

(Charles Wellington Furlong in " The World's Work.")

PART V.

THE " COMBINATION " TRANSPORT.

But the coaches were late and drove rapidly by. Creased between mountains lay the Aconcagua Valley on the other side of the Cumbre, stretching away Chile to Los Andes. Now began the steep descent, mostly at a fast trot. Splendid drivers, these Chilean *cocheros.*

"*Permisso, Senor*!" broke in Antonio, for we were at one of the sharp turns. At the angle a broken wall fringed a precipice. When well in the angle of the turn, Antonio without hesitancy and with consummate skill swung the animals around the sharp bend of thirty-degrees, the inner horse acting as a pivot, the absence of outer traces accelerating the mobility of the outside horses at the turns. These when very sharp caused the outermost horse to brace along the retaining wall, the others setting back splendidly.

The " Combination Transport " or mountain coach service (officially known as *El Servicio Cordillera*) was probably the most efficient service of that kind in existence. Besides one hundred and fifty men for the coach and pack, it consisted of twenty coaches, ten baggage wagons, and five hundred animals. The " Combination" was run six or seven months a year—that is, until the heavy snows buried the roads. Then the traveler between Buenos Aires and Valparaiso made the long journey by sea via the Straits of Magellan In April or May "the Combination" was discontinued; the animals were driven down to the green valleys and kept on feed through the winter. The *Servicio Cordillera* has been maintained at no less than $40,000 a month; now that the railroad is completed, the sturdy little animals have made their last trip over the great, desolate Cumbre and are far down in the verdant valleys of Los Andes. The regular traveler will lose the privilege of ascending the uppermost heights of this pass, but the railroad journey itself will afford a wonderful insight into one of nature's greatest scenic theatres.

With a rush and a cloud of dust we passed under a little bridge amid a crowd of picturesque Chilean tunnel-workers — the day-shift just off duty—and drew up beside the waiting train of the Chilean Trans-andine Railway at Caracoles (10,459 feet), just below the Chilean Summit Tunnel entrance, the coaches having made a record trip of one hour and fifty minutes.

Above the darkened mountain peaks, against the turquoise blue of the sky, a single blaze of cloud shot up in a vigorous saffron swerve, an echo of the departed day, and we plunged into the deep, dark valley and night—on by Juncal, Guardia Vieja, and Salto del Soldado, ever downward to Los Andes, where all changed to the broad guage of the Chilean State Line.

THE CHILEAN SECTION OF THE LINE.

Leaving Santiago shortly after 5 a.m. the following Tuesday, I retraced my journey, meeting Mr McGinnis (the general manager) at Los Andes.

Leaving Los Andes on the Trans-andine Railway, a post showed me that I was one kilometer (nearly a mile) on my way back up the beginning of one of the most remarkable railroad climbs in the world.

" Come back, if you want a better view," suggested McGinnis; so with him and his traction foreman I was seated on a handcar towed by the train.

"Look sharp—there's El Salto del Soldado," and through a tunnel gap I caught a glimpse of a picturesque stone bridge that we had just crossed in a mountain crevice, spanning a gorge.

For the first twenty-eight miles to Rio Blanco (4,822 feet) we puffed along over gradients of 2 1-2 per cent.; then the engine began to strain harder; the heavy cogs dropped into the rack-rail, for, as in Argentina, where the grade exceeds 2 1-2 per cent. the third or rack-rail (Abt system) is employed; so, from Rio Blanco on to the tunnel at Caracoles, it is brought into use fully two-thirds of the way, and at places the grade reaches a maximum of 8 per cent. The hard roble-pine sleepers (eleven to the 8-metre rail, 27 kilos to the metre) do splendid service on the adhesion gradients, and tough steel sleepers are not only on the rock grades, but on all grades above 2 1-2 per cent.

Passing Portillo, with its rock-bordered Inca Lake, which lies calm and still like a polished sapphire in its setting of steep mountains sloping abruptly into its waters, we enter a region (between Juncal and the Summit) whose desolate grandeur baffles description Prodigious masses of andesite tower up to sharp-pointed peaks, snow-covered and sublime against the clear cobalt above, higher than the habitat of the condor or mountain eagle. Here nature has written on the naked, rocky, mountain fastnesses the story of the rise and fall and building again of one of earth's youngest continental ranges. Tremendous landslides have shunned down the precipitous sides, and colossal ledges —poised on a period of time—hang above you, some day to go crashing their way to the depths below. Go back in imagination through geologic ages to a time which cannot be even approximately estimated, but which men are pleased to call the Mesozoic Period—some time then, a few million years one way or the other, as the earth cooled, its crust cracked; from the terrestrial fissures exuded prodigious masses of molten rock, occasionally with convulsions which must have shaken the very foundations of the earth. So, anciently, slowly emerging from the briny sea, the Andes were born.

I looked out on the quiet sunshine, back through the peaceful, hazy distance which hung over the valley, to Santa Rosa de los Andes, and then toward the little atoms of men up beyond, laying rails at railhead a hundred feet from the yawning mouth of the tunnel, for we had reached Caracoles, where the train stops at the end of the train-line. We were now nearly sixty miles from Los Andes, about twenty miles of it on the rack-rail with minimum curves of 165 yards, though all but two are over 220 yards We crossed 118 bridges, passed through no less than twenty-four tunnels, and numerous snow and avalanche sheds.

THE PORTO VELHO
Marconigram

"LA VIDA SIN LITERATURA Y QUININA ES MUERTE"

Published at Porto Velho (Rio Madeira), Amazonas, Brazil

VOLUME 4　　　SATURDAY, APRIL 29, 1911.　　　NUMBER 4

WIDE-REACHING WIRELESS

The Chilian Government is putting up a wireless tower on Juan Fernandez Island, 360 miles distant, and soon the lonely place where Alexander Selkirk was wrecked and where Robinson Crusoe found the tracks in the sand for Defoe's millions of eager readers will get the latest news in thirty seconds from the centres of civilization. The British Postmaster General is linking up the isolated islands on the west coast of Scotland with the mainland by wireless for a daily air-letter service. Germany and England are considering a plan to talk across the Sahara Desert in Arica by means of a chain of wireless poles on the oases. Wireless bulletins from hades itself are not a remote conjecture, says Senator Depew, who suggests asbestos receiving instruments

EARTH SLIDE AT GATUN DAM

Three Killed by Break of Earth at North End of the Big Lock

Colon, Panama, March 11.—Without warning of any sort, 350,000 cubic yards of earth dropped in Culebra cut at Gatun Locks, last night. So sudden was the launching of the avalanche that three of a night gang of laborers were unable to get to safety with their thirty companions and were killed. A steam shovel was buried.

The gang was working under searchlghts, but these were directed on the steam shovel. Only a few arc lamps were on the crest of the cut. One of the laborers glanced up from his work and yelled, "A slide! A slide"

Dropping tools on the instant, the laborers ran. Two Spaniards and an Italian were not fleet enough and were swallowed up in the soft, crumbling earth. This slide is not far from Gold Hill, from the crest of which 500,000 yards slumped into the cut on February 9. At that time there were predictions that the whole cut would have to be widened, making the slope so gradual that slides would be impossible. Colonel Goethals denied this, but the last slide makes it seem he will be forced to change his plans, and the canal work will be delayed.

Gatun Locks are half finished by concrete workers A back fill was to have protected them, but plans may have to be changed.

NEW BRAZIL BANK BRANCH

Rio Janeiro, Brazil, March 11.—President Nilo Pecanha of the Bank of Brazil sailed to-day on his mission of establishing branches of the institution in the United States, France and England.

CAMPS IN CONSTRUCTION DIVISION

Camp 32 1-2, kilometer 211 ; D. E. Kelly, Sub-Foreman, reporting to B. L. Hart at Camp 33.

Camp 33, kilometer 219; Ben L. Hart, Foreman ; K. A. Fry, Timekeeper.

Camp 34, kilometer 229; Ivan Landes, Foreman; John Trimble, Timekeeper.

Camp 35, kilometer 237; M. S. Brown, Foreman; I. Robertson, Timekeeper.

Camp 36, kilometer 247; P. L. Harrison, Foreman; T. M. Greenwood, Timekeeper.

Camp 37, kilometer 250; George P Wright, Foreman; J. B. Fordyce, Timekeeper.

Camp 38, kilometer 267 (Approx); D. P Bailey, Foreman ; T. Garthwaite, Timekeeper.

POST OFFICE NOTICE

DEAD LETTERS

The undermentioned is a list of letters for white men now laying unclaimed at the Post Office. The owners of same cannot be located and any information as to their whereabouts will be thankfully received.

Andersson, Axel.,
Amanawicz, Antoni,
Burney, R. L.,
Clifford, F. M.,
Cogedill, R. W.,
Connors, George A.,
Cornish, F. H.,
Chaplain, John J.,
Dijkmans, C.,
Drummond, A.,
Drayton, Allen,
Delfien, Ernst,
Emery, A. J.,
England, James,
Eichholzer, Charles,
Franklin, George,
Furlow, S. D.,
Farrington, Ludwig,
Frank, Egon,
Feinester, Leo ,
Gardner, David B.,
Gerst, Harry,
Gibson, Harry,
Hill, John,
Hunter, T.,
Hochenzy, Stainslaw,
Hamlin, Joseph R.,
Hellmich, Robert,
Heatley, John R.,
Henderson, V. U.,
Joy, Frank,
Jahn, Theo. W. A.,
Keller, Karl T.,
Kusai, Joseph.

Kopilink, S.,
Kreuger, C. A.,
Leffel, Frank,
Lloyd, A. G.,
Lachlan, W.,
Melville, Thomas,
Moore, F. M.,
Peters, Imas,
Raundoo, John H.,
Reismann, Jacques,
Rupert, Victor,
Reimert, Kai,
Ruhe, Albert,
Steen, Henry,
Schuler, Fred,
Schuler, Fritz,
Saunders, H. T.,
Stalhey, Ernest,
Stout, George W.,
Sztiblo, Franc,
Wade, Elgood,
Wilson, Athelstan J.,
Williams, Thomas,
Watson, N.,
Wollitz, Ernest,
Walker, A. H.,
Weir, James A.,
Wilcox, R. M.,
Walle, E.,
Wernock, W.,
Ward, W.,
Wood, Frank,
Werokenthin, W.,
Walker, A. W.,
Werchenthien, G.,
Zjarnberg, W.,

A Biography

Solomon Grundy,
Born on Monday,
Got rich Tuesday,
Espoused on Wednesday,
Famous on Thursday,
Senate on Friday,
Art collector on Saturday,
Hall of Fame Sunday—
That was the success
Of Solomon Grundy.—*Puck.*

THE PORTO VELHO
MARCONIGRAM

Published at
Porto Velho (Rio Madeira) Brazil

J. H. ARMITAGE—*Editor*
S. WELLWOOD—*Publisher*

SATURDAY, APRIL 29TH, 1911.

YE EDITOR

Our thanks are due to some of the "boys" up the line—and we take this means of extending them, assuring, at the same time, our sincere gratefulness. However, the number is still small and we want to see it larger, much larger. We only have four pages; these can be filled each week with local items and we want them so. Come now, and send in those notes you have been intending to each week. We have an iron or two "in the fire" and, though we won't say how warm they are, still the fire is alright and, in a short time, we will divulge our secret—to the benefit of all our readers.

NOTES FROM THE CAMPS

The Box Culvert at Station 745 is rapidly nearing completion, and excavating at Station 749 for the culvert at that place is well under way.

On completion of the last named culvert, Camp Foreman H. Ferris and his outfit, expect to move to Camp 16 to put in the concrete wing walls for the Caracol bridge.

We understand the "Piums" at 16 are just "alf and alf," but "oh dear" the mosquitoes are beastly. Pertinacious "you know," and it reminds one of that dear "New Joisey" U.S.A. "Bah Jove."

OCEAN STEAMSHIP SAILINGS

Sailings for New York:

Coorense	.	May	7th
Cuthbert	.	"	17th
Benedict	.	"	27th
Clement	.	June	7th
Denis	.	"	17th
Poly Carp (no passengers)	"	27th

Sailings for Germany:

Rio Negro	.	May	1st
Rhaetia	.	"	17th
Rio Grande	.	June	1st
Rugia	.	"	17th

PROVERBS

All my life I have had a grievance against Proverbs. Those little moral maxims that are held over us all in the days of our unruly youth—whenever we leave undone what should have been done, or vice versa. They are all a part of a deep laid plot on the part of designing elderly folks to help them in suppressing the outward expression of almost irrepressible ebullience of spirits in unsophisticated youth. (All rights reserved. Copyright in all languages.)

Let us look at one or two of these "wise sayings," as the dictionary calls them. For instance, "all is not gold that glitters." Does anyone who has a wisdom tooth need to be told that? And why rub it in? We all know it, and yet, in spite of the warning we all fall to the old gold brick when it is properly gilded. Dear old gold bricks of our youth! How we would love to realize on you at thirteen cents on the dollar.

"Spare the rod and spoil the child." There's another one for you! What does it mean anyhow. Why should you spare the rod? Of course if it's the only walking cane you have, why then by all means save it for Sundays. Besides—any competent grown-up can spoil a kid good and plenty with a carpet slipper, without having to fall back on a rod. The child may say, "it all depends on the point of view," but that has nothing to do with it. It's the point of *contact* that counts. And who cares what a kid thinks anyway.

"The pitcher goes off to the *well*." Well, well, now I always thought the pitcher went into the *box*. That's my ignorance, I suppose, if we are to rely on these "wise sayings."

"A rolling stone gathers no moss." Who wants to gather moss anyhow? Let's take this up in more serious vein. The proverb discredits the "rolling stone," and yet, in all the world's history, who have been the great pioneers of civilization, the builders of empire, the forces making for the general advancement of our common destiny? Who but the rolling stones? What made Rome the greatest Empire of her day, when the proudest boast a man could utter, was, "I am a Roman citizen." Simply the rolling stones of the Roman legions, with their colonizing and civilizing effects. From their one little City on the seven hills the stones of Roman civilization spread and spread and spread until—*the stones cease to roll* and the militant soldier became the effeminate, stay-at-home courtier, who took his ease, and gathered the moss which inevitably overgrows neglected activities. History tells us what happened then. The despised Barbarian swept down upon Imperial Rome while she gathered *moss*—and Rome went out—as a name and as a glorious tradition only, does the Roman Empire remain to-day, whilst the rolling stones have continued to roll. And wherever they have rolled and continue to roll, will be found always, what we believe to be, and love to call—"Gods' Country."—*Pedro.*

LEVEL AND TRANSIT NOTES

Mr. M. V. Powell came in from up the line Sunday evening.

The Preliminary Party: Mr. J. Bolton (Chief of Party) consisting of Messrs. J. C. Bolton, C. J. Kalbfell, C. H. Eaton, R. C. Mount and M. S. Reatiqui, together with twenty-two laborers, after having completed their survey, arrived from Guajaramiram Monday evening. Everyone is in the pink of health and, though expecting to leave on their vacations shortly, are enthusiastic over the splendid improvements in Porto Velho, as well as it growth and are enjoying themselves thoroughly, after the trying times at the front. As will be recalled by many, this party left Porto Velho about the first of last October and have made somewhat of a record in their work, which deserves the congratulations being extended them from every side.

Messrs. O. L. Pyles, R. A. Bowman and L. G. Trenary, of Party No. 7 (Mr. E. B. Karnopp's Party), arrived here Monday afternoon, after an eight day trip from Guajaramirm. Mr. Bowman left Thursday for Camp 23 (Mr. Jenkins in charge) and Mr. Trenary to Camp 16 (Mr. Mullen, Resident Engineer), Mr. Pyles left Friday for vacation, on the *Barbosa.*

Mr. William Greenslade was transferred to Engineering Department, April 11th, and will assist Mr. A. Harwell, Resident Engineer at Camp 37.

Mr. W. E. Lord, of Camp 16, came down to Candelaria Monday, to spend a few days, returning Friday morning.

Mr. L. L. DeForrest of Camp 23 has been assigned work at Camp 21 1-2.

Mr. F. M. Gibson, of Location Party (Mr. F. C. Kyte, chief) has been assigned to Party 7, Guajaramirim.

Messrs J. M. Robinson, Assistant Chief Engineer and A E Hess arrived here Tuesday afternoon after a trip to the front.

Messrs J C. Bolton, C. H Eaton, R. C Mount, C. J. Kalbfell and M. S. Reatiqui, the Engineers comprising "Boltons' Party," left on the *Barbosa* on their vacations.

Mr. S. S. Bunker, Division Engineer, with office at Camp 33, left on *Barbosa* Friday morning for his vacation.

Mr. D. B. Merrill, Photographer, left for a trip up the line Thursday morning

Mr. H. O Weiss, of Terminal Engineer Hendrickson's staff, who has been spending a few days as a guest at Cantelaria, is again among us and in harness.

The screening of the old quarters is complete, and painters are now at work giving it an attractive dressing. "Solid Ivory"—and comfort.

Mr J M. Robinson, Assistant Chief Engineer, who has been "in harness" here for over sixteen months, left on his vacation on the *Barbosa.*

Will "Port" Arthur kindly explain "why?" 5 shillings means more "dough" in Barbados than $6 00

Mr. F S. Weston, of Terminal Engineer's force, left on his vacation on *Barbosa.* During Mr. Hendrickson's absence, while on vacation, Mr, Weston was acting Terminal Engineer.

BULLETIN
April 26, 1911.

To all concerned :—Mr. A. E. Hess, Assistant Engineer, has been placed in charge of all Construction. Resident and Division Engineers will in the future please report to him instead of the Chief Engineer.

H. F. DOSE,
Chief Engineer.

April 28, 1911.

To all concerned :—Effective this date all Resident Engineers from Camp 33 ahead will report to and receive their instructions from Mr. M V Powell, who has been appointed Division Engineer, vice Mr. S. S. Bunker, on leave of absence.

H F DOSE,
Chief Engineer.

THE WEATHER
April 21-.27

	Temperature		Rainfall
	High	Low	(Inches)
Fri.	86 deg.	71 deg.	0.00
Sat.	89 ,,	77 ,,	2.06
Sun.	88 ,,	75 ,,	0.00
Mon.	84 ,,	77 ,,	0.00
Tues.	86 ,,	77 ,,	0.00
Wed.	86 ,,	76 ,,	0.10
Thurs.	87 ,,	77 ,,	0.00

NOTES ABOUT TOWN

April 26:—Rails are down to Kilometer 200. It looks as though the people up that way were keeping busy.

Messrs. Mays, Marshall and McCloud, of Material Department, and Mr. Liggett, of Transportation Department, are now quartered in Quarters No. 1 (Commissary).

Preparations are being made to give the electric transmission towers a coat of preservative paint, adding to attractiveness, and greater durability to these well-made fixtures.

A cable of the 21st, reaching here Sunday (23rd) announced the arrival of Mr. Stork, with a little girl, at the home of our popular citizen (and esteemed editor) Mr. J H Armitage. Many have been the congratulations from his scores of friends here and we warn the Postmaster to prepare for heavy mail from the States.

Jim Stephens had a very painful accident in the yards this week. While throwing a switch the lever slipped and he fell forward his hand striking the railroad track just as the car happened along. One of the wheels passed over one of his fingers cutting it off to the first joint Jim is taking life easy these days waiting for the time when his finger will allow him to get into the "hustle" again.

J. C. Burgess, while out walking one evening last week stepped into a hole in the dark, turning his ankle and spraining it severely. He is having the injured member treated at Candelaria

The number of meals served during the month of March, 1911, at the General Mess were :

First Class	16,697
Second Class	2,968

Souvenir hunters can secure no better relic of the Madeira-Mamore Railway than the collection of photographs offered by Mr. Merrill The collection contains all of the familiar scenes in and around Porto Velho and of life up the line in and about the Camps. The selection of views to choose from in an extensive one and well worth a visit to see alone.

A new station was opened at Camp 28 this week.

Mr. Gilbert of Camp 25 is spending a few days in town.

The painters have finished with Quarters No. 2 and they are a fine illustration of what a little paint, applied by a man who knows now, can accomplished If Mr. Seaman keeps the good work up Porto Velho will be a rival of "Spotless Town."

The *Rio Machado* left Itacoatiara, Thursday, April 20th, for Porto Velho, with four sacks of mail on board

A PRETTY ROMANCE AT CANDELARIA

Although the secret has been carefully guarded, Cupid was so overjoyed, happy and elated that he couldn't contain himself and whispered to us. Knowing the popularity of the two parties and the genuine interest that will be taken by their scores of friends here, we cannot conscientiously withhold the good news and, congratulating the happy pair, as well as being glad to spread the pleasure-laden news, we must 'fess up and tell.

Mrs. Bertha Fairall has yielded to Dan Cupid and the love of Mr. J. C. Burgess and, upon the arrival of the steamer *Rio Machado*, the happy couple will be united in matrimony. As planned at present, the honeymoon will extend to Europe, via Bridgetown, Barbados, where a few days—or weeks—will be spent among the balmy breezes and perfumed bowers, an ideal spot for a honeymoon. We cannot say with authority, as to the scope of the European tour. However, the continent is full of little quiet, "spooning" spots and, among these, we expect the blushing bride and happy groom will wend their way.

Mrs. Fairall, has won many friends during her short stay here; friends who wish her the happiest happiness Mr Burgess, who was already known to many from association elsewhere, has added hosts to his army of friends One and all will join heartily in extending the happy pair felicitations.

"Bless you, my children, and joy go with you."

MARINE INTELLIGENCE
April 22-28

River Gauge (Meters)

		1911	1909
April	22nd	92.21	93.54
	23rd	92.08	93.54
	24th	91.96	93.52
	25th	91.86	93.35
	26th	91.86	93.21
	27th	91.86	93.11
	28th	91.72	93.06

ARRIVALS

April 23rd.—Freighter *Borborema* (Br.) from Santo Antonio. Railroad ties.

April 27th.—Madeira-Mamoré Railway Co's. tug *Barbosa*, with barges *Purus* and *Guapore*, from Itacoatiara. Provisions and structural materials.

April 28th.—Madeira Mamoré Railway Co's. tug *Uncle Tom*, with barge *Cameta*, from Itacoatiara. Passengers.

SAILINGS

April 28th.—Madeira-Mamoré Railway Co's. tug *Barbosa*, with barge *Jaci-Parana*, for Itacoatiara. Mail and passengers.

TO LOWER PRICE OF BEEF

Brazilian Trade Corporation Gets Concessions

Designed to sell fresh beef in New York at a price from six to eight cents a pound lower than present prices, the Brazilian Trade Corporation—which has a Maine charter and whose head offices are located in New York—has been formally admitted to do business in Brazil. It is stated that with the exception of the Singer Sewing Machine Co., which devotes itself exclusively to selling its own product, this is the only American company domiciled in Brazil for the purpose of representing American interests there.

"Under the law," said John R. Henneberry, secretary and treasurer of the new company, "the Brazilian Government may only enter into contracts or business negotiations with Brazilian firms or with foreign firms domiciled in Brazil and authorized to do business by federal decree. Individual salesmen traveling as representatives of firms not so authorized, are virtually prohibited from soliciting business, except through a registered firm to which, of course, they must pay a commission

"French, English and German houses have taken fullest advantage of this law. Such establishments as the United States Steel Corporation, the Standard Oil, the Westinghouse Co., the Baldwin Locomotive Co. and other great American enterprises, are, without exception, represented by European firms because there is not one authorized American house that could serve their purpose."

"No American organization has existed which could bid upon government contracts or the loans which are offered from time to time by the various states and municipalities. Frequently the 6 per cent bonds on these loans are offered at 95 and the 5 per cents are offered at prices ranging from 88 to 92 with the best of securities. The French and English contest eagerly for these loans and their domination in the country's affairs may be directly attributed to the vast sums which

they have raised through the medium of these loans."

Want American Capital.

"All other things being equal, the Brazilians would prefer to place their business in the hands of Americans to equalize in some measure the trade balance, which shows $100,000,000 in Brazil's favor and for the purpose of diversifying the foreign interests in their country. They look with concern upon the growing domination of the French, English and Germans in their affairs."

"Because of this sentiment the French are in some cases actually operating under American charters. For instance the Socorabana Railway, incorporated under the laws of Maine, operating 800 miles of railroad, is all owned by French and with only one American, the superintendent, in a position of responsibility. The Brazilian Railway operates 5,000 miles, is a Maine corporation and has two Canadian, three Brazilian, two English one French and one American director. It has between $75,000,000 and $100,000,000 of European capital and not one dollar of American money invested. Other Maine companies, representing in no instance one dollar of American capital, are the Port of Para, the Madeira and Mamore Railway Co., and the Bahia Light & Power Co."

"Our company was incorporated last June with a capital of $500,000 and we have secured concessions which will give us an opportunity to develop the cattle interests of Brazil, both domestic and foreign. Up to this time there has not been one cold storage plant in the country with the exception of a small one for local use in Rio Janeiro. It has been estimated that there at present 30,000,000 cattle existing in the country, millions of them running wild They are of fine quality, descended from blooded stock, and the government is constantly improving them by registered European cattle "

"Because of the crude method of handling, the lack of railroad facilities and proper cold storage plants, the meat staple is dried beef. Fresh meat is a luxury.'

"It is our purpose to erect abba-

toirs and cold storage plants at various points, and to use for export the same freezing process as that of the Australian shippers. The length of the voyage from Australia to England is 42 days. From Brazil it is 20 days And we are 1,200 miles nearer New York and London than are the Argentine shippers from Buenos Aires "

Will Ship From Four Ports.

"As soon as we can get the facilities we propose to export from the ports of San Luiz, Fortaleza, Salvador da Bahia and Rio We are certain that we can lay beef down in New York despite the freight charges, and import duty of 1 1-2 cents a pound, at from six to eight cents below the present prices, and we can also meet the competition on American beef in England, even though American packers now own the beef industry of the Argentine Republic This is because they have lifted the English prices on Argentine beef so that it cannot compete with American beef, and that American beef is sold in the Smithfield market in London at five cents a pound less than in New York We expect also to deal in hides and by-products."

"You can get a good idea of the lack of development in the beef industry in Brazil from the manner in which it is sold in Rio Janeiro, noted as the most sanitary city in the world. The cattle are shipped without provision for watering or feeding, and it is easy to imagine their condition when they arrive at the abbatoir after a journey of four days They lose on an average of 33 pounds, many are trodden to death and many more are condemned by the city's medical inspectors because of bruises and other developments."

"The city regulations require the butchers, whose shops must be lined with porcelain and marble, and which are absolutely sanitary, to buy their supply of fresh meat for the day at 4 o'clock in the morning. At 3 o'clock in the afternoon the shop must be closed and the unsold meat must be thrown away It is easy to gather that the waste in the business makes it a decidedly costly proposition "

"It is easy also to be seen that with every natural advantage for the raising of cattle of the finest quality, the introduction of modern methods will make an enterprise of this sort decidedly worth while "—(N Y Commercial.)

Dana Merrill:
Other Images from the Chronicler of the Jungle

PEDRO RIBEIRO MOREIRA NETO

Back in 1999, I expressed somewhat contradictory emotions. On the one hand, I was very happy that the Museu Paulista at the University of São Paulo had recently acquired Dana B. Merrill's photographs of the construction of the Madeira-Mamoré Railroad. On the other hand, I mourned the fact that these still-preserved images represented only about 10 percent of the entire set of photographs. My words closed with the statement that—after the fire at the railway archives—nothing remained except for the 189 negatives obtained by the museum—these lost images from the photographer, like so many lives, had disappeared anonymously and now raised the curtain of legend and mystery from a hidden story and magnified the tragic aura of the *ferrovia do diabo*.

More than a decade has passed. Even outside the museum's archives, the photographs were subjects of great discussion and inquiry; they were as engrossing as a movie, a televised novel whose plot follows the construction of the railway. Dana Merrill's forceful images—even if only indirectly—attracted the general public's attention, and the museum's collection began to take on a social purpose. Today we live in a time of political and economic reorganization where issues that were once considered absolute priorities face growing attacks. Countries that more recently have become part of the hegemonic base of the global system are forced to make split decisions that impact human destiny with their new partners, the so-called ascenders, which are scattered in other regions. Capitalism, which concentrates on the production of consumer goods and accumulation of capital but also effects humanity's heritage—as well as the planet's future—is being questioned, paradoxically, from the very center of its system. Environmental questions and climate change are matters that have become social and economic issues. Brazil is among the countries in the middle of this debate.

Brazil was long considered a major supplier of raw materials, including those from its rain forests, but it has recently assumed a more important role in this new debate. In the case of the Amazon—which Brazil shares with several neighboring countries—certain controversial questions have acquired international importance, including its preservation and conservation and the presence of activities that are not always compatible with the health of its ecosystem.

If these environmental and economic questions seem news to Brazil, it is only because they have moved from peripherally important issues to more central ones that impact the preservation of planet Earth itself. Today what is best for Brazil affects all of humanity. But this story is not quite as recent as it seems. Rather, it dates back to the mid-nineteenth century and the start of the great march to the Brazilian hinterland searching, principally, for latex, the product destined to initiate and greatly influence industrialization on a global scale.

The major milestone in occupying the Brazilian countryside is generally credited to the creation of Brasilia. In part this is true. However, the nineteenth and twentieth centuries had already witnessed a territorial event almost as important as founding a new capital—the construction of the Madeira-Mamoré Railroad. This project moved the most refined infrastructural engineering technology available closer to the geographic center of South America.

Documenting great civil-engineering accomplishments has been a common practice since the earliest days of photography. Many photo collections portray these construction projects and highlight, in particular, the great icon of the modern age: the railways. Therefore, hiring a photographer to record the development of the Madeira-Mamoré Railroad was not a new idea. As for the work environment, it was stressful—a multitude of adventurers from the most diverse ethnicities were fighting against the untamable forces of nature that repelled—and still repel, in their own way—the progress of humanity. It therefore seems logical to speculate that the interaction between the photographer and his environment provided the incentive to create original work. This situation by itself, however, is not enough to explain the uniqueness of the photographs of Madeira-Mamoré. The construction of railroads in inhospitable environments—such as Siberia or the Congo jungles— did not result in important collections like the images of this Amazonian railway.

How then did these dramatic and powerful images emerge—since we find no precedent—if not from the genius of the photographer? What other photographer could have produced images of such sophisticated technical quality, judiciously processed to allow them to survive the adverse heat and humidity in the Amazonian rain forest? Dana Merrill, the official photographer of the Madeira-Mamoré Railroad, was only identified by Frank Kravigny, the surviving scribe of the construction, in his book, *The Jungle Route*. We know little about this photographer except that he worked for the city of New York and later returned there, as confirmed by the bulletins of the Madeira-Mamoré Association. Probably his previous experience prepared him for this assignment, providing the technical expertise that he brought with him to Porto Velho.

The photographic equipment Dana Merrill used was practically identical to what was available to most professionals at the time. The choice of the 13-by-18-centimeter negative format—considered small and light then—was best suited for frequent travel from one site to the next over difficult terrain. In addition to the more common glass plates, Merrill also adopted a chassis utilizing the recently developed film pack. These packs were composed of a plate with a flexible base and an emulsion coating; they were much lighter than glass plates and usually came in packages of a dozen plates. This choice considerably lightened the equipment weight for the photographer and made it much easier for him to change plates.

However, the camera Merrill used was still a conventional one, more appropriate for traditional photography with the subjects placed at medium distance from the camera, carefully framed, and most often posed, a result of the necessary use of a tripod due to long exposure times.

It appears that many of Merrill's surviving images fall into the category of early twentieth-century photography. However, Merrill was not a typical photographer but a pioneer, not bound by the technical limitations or aesthetic standards of his day. By taking the limits of his equipment to the extreme, he was able to explore a variety of camera angles and, in many instances, did not conform to the photographic conventions of his era, for example, when he purposefully used long exposure times for scenes involving movement. He placed priority on not losing the moment.

His images suggest that he selected the point of view that best captured the feelings that struck him at that moment, even though this often meant he had to photograph from ditches, boats, or scaffolding, knee-deep in mud, or from the tops of train cars or trees. Such practices—quite common in today's photography—marked Merrill as a pioneer. The scenes in his images are so dynamic that they seem to have been taken with a 35 mm camera that didn't even appear until twenty years later.

Merrill's job was to document the progress of the railroad construction. Analysis of his photographs indicates that he did not have a planned routine. He probably developed an arbitrary narrative in accordance with the opportunities that arose as the project progressed. Each negative—systematically numbered in India ink—implies a chronological order, although this cannot be confirmed.

But the photographer—in addition to documenting the construction work—recorded the endless procession of every type of person who participated in the railroad project. Those not portrayed in groups, such as bureaucrats or the laundry or hospital staff, appear in individual photos or in pairs with the omnipresent background of their work environment. Others are depicted in individual portraits that highlight their physical attributes or distinctive traits.

But these photographs are only a small part of Merrill's work. The surviving photographs come from a selection made by Manoel Rodrigues Ferreira, who—with his engineering training—probably leaned toward images directly related to construction. If Ferreira had been a botanist or biologist, what other photographs would have withstood the test of time?

Into this search for answers come the new images— until now unknown—that have resurfaced in the Oscar Pyles collection, now available to the public. These add to the legacy of new images attributed to Dana Merrill, like those in the National Library of Brazil. If the spell cast by the legends and mysteries continues to intensify the tragic aura of the *ferrovia do diabo,* then these resurrected photographs will reshape what we know and bring us to a new vision of a lost story.

Pedro Ribeiro Moreira Neto received his doctorate degree in social history from the University of São Paulo. His areas of interest are photography, video, and the visual arts. He is considered an expert on the photographs of Dana Merrill. He currently teaches at the University of São José dos Campos.

Notes

ACKNOWLEDGMENTS

1. Rose Houk, *Golden Spike National Historic Site* (Tucson: Western National Parks Association, 1990), 1.

INTRODUCTION

1. Theodore Roosevelt, *Through the Brazilian Wilderness* (New York: Charles Scribner's Sons, 1914), 236.

2. On May 25, 1966—with Decree No. 58,501—President Castello Branco transferred responsibility for the Madeira-Mamoré Railroad to the transportation division of the Brazilian Ministry of War. The decree made the 5th Engineering and Construction Battalion, stationed in Porto Velho, responsible for the deactivation of the railroad.When we interviewed Luiz Leite de Oliveira in Porto Velho, he told us he believes that the army's demolition of the railroad was connected to maintaining security along the vulnerable border between Brazil and Bolivia.

3. Frank W. Kravigny, *The Jungle Route* (New York: Orlin Tremaine Company, 1940), 175.

CHAPTER 1

1. Neville B. Craig, *Recollections of an Ill-Fated Expedition to the Headwaters of the Madeira River in Brazil* (Philadelphia and London: J. B. Lippincott Company, 1907), 18.

2. Ibid.

3. Ibid., 20–21.

4. Ibid., 75.

5. Ibid., 77.

6. Ibid.

7. Ibid., 459–60.

8. Earl P. Hanson, "The Depression Comes to the Jungle," *Harper's,* May 1935, as quoted in Frank J. Kravigny, *The Jungle Route* (New York: Orlin Tremaine Company, 1940), 65–66.

CHAPTER 2

1. Frank W. Kravigny, *The Jungle Route* (New York: Orlin Tremaine Company, 1940), 115.
2. Ibid., 115–16.
3. Ibid., 113–14.
4. Ibid., 114.
5. "Across South America by Water," *Porto Velho Marconigram,* December 17, 1910.
6. The Dana Merrill collection, including this album, is housed in the New York City Public Library.
7. Dana B. Merrill, *Views of the Estrada de Ferro Madeira e Mamoré, Amazonas & Matto Grosso, Brasil SA (1909–1912),* Stephen A. Schwarzman Building/Photography Collection, Miriam and Ira D. Wallach Division of Art, Prints and Photographs, New York City Public Library, New York.
8. Dr. Henry Wickham carried the seeds in 1876. Kravigny, 114–15.
9. James A. Brooke, "Manaus Journal; For the Rubber Soldiers of Brazil, Rubber Checks," *New York Times,* May 15, 1991, available online at http://www.nytimes.com/1991/05/15/world/manaus-journal-for-the-rubber-soldiers-of--brazil-rubber-checks.html

CHAPTER 3

1. Frank W. Kravigny, *The Jungle Route* (New York: Orlin Tremaine Company, 1940), 169.
2. Ibid., 37–38.
3. "Progress on the Madeira," *Porto Velho Marconigram,* November 17, 1910.
4. "A Fitting Comparison," *Porto Velho Marconigram,* November 19, 1910.
5. Kravigny, 40–43.
6. Ibid., 72.
7. Ibid., 70–71.
8. *Pan American Bulletin,* December 1912, quoted in Kravigny, 70.
9. Dana B. Merrill, *Views of the Estrada de Ferro Madeira e Mamoré, Amazonas & Matto Grosso, Brasil SA (1909–1912),* Stephen A. Schwarzman Building/Photography Collection, Miriam and Ira D. Wallach Division of Art, Prints and Photographs, New York City Public Library, New York.

10. Kravigny, 28–29.

11. "Across South America by Water," *Porto Velho Marconigram,* December 17, 1910.

12. Kravigny, 38.

13. "Christmas at Candelaria," *Porto Velho Marconigram,* December 31, 1910.

14. Merrill, *Views of the Estrada,* New York City Public Library.

15. Ibid.

16. Ibid.

CHAPTER 4

1. Frank J. Kravigny, *The Jungle Route* (New York: Orlin Tremaine Company, 1940), 48–49.

2. "Moving Day in Porto Velho," *Porto Velho Marconigram,* January 14, 1911.

3. Kravigny, 107–8.

4. Ibid., 112.

5. Ibid., 104.

6. Ibid., 123.

7. Ibid., 124–25.

8. "Notes from Jaci-Parana," *Porto Velho Marconigram,* November 19, 1910.

9. Kravigny, 68.

10. "The Woman Who Understands," *Porto Velho, Marconigram,* January 14, 1911.

11. Dana B. Merrill, *Views of the Estrada de Ferro Madeira e Mamoré, Amazonas & Matto Grosso, Brasil SA (1909–1912),* Stephen A. Schwarzman Building/Photography Collection, Miriam and Ira D. Wallach Division of Art, Prints and Photographs, New York City Public Library, New York.

12. Ibid.

13. Ibid.

14. "Lines on a Railroad Time-Table," *Porto Velho Marconigram,* October 15, 1910.

15. Merrill, *Views of the Estrada,* New York City Public Library.

16. Ibid.

CHAPTER 5

1. "Seeing Civilization," *Porto Velho Marconigram,* November 19, 1910.

2. "A Night in the Jungle," *Porto Velho Marconigram,* October 22, 1910.

3. "Strenuous Times up the Line," *Porto Velho Marconigram,* October 22, 1910.

4. "A Large Fish Caught," *Porto Velho Marconigram,* January 14, 1911.

5. "Perilous Encounter with an Ant Bear," *Porto Velho Marconigram,* November 19, 1910.

6. "Big Snake Killed," *Porto Velho Marconigram,* October 15, 1910.

7. Frank J. Kravigny, *The Jungle Route* (New York: Orlin Tremaine Company, 1940), 127–28.

8. "Notes from Jaci-Parana," "How They Didn't Kill the Hog," *Porto Velho Marconigram,* October 15, 1910.

9. "Dope," *Porto Velho Marconigram,* November 19, 1910.

10. "Food and Amazon Rubber," *Porto Velho Marconigram,* January 7, 1911.

11. Dana B. Merrill, *Views of the Estrada de Ferro Madeira e Mamoré, Amazonas & Matto Grosso, Brasil SA (1909–1912),* Stephen A. Schwarzman Building/Photography Collection, Miriam and Ira D. Wallach Division of Art, Prints and Photographs, New York City Public Library, New York.

CHAPTER 6

1. Charles Darwin, quoted in Frank J. Kravigny, *The Jungle Route* (New York: Orlin Tremaine Company, 1940), 186.

2. "Across South America by Water," *Porto Velho Marconigram,* December 17, 1910.

3. "New Avenue to Bolivia—The Madeira-Mamoré Railway," *Porto Velho Marconigram,* October 15, 1910.

4. Kravigny, 66, 68.

5. "New Avenue to Bolivia," "Life in a Railroad Camp," *Porto Velho Marconigram,* October 15, 1910.

6. Dana B. Merrill, *Views of the Estrada de Ferro Madeira e Mamoré, Amazonas & Matto Grosso, Brasil SA (1909–1912),* Stephen A. Schwarzman Building/Photography Collection, Miriam and Ira D. Wallach Division of Art, Prints and Photographs, New York City Public Library, New York.

7. "Does the Wireless Work?" *Porto Velho Marconigram,* January 7, 1911.

8. Merrill, *Views of the Estrada de Ferro,* New York City Public Library.

CHAPTER 7

1. "South America's First Transcontinental," *Porto Velho Marconigram,* December 24, 1910.

2. "The Madeira-Mamoré Railway Brazil," *Engineering News Record,* May 12, 1939.

3. Peter Eisner, "Amazon's Mad Maria Back on Track," *Newsweek,* July 8, 1991, p. 27.

Bibliography

Ambrose, Stephen E. *Nothing Like It in the World: The Men Who Built the Trans-continental Railroad 1863–1869.* New York: Simon & Schuster, 2000.

Brooke, James A. "Manaus Journal; For the Rubber Soldiers of Brazil, Rubber Checks." *New York Times,* May 15, 1991. Available online at http://www.ny-times.com/1991/05/15/world/manaus-journal-for-the-rubber-soldiers-of--brazil-rubber-checks.html

Copeland, Martin. *River of Doubt.* N.p.: Booklocker.com, Inc., 2001.

Craig, Neville B. *Recollections of an Ill-Fated Expedition to the Headwaters of the Madeira River in Brazil.* Philadelphia and London: J. B. Lippincott Company, 1907.

Eisner, Peter. "Amazon's Mad Maria Back on Track." *Newsweek,* July 8, 1991, p. 27.

Ferreira, Manoel Rodrigues. *A Ferrovia do Diabo.* São Paulo: Melhoramentos, 2005.

Gauld, Charles A. *The Last Titan: Percival Farquhar, American Entrepreneur in Latin America.* Stanford, CA: Stanford University, Institute of Hispanic--American and Luso-Brazilian Studies, 1964.

Grann, David. *The Lost City of Z: A Tale of Deadly Obsession in the Amazon.* New York: Vintage Books, 2009.

Hanson, Earl P. "The Depression Comes to the Jungle." *Harper's,* May 1935, pp. 746–54.

Jones, Judith MacKnight. *Soldado descansa! Uma epopéia Norte Americana sob os céus do Brasil.* São Paulo: Jarde, 1967.

Kravigny, Frank W. *The Jungle Route.* New York: Orlin Tremaine Company, 1940.

London, Mark, and Brian Kelly. *The Last Forest: The Amazon in the Age of Global-ization.* New York: Random House, 2007.

Merrill, Dana B. *Views of the Estrada de Ferro Madeira e Mamoré, Amazonas & Matto Grosso, Brasil SA (1909–1912).* Stephen A. Schwarzman Building/Photography Collection, Miriam and Ira D. Wallach Division of Art, Prints and Photographs, New York City Public Library, New York.

Roosevelt, Theodore. *Through the Brazilian Wilderness.* New York: Charles Scribner's Sons, 1914.

Teixeira, Marco Antonio Domingues, and Dante Ribeiro da Fonseca. *História Regional: Rondônia*. 4th ed. Porto Velho: Editoria Rondôniana, 2003.

Tomlinson, H. M. *The Sea and the Jungle*. New York: E. P. Dutton & Co., 1928.

ADDITIONAL NON-ENGLISH BIBLIOGRAPHY

Estrada de Ferro Madeira-Mamoré:EFMM. São Paulo: Museu da Imagem e do Som São Paulo, 1993.

Foot, Francisco. *Trem-fantasma: a ferrovia Madeira-Mamoré e a modernidade na selva*. 2d ed. São Paulo: Companhia das Letras, 2005.

Góes, Hércules. *Odisséia da ocupação Amazônica: Rondônia terra de migrantes, histórias de sucessos*. 3d ed. Porto Velho: Editora Ecoturismo, 1997.

Kaarsberg, Christian. *Djævelens jernbane: en rejse i Amazonas historie*. Copenhagen: Gyldendal, 1995.

Nogueira, Julio. *Estrada de Ferro Madeira-Mamoré*. Rio de Janeiro: Superintendência do Plano de Valorização Econômica da Amazônia, 1959.

Santilli, Marcos. *Madeira-Mamoré:imagem & memória = image & memory*. São Paulo: Memória Discos e Edições, Mundo Cultural, 1988.

A collection of postcards, photographs, and newspaper and magazine clippings about the Madeira-Mamoré expeditions, assembled by Robert Hopewell Hepburn, is also available in the Princeton University archives.

About the Authors

Gary and Rose Neeleman are native Utahns. Gary graduated from the University of Utah, and Rose received her bachelor's and master's degrees from Brigham Young University. The couple have been involved with Brazil most of their lives and speak, read, and write Portuguese. Gary served as a missionary for the Church of Jesus Christ of Latter-day Saints and later returned with Rose as a correspondent for United Press International, covering events in Brazil and other parts of South America. Many of the couple's seven children, thirty-four grandchildren, and nine great-grandchildren have dual citizenship.

In addition to a lengthy career with United Press International, Gary spent seventeen years working in international syndication for the *Los Angeles Times.* He has also written for *The Saturday Evening Post, Time,* and *Sports Illustrated.* The Neelemans currently operate their own international media consulting company.

Rose is the author of two books, *Far above Rubies* and *A Man for Every Woman,* published by Brigham Young University Press. Gary coauthored *Farewell My South,* a novel about the thousands of Confederate soldiers who migrated to Brazil at the end of the Civil War. The couple are presently working on a nonfiction version of the book as well as a history of the fifty-five thousand rubber tappers in Brazil who supported the Allied effort during World War II. They are also coauthors of an English-language Brazilian cookbook, *A Taste of Brazil.*

Tracks in the Amazon was first published in Portuguese in Brazil in 2011 as *Trilhos na selva* and received praise from the Brazilian press.

The Neelemans have lectured and written extensively about Brazil and the Brazilian people, and Gary currently serves as the honorary consul of Brazil for Utah.